Smith · Lustgarten · Franquiz · Peer

MISFIT CITY™

Volume Two

BOOM! BOX™

BOOm! BOX™

MISFIT CITY Volume Two, May 2018. Published by BOOM! Box, a division of Boom Entertainment, Inc. Misfit City is ™ & © 2018 Kiwi Loves You, Inc. and Kurt Lustgarten. Originally published in single magazine form as MISFIT CITY No. 5-8. ™ & © 2017 Kiwi Loves You, Inc. and Kurt Lustgarten. All rights reserved. BOOM! Box™ and the BOOM! Box logo are trademarks of Boom Entertainment, Inc., registered in various countries and categories. All characters, events, and institutions depicted herein are fictional. Any similarity between any of the names, characters, persons, events, and/or institutions in this publication to actual names, characters, and persons, whether living or dead, events, and/or institutions is unintended and purely coincidental. BOOM! Box does not read or accept unsolicited submissions of ideas, stories, or artwork.

For information regarding the CPSIA on this printed material, call: (203) 595-3636 and provide reference #RICH – 777366.

BOOM! Studios, 5670 Wilshire Boulevard, Suite 400, Los Angeles, CA 90036-5679. Printed in USA. First Printing.

ISBN: 978-1-68415-172-1, eISBN: 978-1-61398-987-6

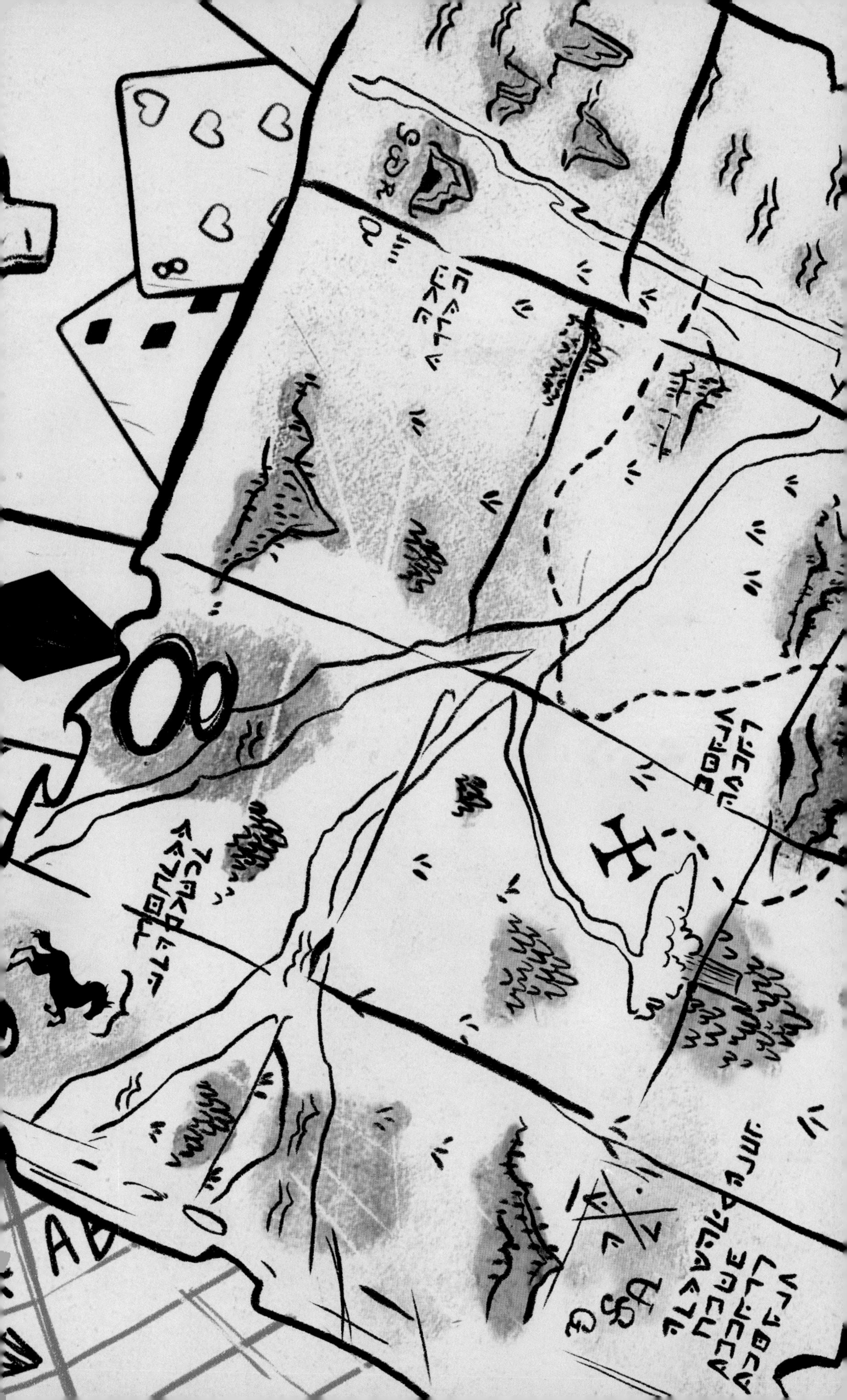

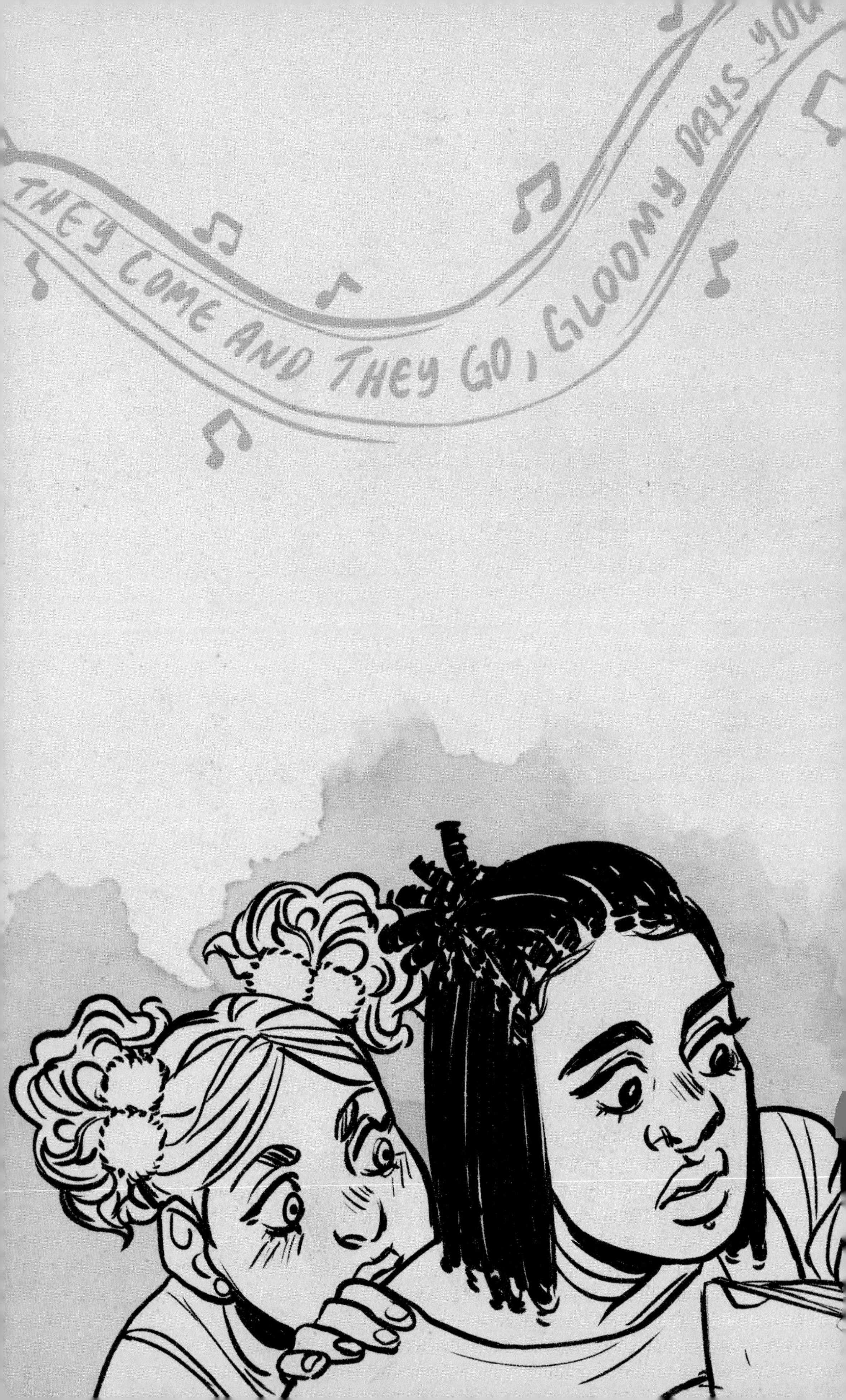
THEY COME AND THEY GO, GLOOMY DAYS YOU

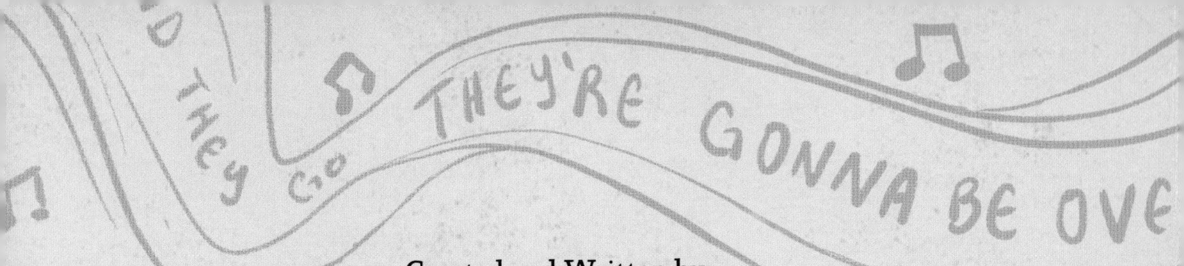
THEY GO
THEY'RE GONNA BE

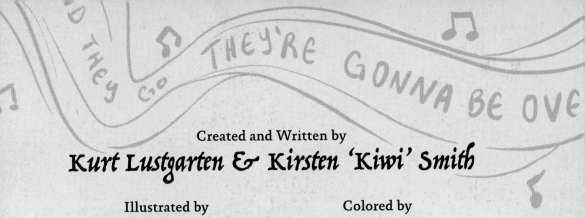

Created and Written by
Kurt Lustgarten & Kirsten 'Kiwi' Smith

Illustrated by
Naomi Franquiz
Additional Inks by
Raven Warner (issues 5-6)

Colored by
Brittany Peer
With Kieran Quigley (issue 5)

Lettered by
Jim Campbell

Cover by
Naomi Franquiz
Colors by Brittany Peer

Designer Marie Krupina
Logo Design Kelsey Dieterich
Assistant Editor Sophie Philips-Roberts
Editor Shannon Watters

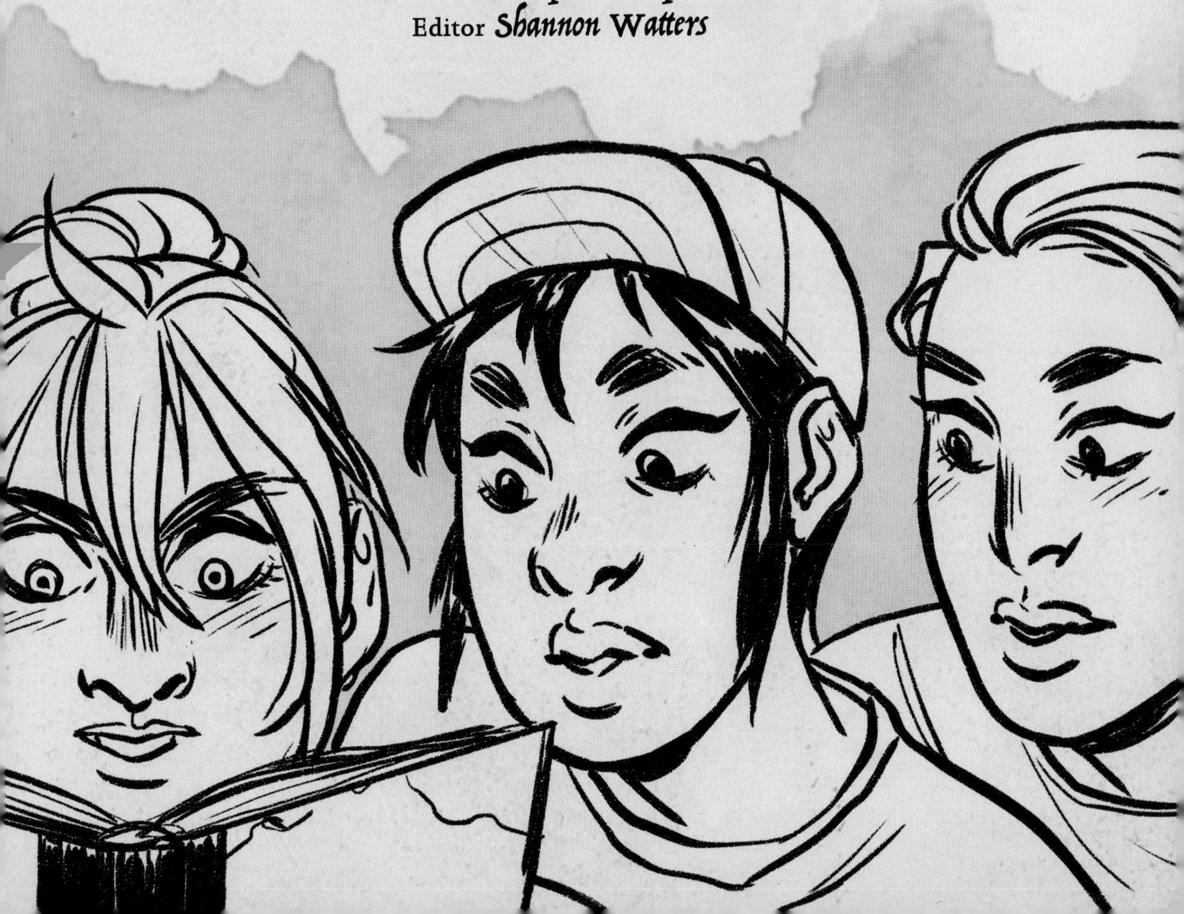

CHAPTER

V

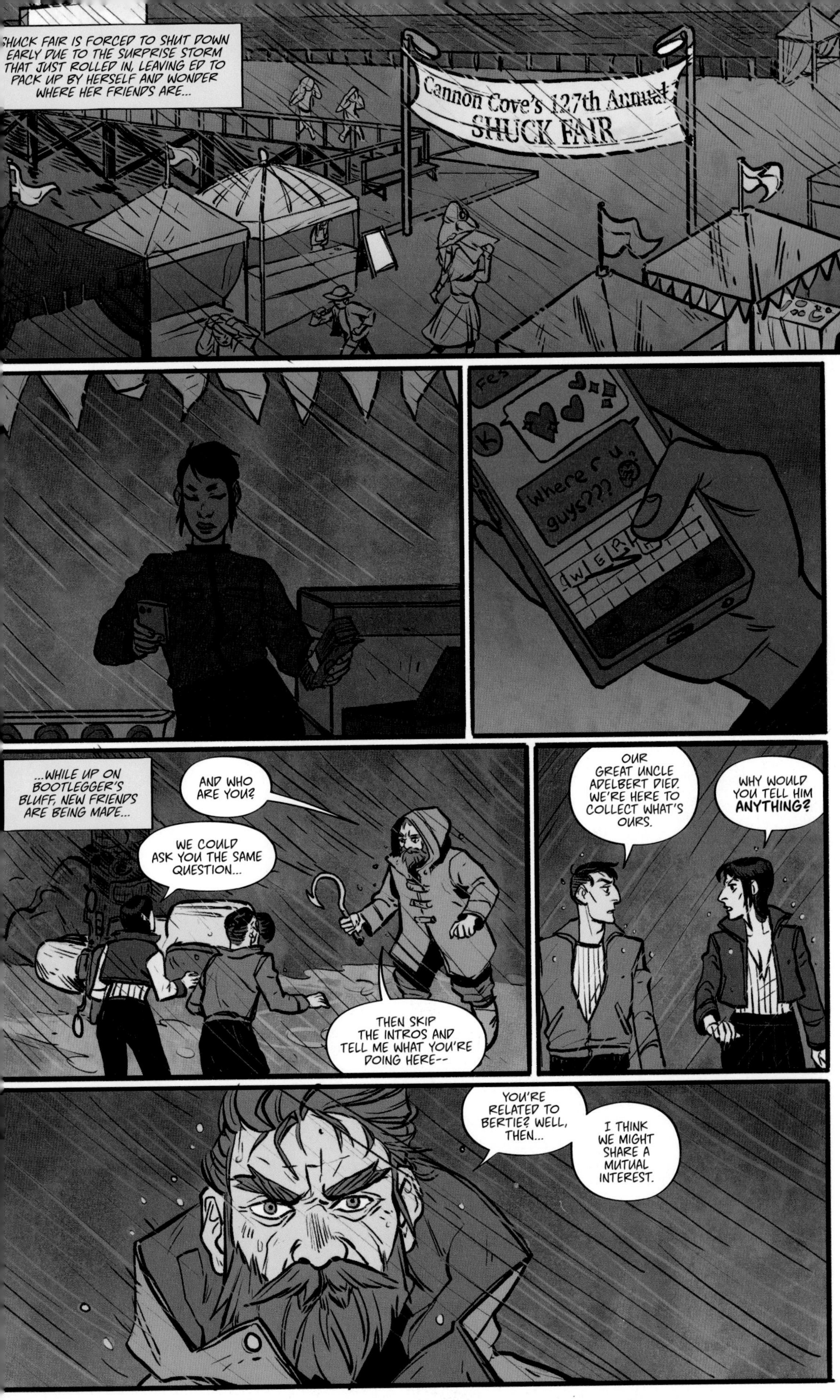
SHUCK FAIR IS FORCED TO SHUT DOWN EARLY DUE TO THE SURPRISE STORM THAT JUST ROLLED IN, LEAVING ED TO PACK UP BY HERSELF AND WONDER WHERE HER FRIENDS ARE...
Cannon Cove's 127th Annual SHUCK FAIR
Where r u guys???
...WHILE UP ON BOOTLEGGER'S BLUFF, NEW FRIENDS ARE BEING MADE...
AND WHO ARE YOU?
WE COULD ASK YOU THE SAME QUESTION...
THEN SKIP THE INTROS AND TELL ME WHAT YOU'RE DOING HERE--
OUR GREAT UNCLE ADELBERT DIED. WE'RE HERE TO COLLECT WHAT'S OURS.
WHY WOULD YOU TELL HIM ANYTHING?
YOU'RE RELATED TO BERTIE? WELL, THEN...
I THINK WE MIGHT SHARE A MUTUAL INTEREST.

...AND INSIDE THE SECRET CAVES, FRIENDSHIPS ARE ABOUT TO GET TESTED.

HOW ARE YOU ALIVE EXACTLY?

YOU'RE NOT...*UNDEAD*, ARE YOU?

LET'S HOLD THE QUESTIONS FOR LATER. JUST WATCH YOUR STEP...

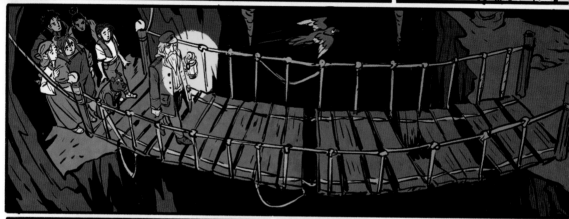

I AM **NOT** ABOUT THIS LARA CROFT LIFE...

IS THIS EVEN SAFE?

I MEAN, HOW **OLD** ARE THESE ROPES?

I WONDER HOW FAR THE DROP IS...

⸎GULP⸎

YOU KIDS COMING OR NOT?

WILDER, NO!

COME ON, GUYS. IF HE CAN DO IT, SO CAN WE.

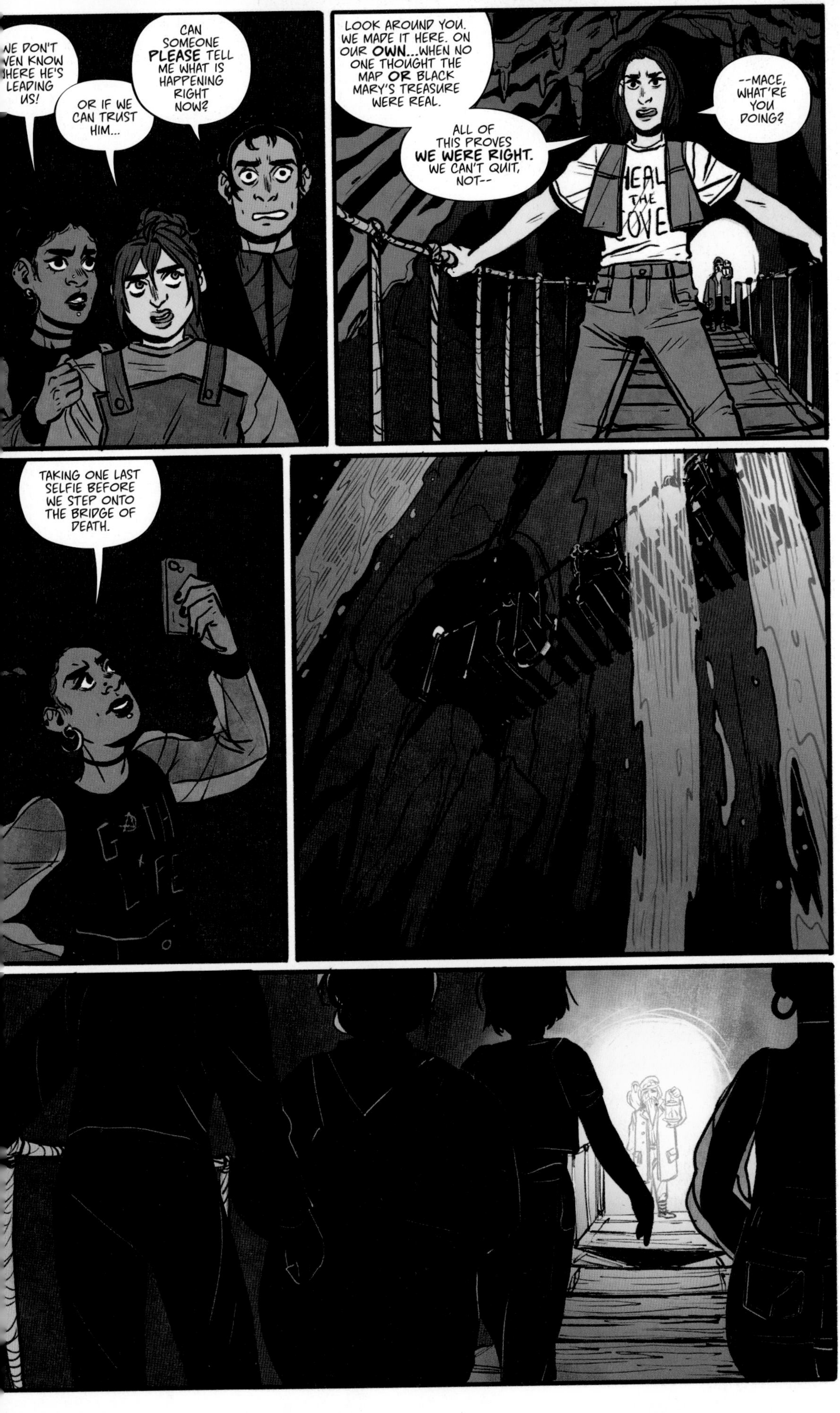
NE DON'T VEN KNOW HERE HE'S LEADING US!
OR IF WE CAN TRUST HIM...
CAN SOMEONE **PLEASE** TELL ME WHAT IS HAPPENING RIGHT NOW?
LOOK AROUND YOU. WE MADE IT HERE. ON OUR **OWN...**WHEN NO ONE THOUGHT THE MAP **OR** BLACK MARY'S TREASURE WERE REAL.
ALL OF THIS PROVES **WE WERE RIGHT.** WE CAN'T QUIT, NOT--
--MACE, WHAT'RE YOU DOING?
HEAL THE COVE
TAKING ONE LAST SELFIE BEFORE WE STEP ONTO THE BRIDGE OF DEATH.

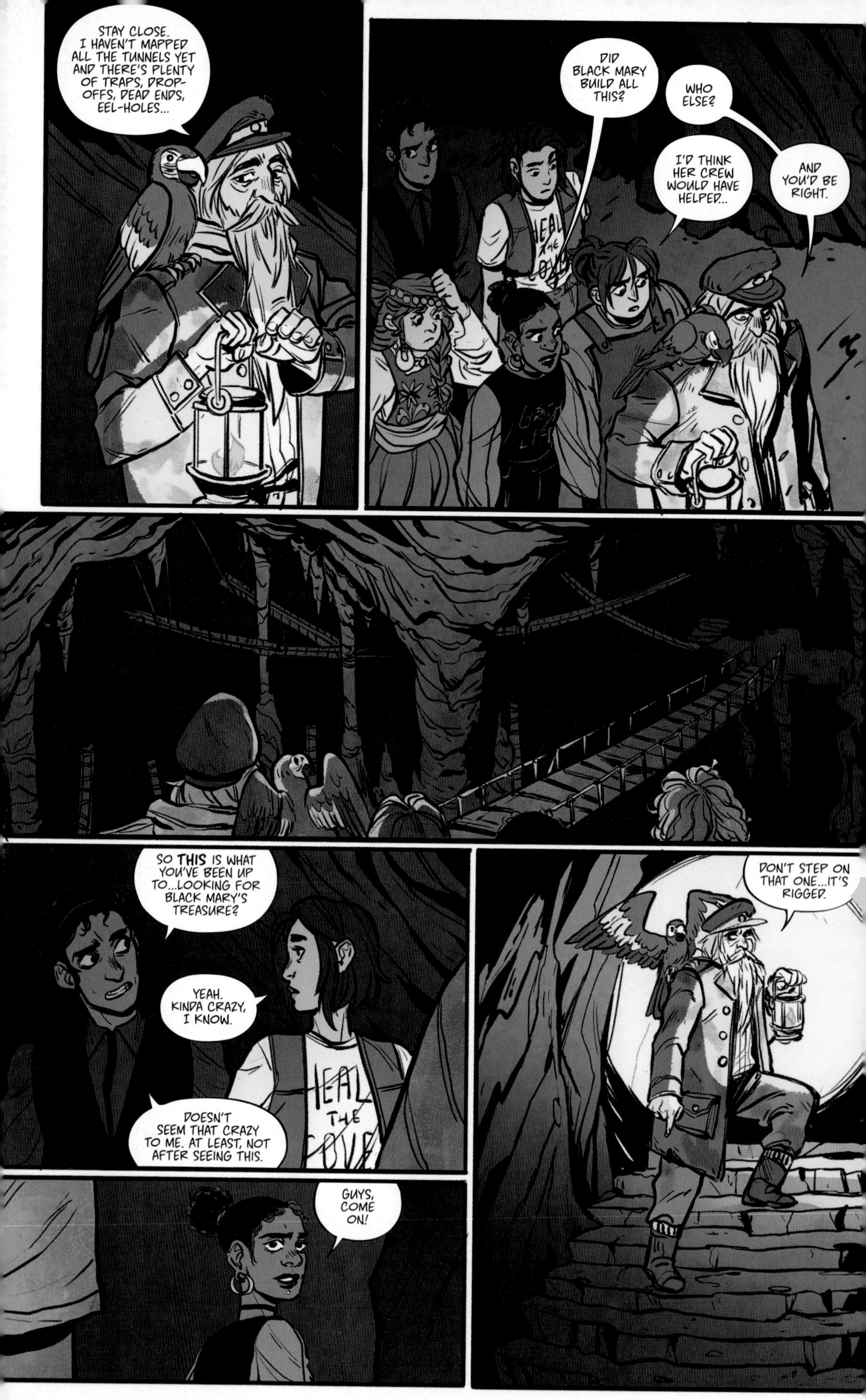
STAY CLOSE. I HAVEN'T MAPPED ALL THE TUNNELS YET AND THERE'S PLENTY OF TRAPS, DROP-OFFS, DEAD ENDS, EEL-HOLES...
DID BLACK MARY BUILD ALL THIS?
WHO ELSE?
I'D THINK HER CREW WOULD HAVE HELPED...
AND YOU'D BE RIGHT.
SO THIS IS WHAT YOU'VE BEEN UP TO...LOOKING FOR BLACK MARY'S TREASURE?
YEAH. KINDA CRAZY, I KNOW.
DOESN'T SEEM THAT CRAZY TO ME. AT LEAST, NOT AFTER SEEING THIS.
GUYS, COME ON!
DON'T STEP ON THAT ONE...IT'S RIGGED.

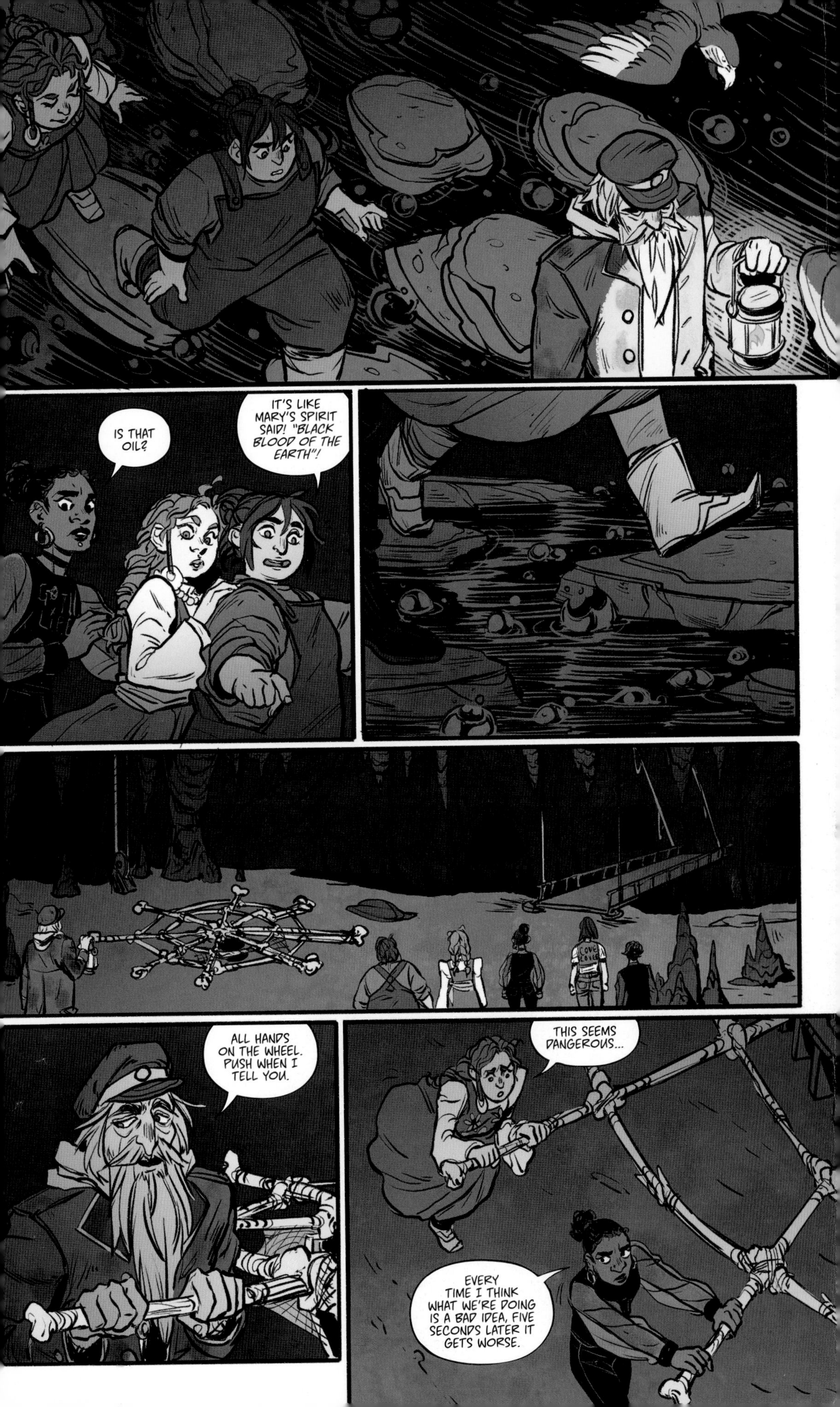
IS THAT OIL?
IT'S LIKE MARY'S SPIRIT SAID! "BLACK BLOOD OF THE EARTH"!
COVE RAVE
ALL HANDS ON THE WHEEL. PUSH WHEN I TELL YOU.
THIS SEEMS DANGEROUS...
EVERY TIME I THINK WHAT WE'RE DOING IS A BAD IDEA, FIVE SECONDS LATER IT GETS WORSE.

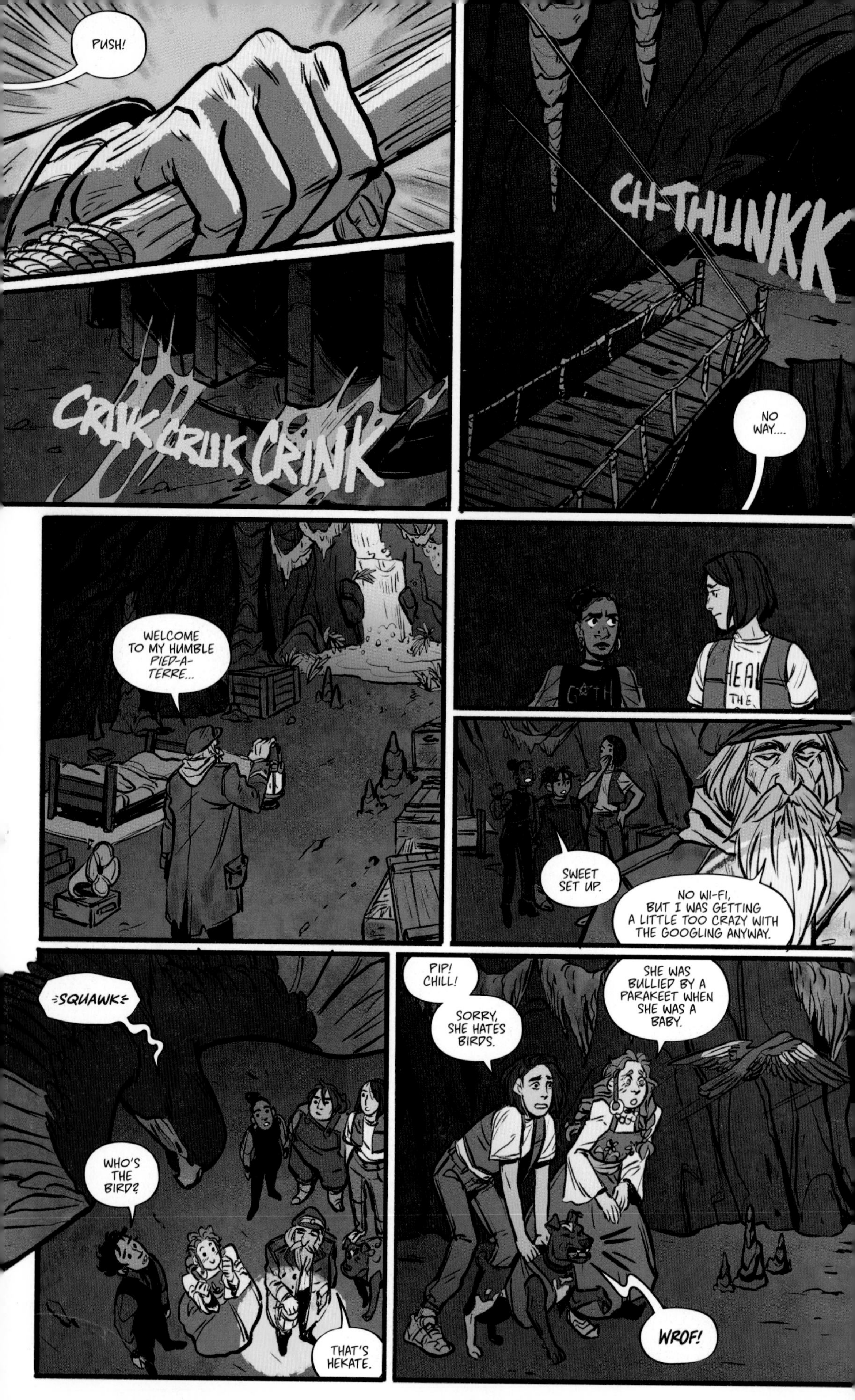
PUSH!
CRIK CRIK CRINK
CH-THUNKK
NO WAY....
WELCOME TO MY HUMBLE PIED-A-TERRE...
SWEET SET UP.
NO WI-FI, BUT I WAS GETTING A LITTLE TOO CRAZY WITH THE GOOGLING ANYWAY.
SQUAWK
WHO'S THE BIRD?
THAT'S HEKATE.
PIP! CHILL!
SORRY, SHE HATES BIRDS.
SHE WAS BULLIED BY A PARAKEET WHEN SHE WAS A BABY.
WROF!

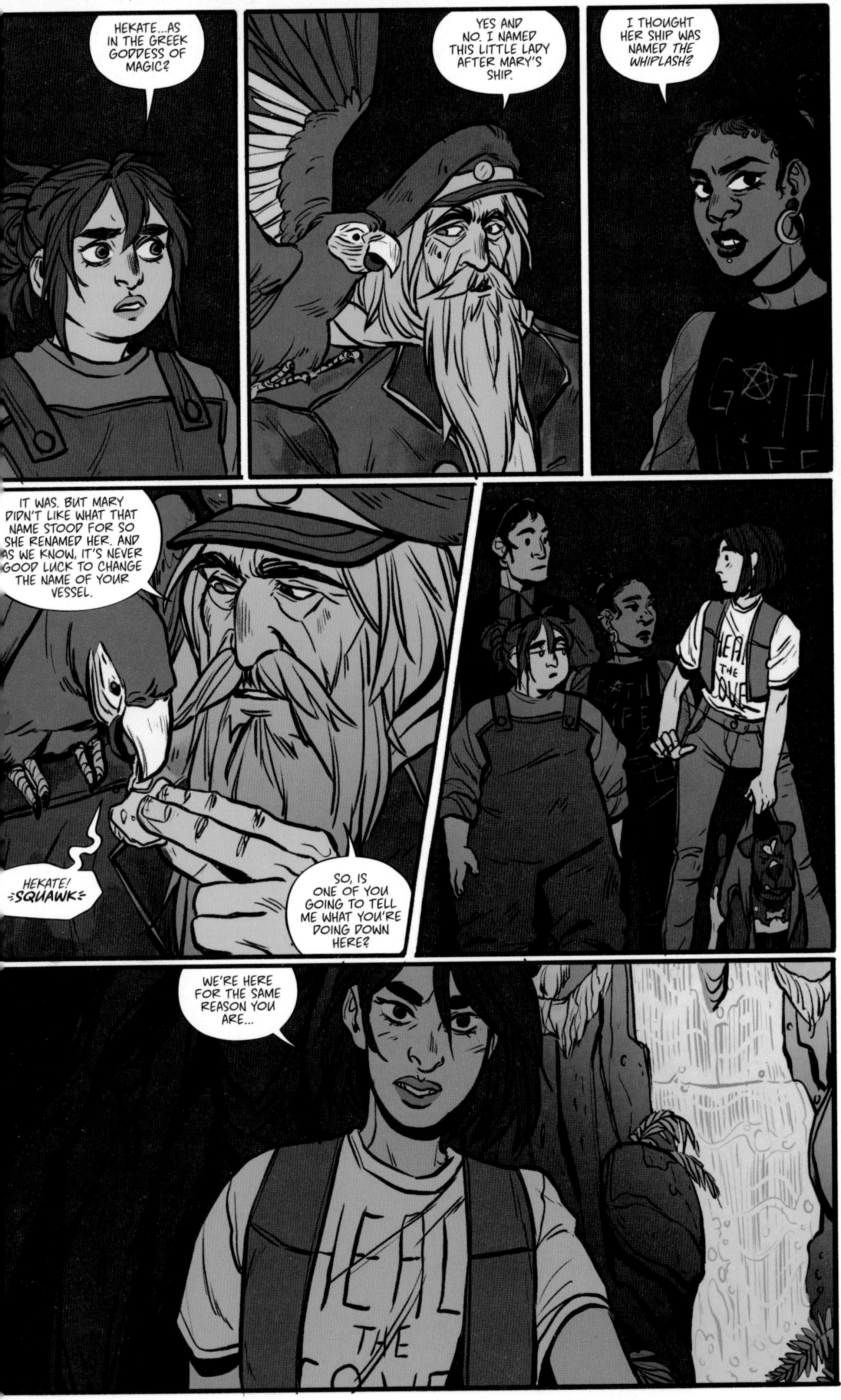
HEKATE...AS IN THE GREEK GODDESS OF MAGIC?
YES AND NO. I NAMED THIS LITTLE LADY AFTER MARY'S SHIP.
I THOUGHT HER SHIP WAS NAMED *THE WHIPLASH*?
IT WAS. BUT MARY DIDN'T LIKE WHAT THAT NAME STOOD FOR SO SHE RENAMED HER. AND AS WE KNOW, IT'S NEVER GOOD LUCK TO CHANGE THE NAME OF YOUR VESSEL.
HEKATE! SQUAWK
SO, IS ONE OF YOU GOING TO TELL ME WHAT YOU'RE DOING DOWN HERE?
WE'RE HERE FOR THE SAME REASON YOU ARE...

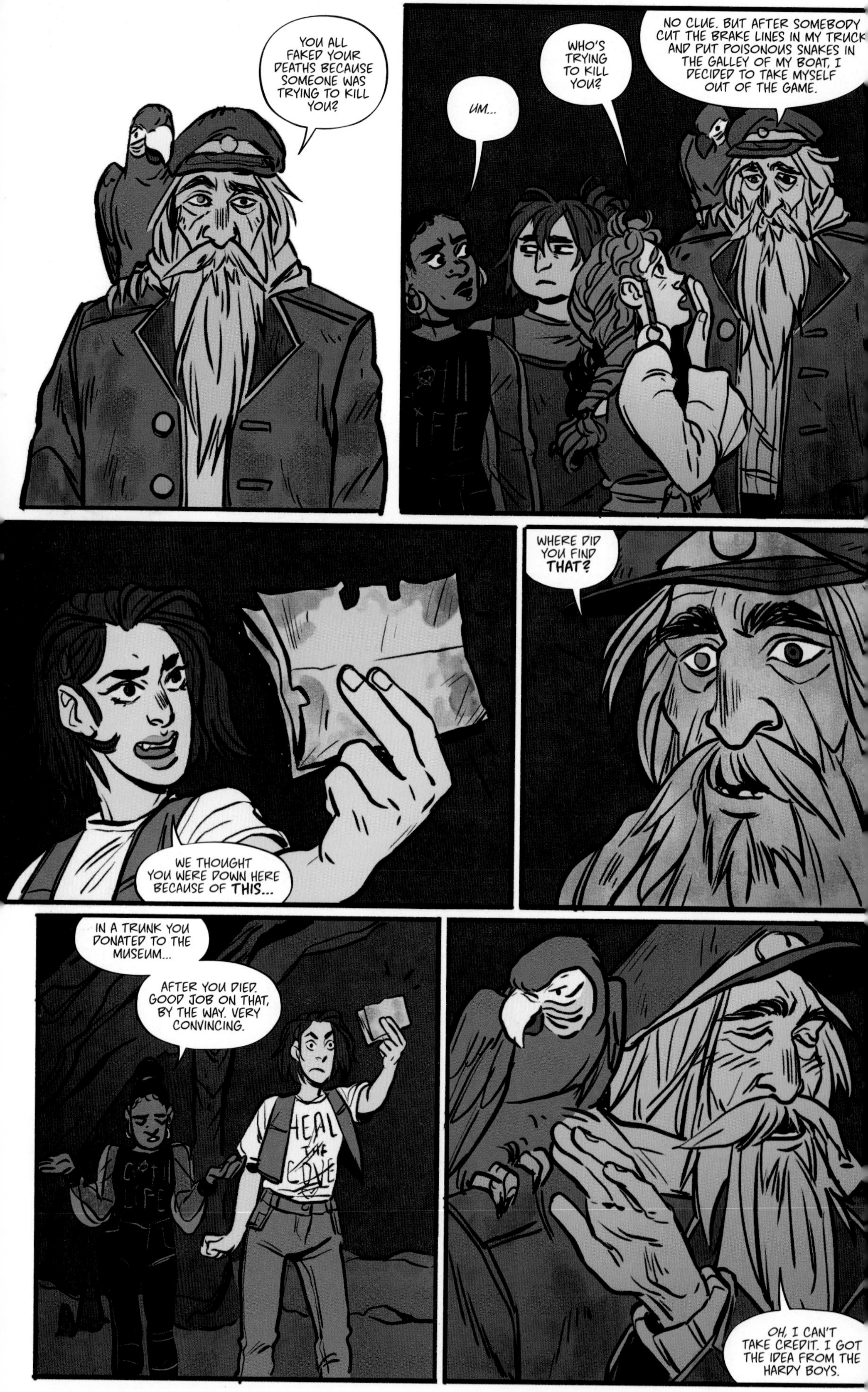
YOU ALL FAKED YOUR DEATHS BECAUSE SOMEONE WAS TRYING TO KILL YOU?
UM...
WHO'S TRYING TO KILL YOU?
NO CLUE. BUT AFTER SOMEBODY CUT THE BRAKE LINES IN MY TRUCK AND PUT POISONOUS SNAKES IN THE GALLEY OF MY BOAT, I DECIDED TO TAKE MYSELF OUT OF THE GAME.
WE THOUGHT YOU WERE DOWN HERE BECAUSE OF **THIS...**
WHERE DID YOU FIND **THAT?**
IN A TRUNK YOU DONATED TO THE MUSEUM...
AFTER YOU DIED. GOOD JOB ON THAT, BY THE WAY. VERY CONVINCING.
OH, I CAN'T TAKE CREDIT. I GOT THE IDEA FROM THE HARDY BOYS.

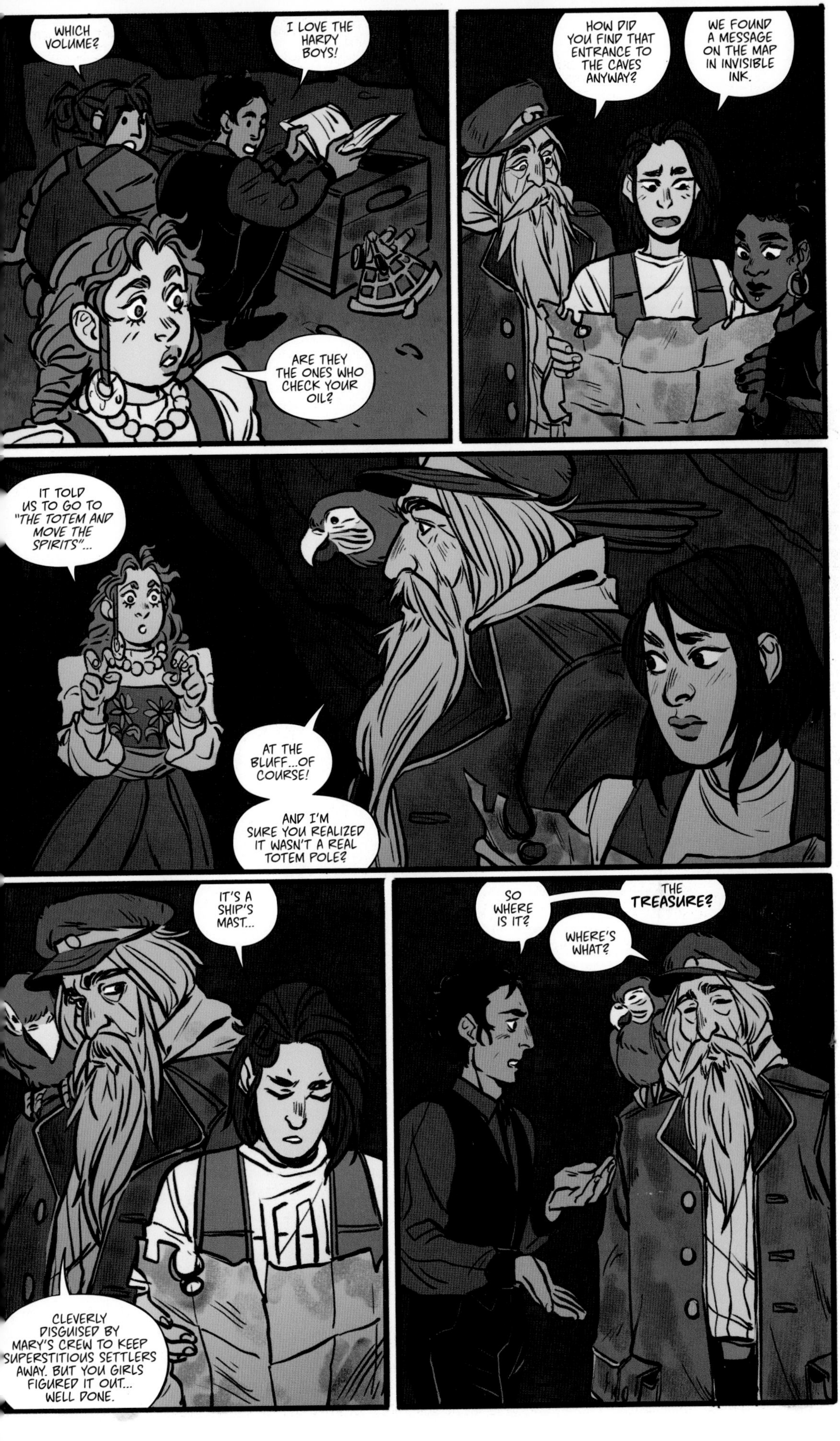
WHICH VOLUME?
I LOVE THE HARDY BOYS!
ARE THEY THE ONES WHO CHECK YOUR OIL?
HOW DID YOU FIND THAT ENTRANCE TO THE CAVES ANYWAY?
WE FOUND A MESSAGE ON THE MAP IN INVISIBLE INK.
IT TOLD US TO GO TO "THE TOTEM AND MOVE THE SPIRITS"...
AT THE BLUFF...OF COURSE!
AND I'M SURE YOU REALIZED IT WASN'T A REAL TOTEM POLE?
IT'S A SHIP'S MAST...
CLEVERLY DISGUISED BY MARY'S CREW TO KEEP SUPERSTITIOUS SETTLERS AWAY. BUT YOU GIRLS FIGURED IT OUT... WELL DONE.
SO WHERE IS IT?
WHERE'S WHAT?
THE TREASURE?

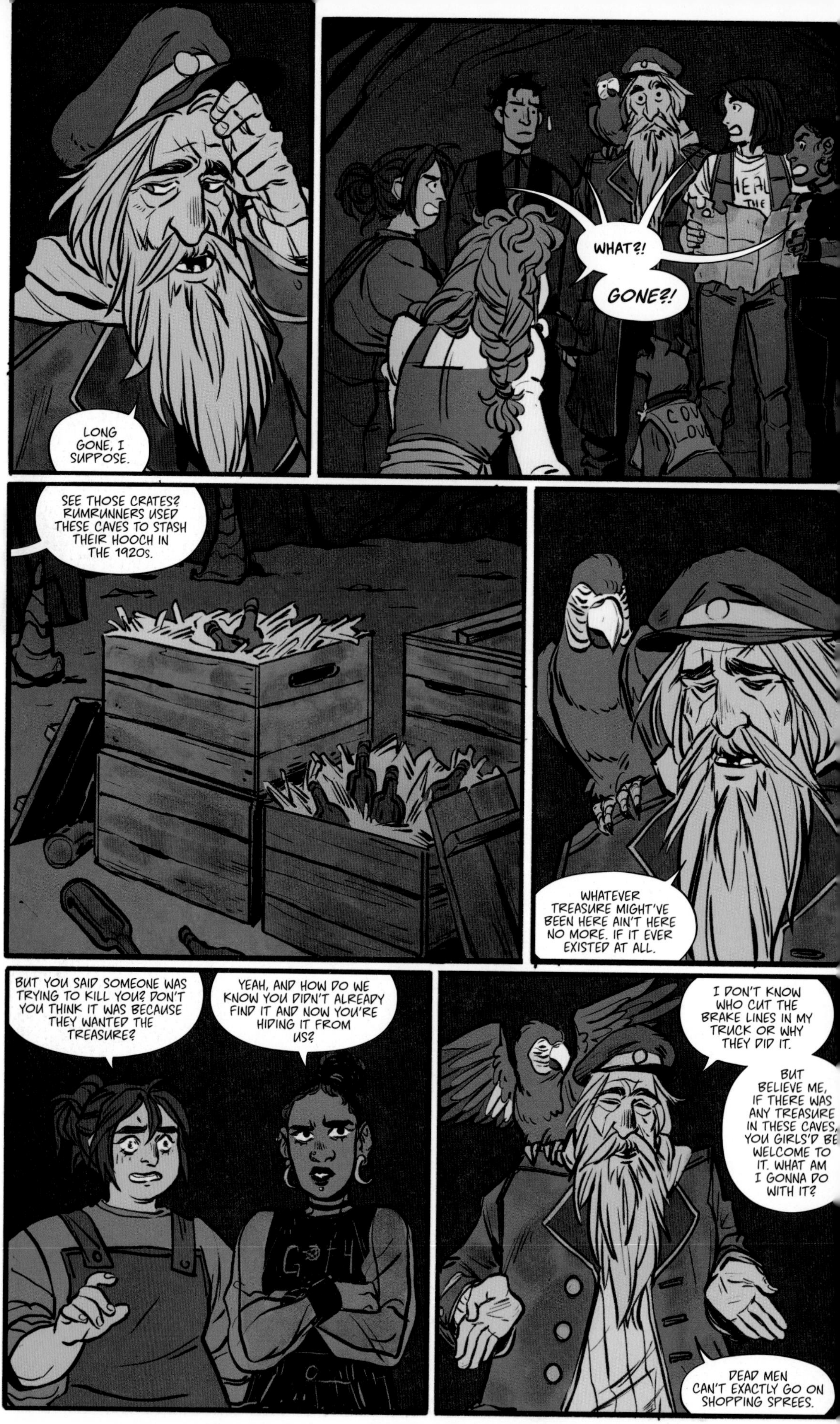
LONG GONE, I SUPPOSE.
WHAT?!
GONE?!
SEE THOSE CRATES? RUMRUNNERS USED THESE CAVES TO STASH THEIR HOOCH IN THE 1920s.
WHATEVER TREASURE MIGHT'VE BEEN HERE AIN'T HERE NO MORE. IF IT EVER EXISTED AT ALL.
BUT YOU SAID SOMEONE WAS TRYING TO KILL YOU? DON'T YOU THINK IT WAS BECAUSE THEY WANTED THE TREASURE?
YEAH, AND HOW DO WE KNOW YOU DIDN'T ALREADY FIND IT AND NOW YOU'RE HIDING IT FROM US?
I DON'T KNOW WHO CUT THE BRAKE LINES IN MY TRUCK OR WHY THEY DID IT.
BUT BELIEVE ME, IF THERE WAS ANY TREASURE IN THESE CAVES, YOU GIRLS'D BE WELCOME TO IT. WHAT AM I GONNA DO WITH IT?
DEAD MEN CAN'T EXACTLY GO ON SHOPPING SPREES.

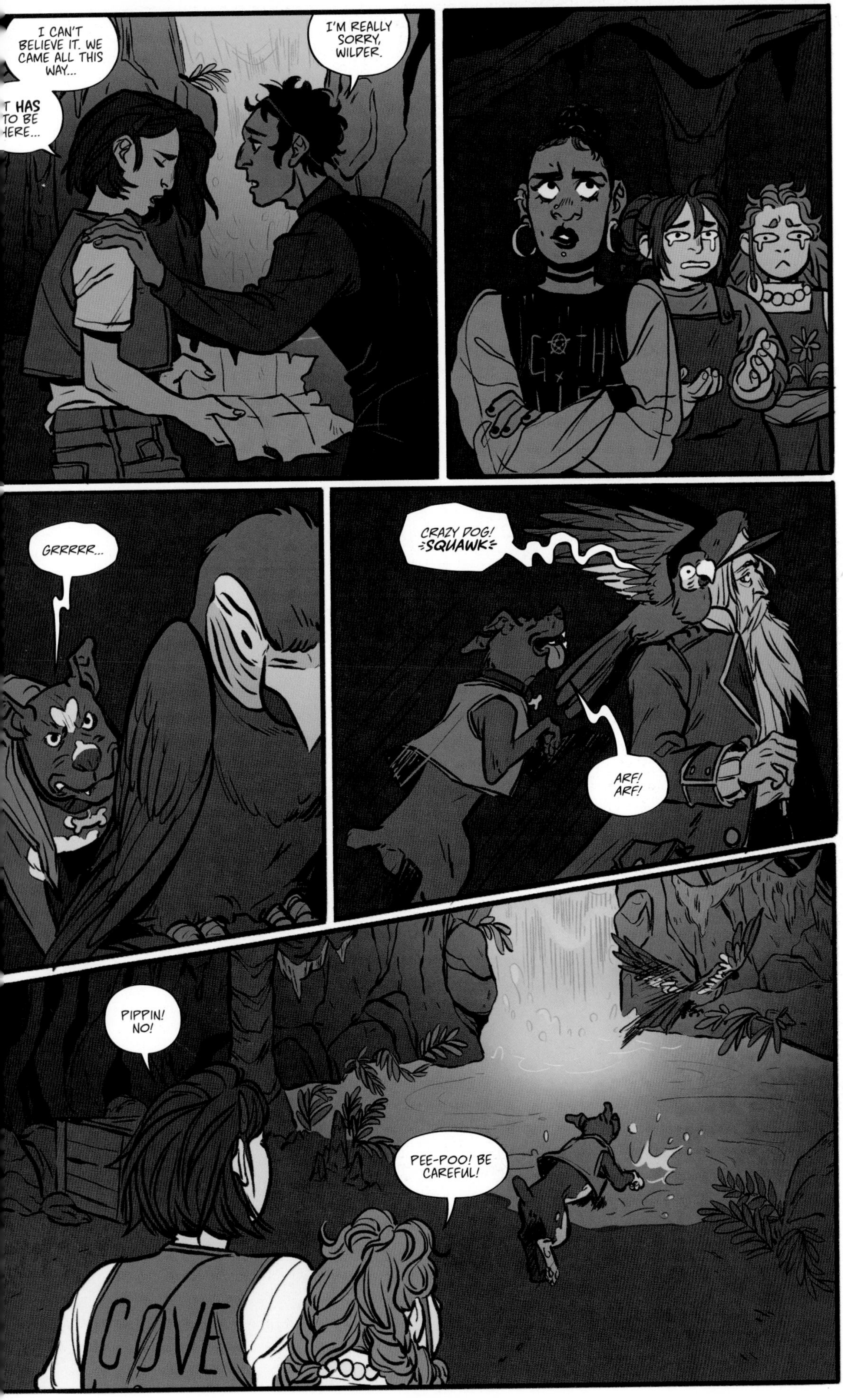
I CAN'T BELIEVE IT. WE CAME ALL THIS WAY...
T HAS TO BE HERE...
I'M REALLY SORRY, WILDER.
GRRRRR...
CRAZY DOG! SQUAWK
ARF! ARF!
PIPPIN! NO!
PEE-POO! BE CAREFUL!
COVE

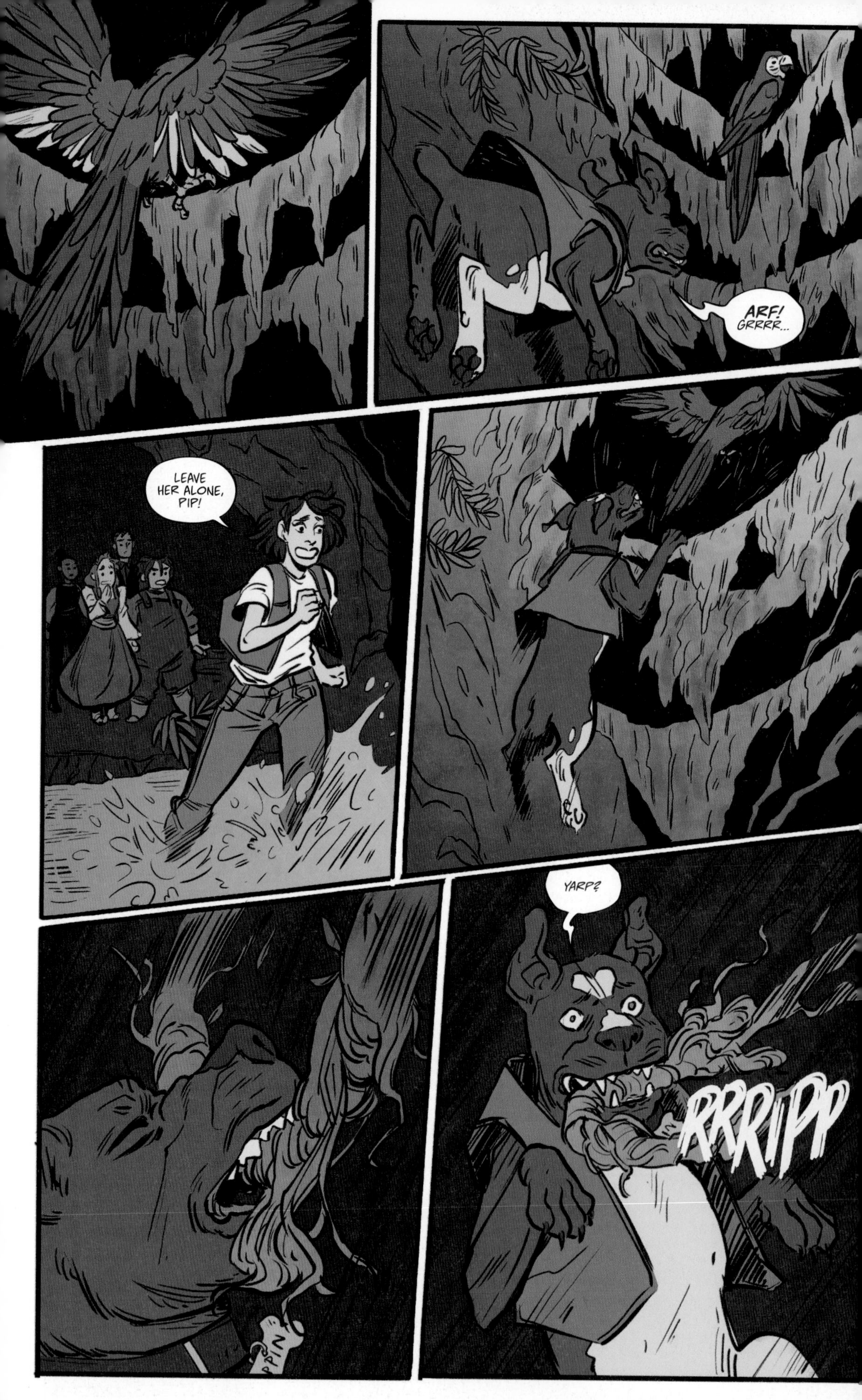
ARF! GRRRR...
LEAVE HER ALONE, PIP!
YARP?
RRRIPP

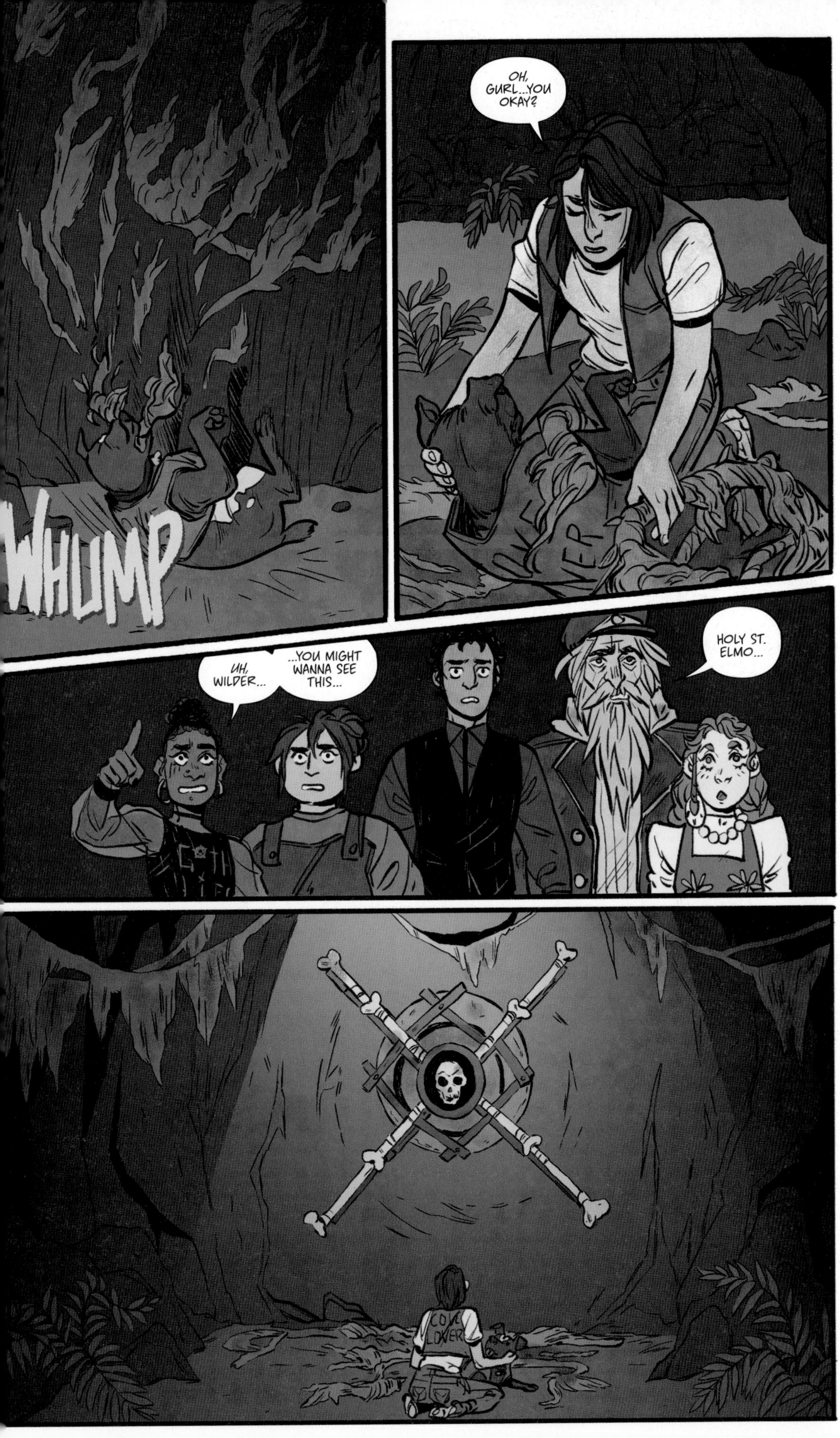
WHUMP
OH, GURL...YOU OKAY?
UH, WILDER...
...YOU MIGHT WANNA SEE THIS...
HOLY ST. ELMO...

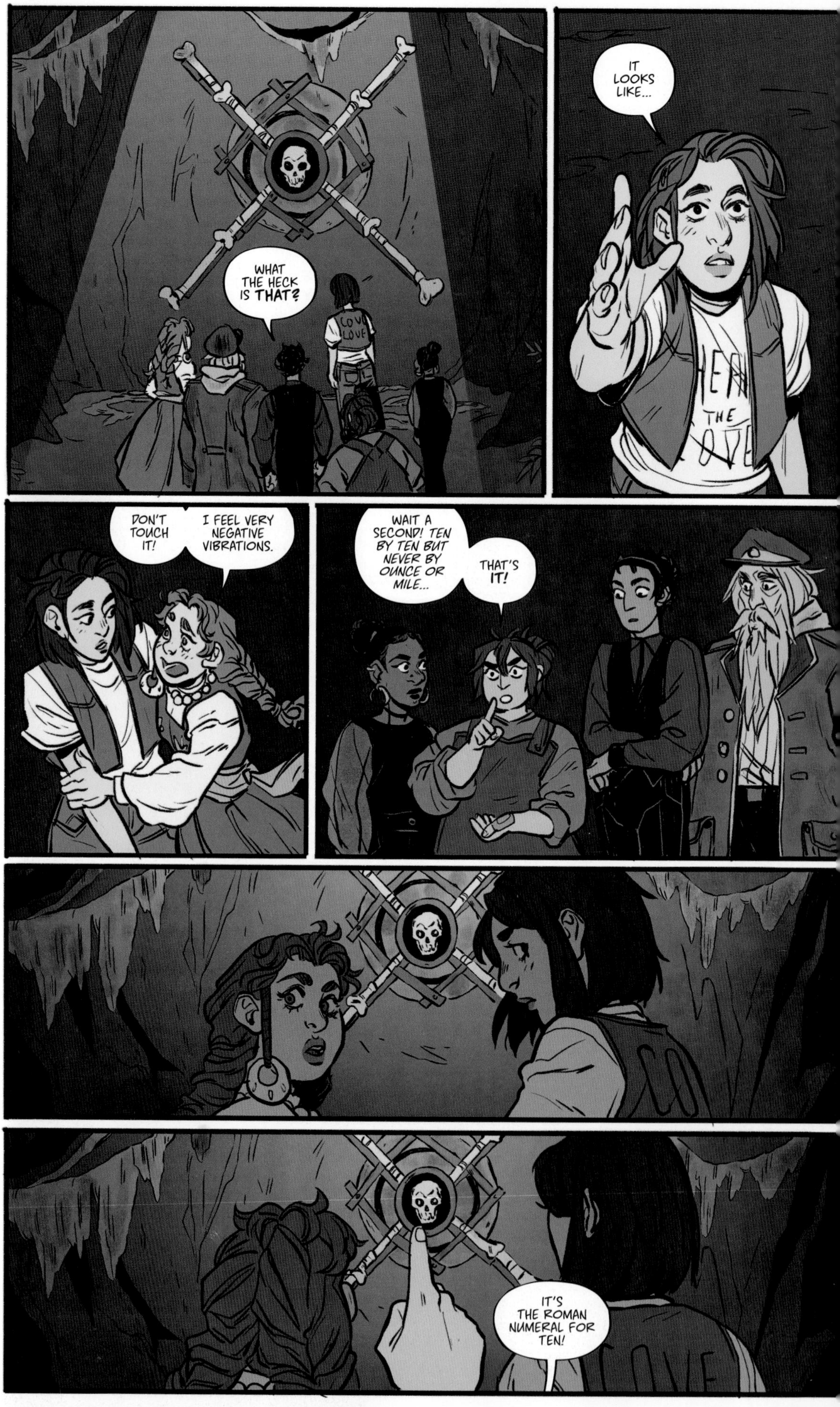
WHAT THE HECK IS THAT?
IT LOOKS LIKE...
DON'T TOUCH IT!
I FEEL VERY NEGATIVE VIBRATIONS.
WAIT A SECOND! TEN BY TEN BUT NEVER BY OUNCE OR MILE...
THAT'S IT!
IT'S THE ROMAN NUMERAL FOR TEN!

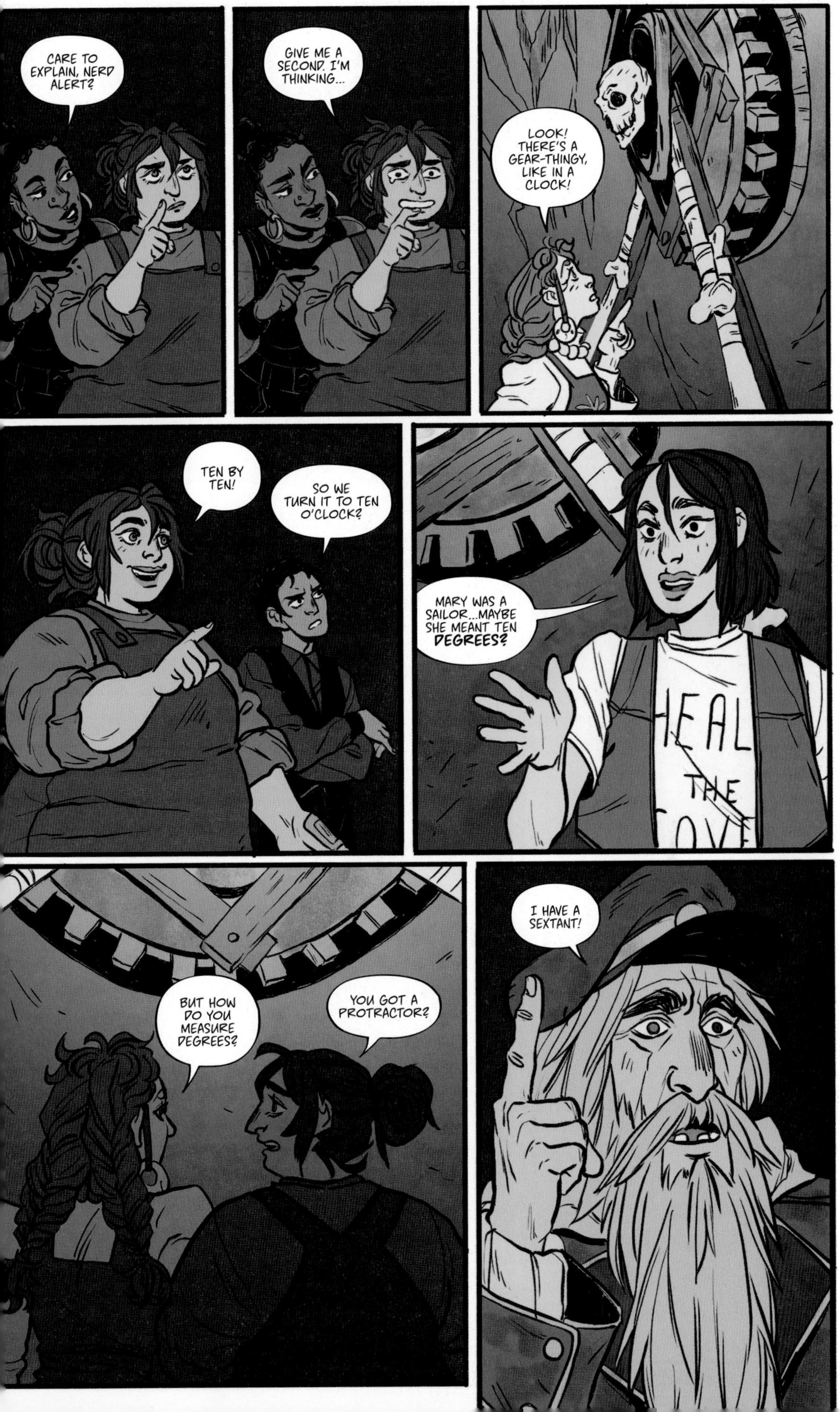
CARE TO EXPLAIN, NERD ALERT?
GIVE ME A SECOND. I'M THINKING...
LOOK! THERE'S A GEAR-THINGY, LIKE IN A CLOCK!
TEN BY TEN!
SO WE TURN IT TO TEN O'CLOCK?
MARY WAS A SAILOR...MAYBE SHE MEANT TEN DEGREES?
HEAL THE COVE
BUT HOW DO YOU MEASURE DEGREES?
YOU GOT A PROTRACTOR?
I HAVE A SEXTANT!

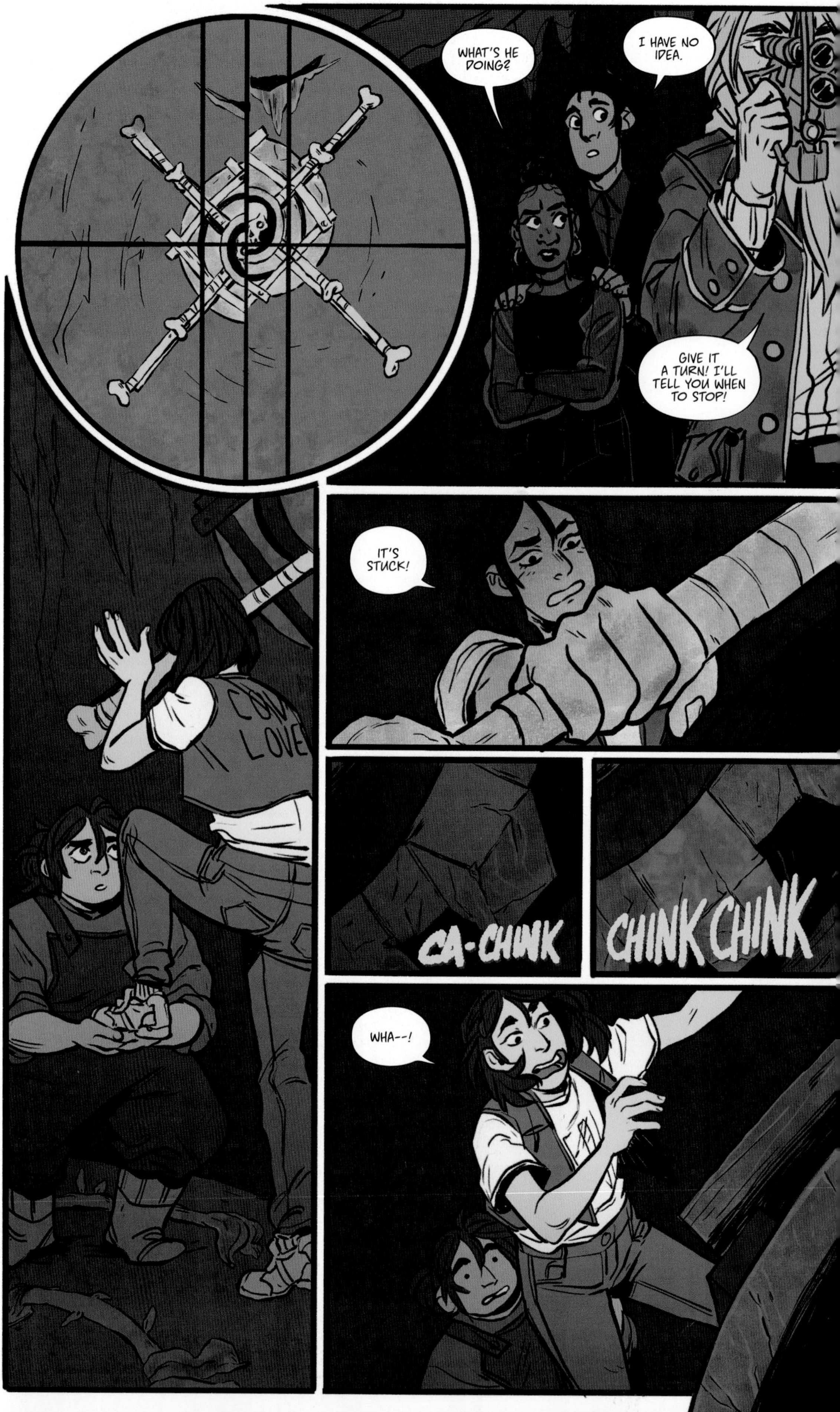
WHAT'S HE DOING?
I HAVE NO IDEA.
GIVE IT A TURN! I'LL TELL YOU WHEN TO STOP!
COW LOVE
IT'S STUCK!
CA-CHUNK
CHINK CHINK
WHA--!

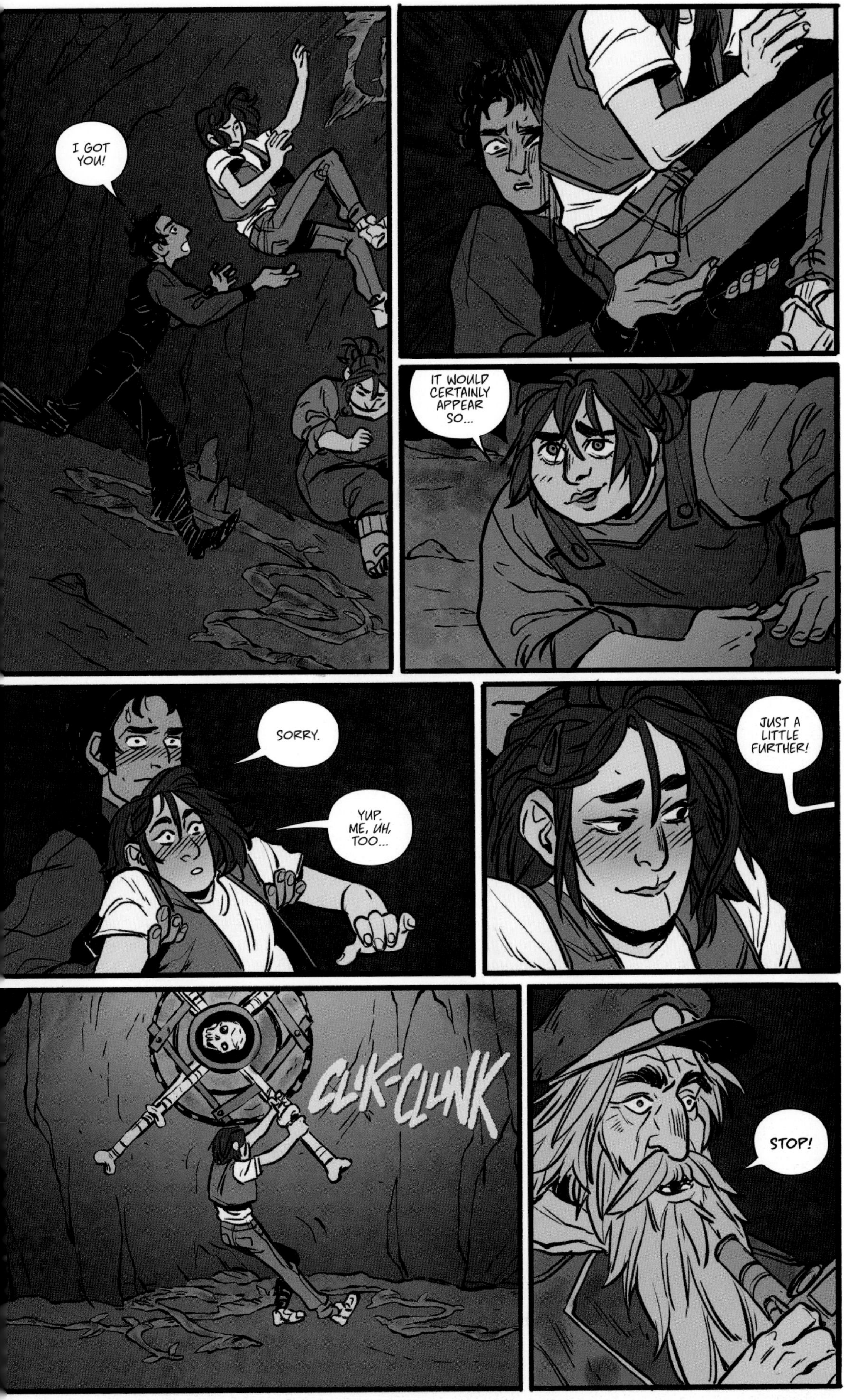
I GOT YOU!
IT WOULD CERTAINLY APPEAR SO...
SORRY.
YUP. ME, UH, TOO...
JUST A LITTLE FURTHER!
CLIK-CLUNK
STOP!

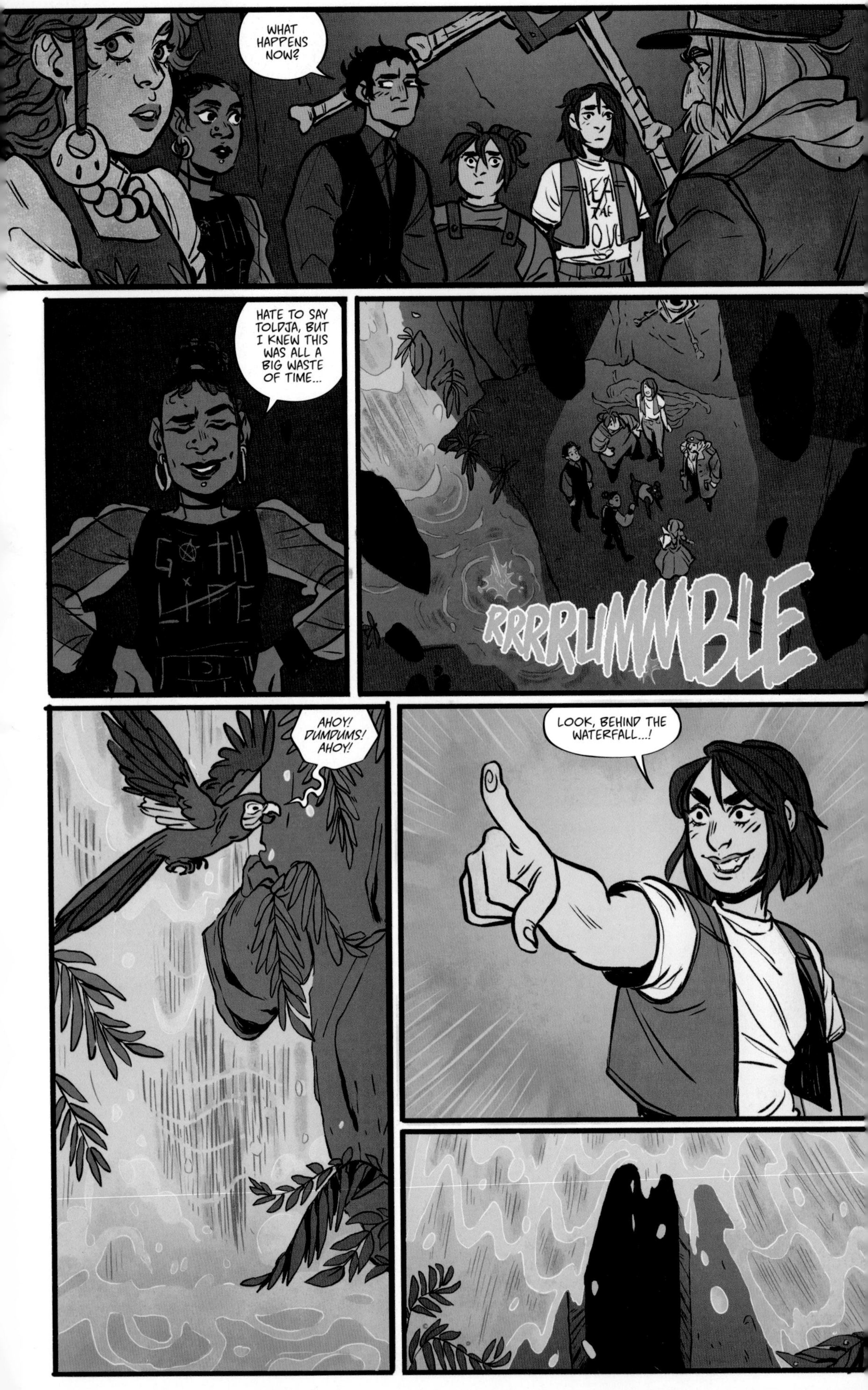

WHAT HAPPENS NOW?
HATE TO SAY TOLDJA, BUT I KNEW THIS WAS ALL A BIG WASTE OF TIME...
RRRRUMMBLE
AHOY! DUMDUMS! AHOY!
LOOK, BEHIND THE WATERFALL...!

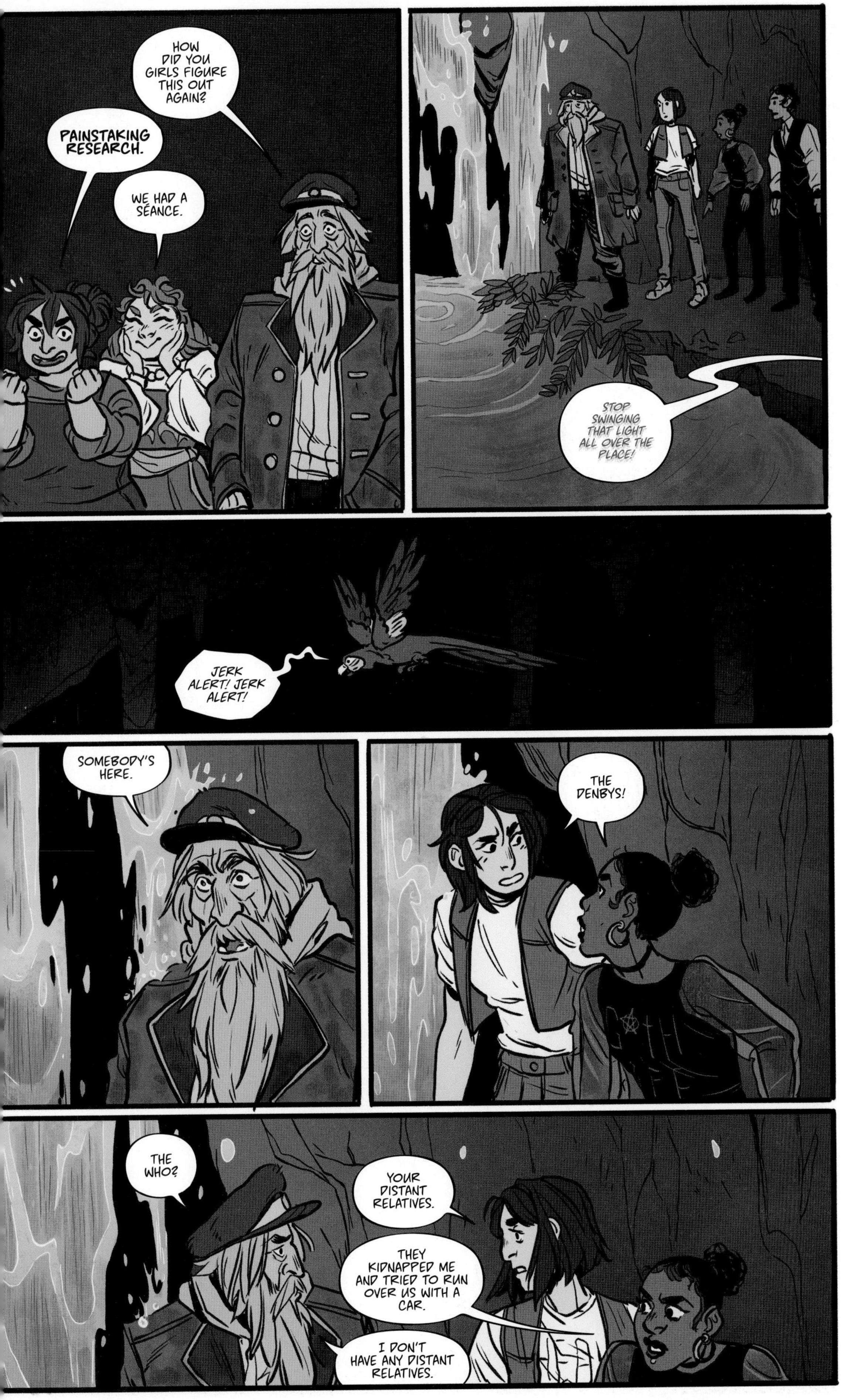
HOW DID YOU GIRLS FIGURE THIS OUT AGAIN?
PAINSTAKING RESEARCH.
WE HAD A SÉANCE.
STOP SWINGING THAT LIGHT ALL OVER THE PLACE!
JERK ALERT! JERK ALERT!
SOMEBODY'S HERE.
THE DENBYS!
THE WHO?
YOUR DISTANT RELATIVES.
THEY KIDNAPPED ME AND TRIED TO RUN OVER US WITH A CAR.
I DON'T HAVE ANY DISTANT RELATIVES.

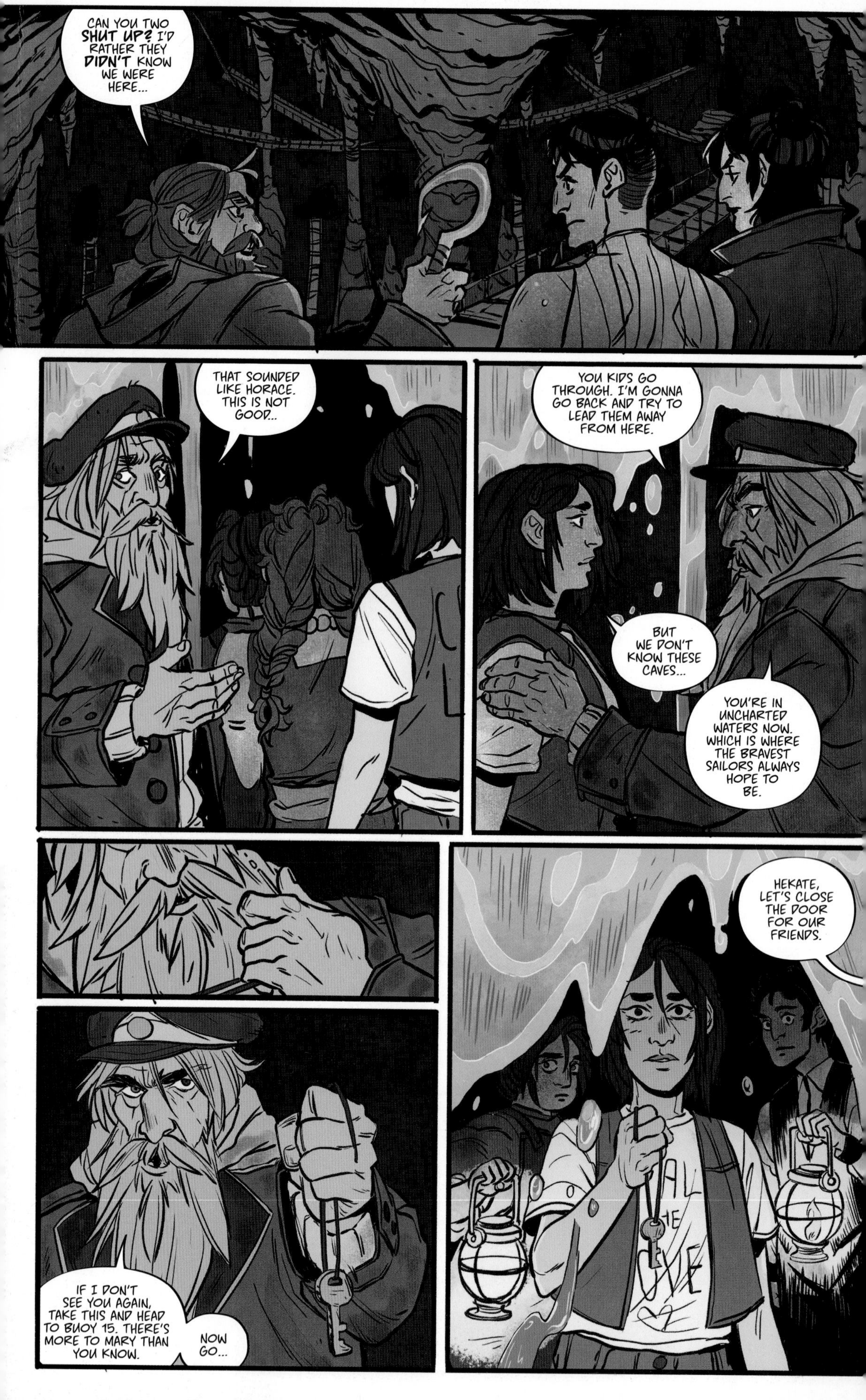
CAN YOU TWO **SHUT UP?** I'D RATHER THEY **DIDN'T** KNOW WE WERE HERE...
THAT SOUNDED LIKE HORACE. THIS IS NOT GOOD...
YOU KIDS GO THROUGH. I'M GONNA GO BACK AND TRY TO LEAD THEM AWAY FROM HERE.
BUT WE DON'T KNOW THESE CAVES...
YOU'RE IN UNCHARTED WATERS NOW. WHICH IS WHERE THE BRAVEST SAILORS ALWAYS HOPE TO BE.
IF I DON'T SEE YOU AGAIN, TAKE THIS AND HEAD TO BUOY 15. THERE'S MORE TO MARY THAN YOU KNOW.
NOW GO...
HEKATE, LET'S CLOSE THE DOOR FOR OUR FRIENDS.

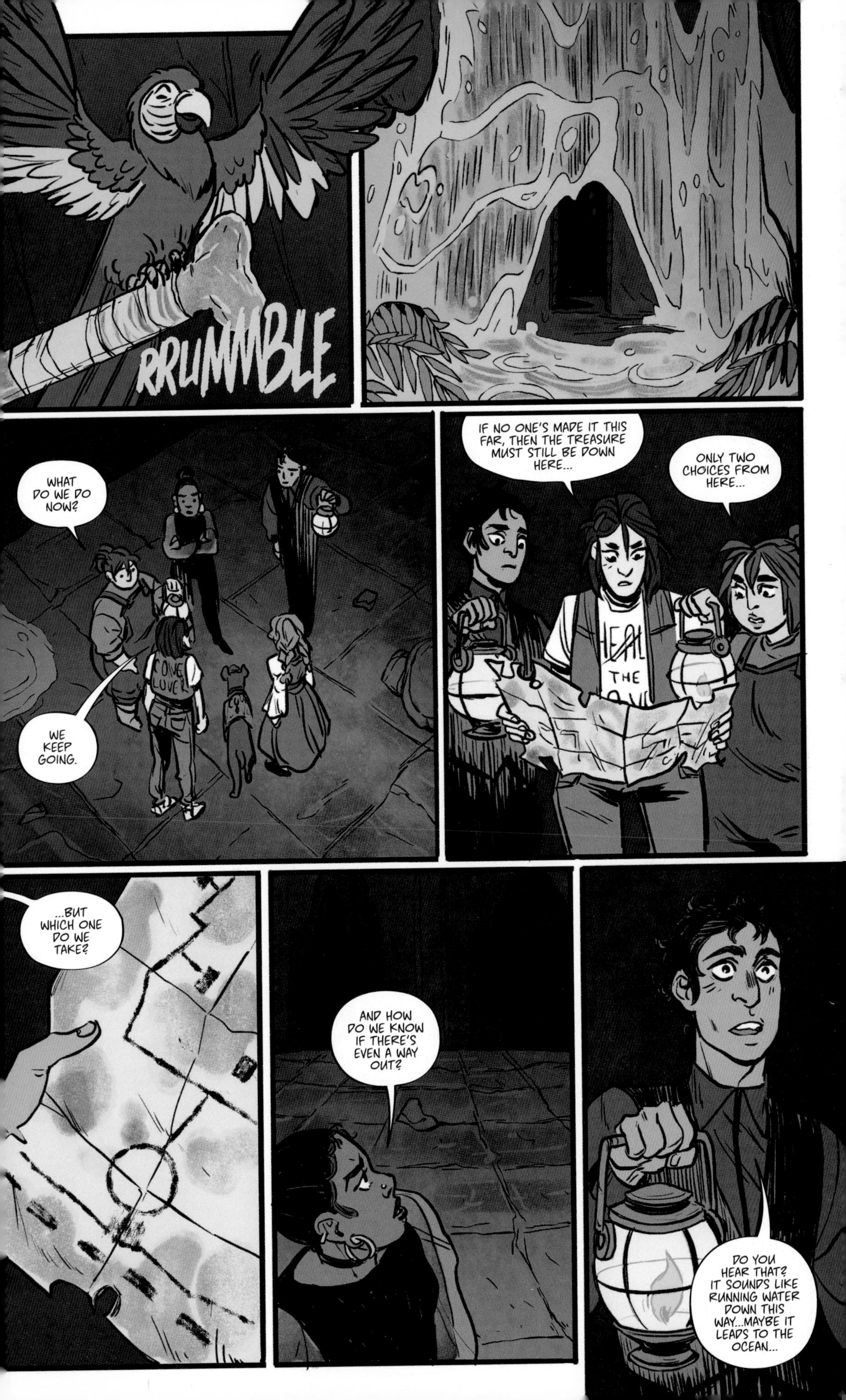
RRUMMBLE
WHAT DO WE DO NOW?
WE KEEP GOING.
IF NO ONE'S MADE IT THIS FAR, THEN THE TREASURE MUST STILL BE DOWN HERE...
ONLY TWO CHOICES FROM HERE...
...BUT WHICH ONE DO WE TAKE?
AND HOW DO WE KNOW IF THERE'S EVEN A WAY OUT?
DO YOU HEAR THAT? IT SOUNDS LIKE RUNNING WATER DOWN THIS WAY...MAYBE IT LEADS TO THE OCEAN...

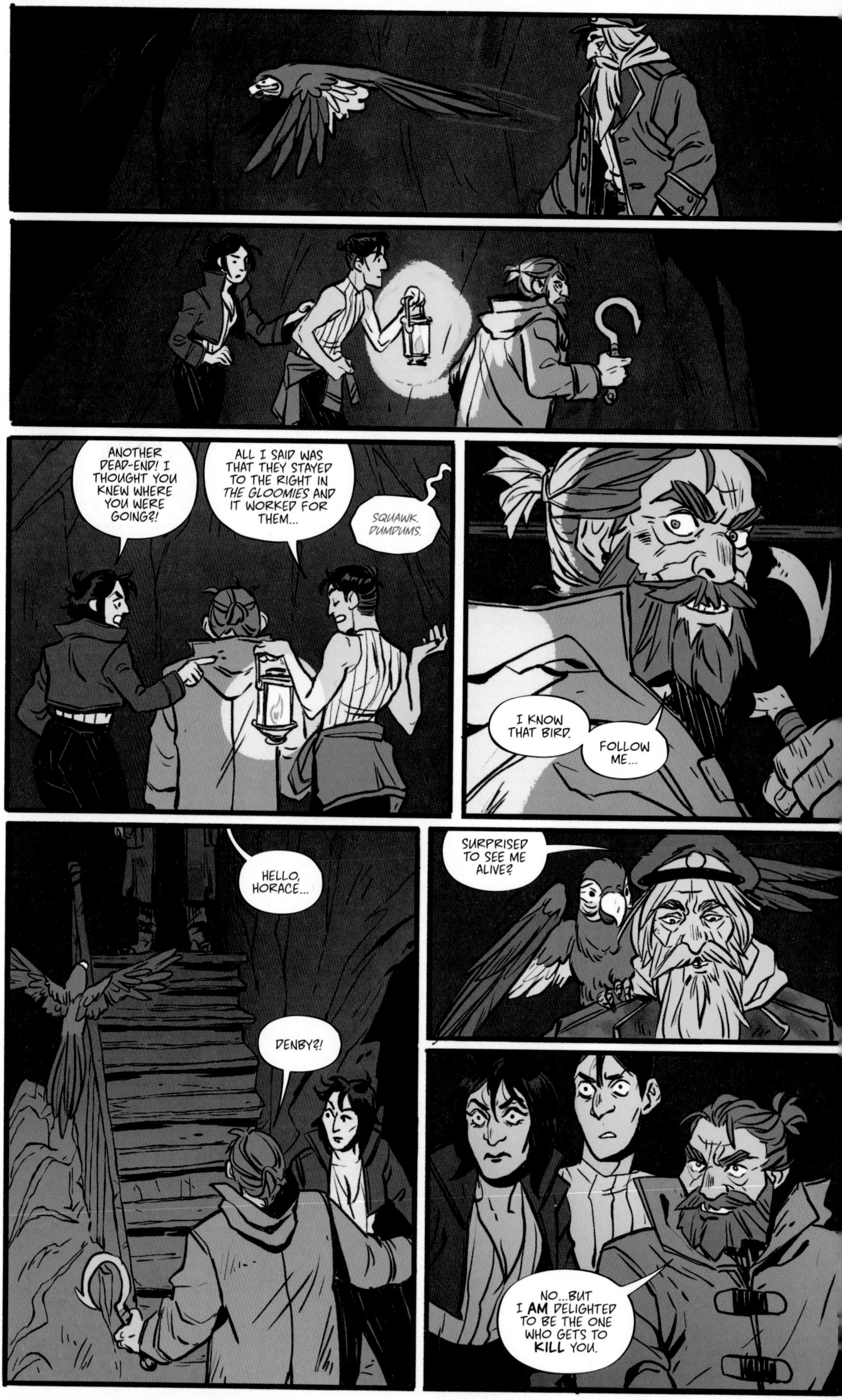
ANOTHER DEAD-END! I THOUGHT YOU KNEW WHERE YOU WERE GOING?!
ALL I SAID WAS THAT THEY STAYED TO THE RIGHT IN *THE GLOOMIES* AND IT WORKED FOR THEM...
SQUAWK. DUMDUMS.
I KNOW THAT BIRD.
FOLLOW ME...
HELLO, HORACE...
DENBY?!
SURPRISED TO SEE ME ALIVE?
NO...BUT I **AM** DELIGHTED TO BE THE ONE WHO GETS TO **KILL** YOU.

CHAPTER
VI

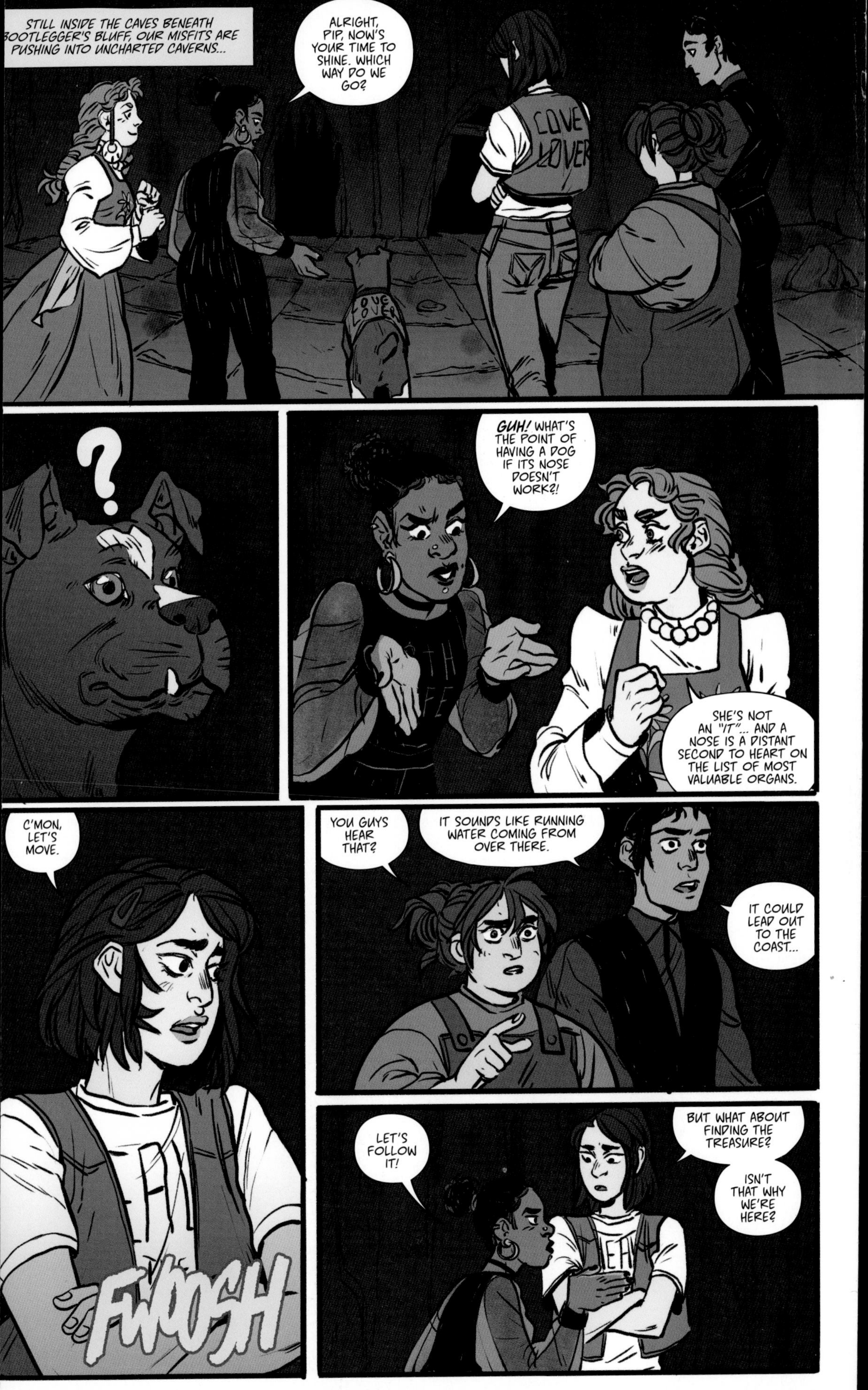
STILL INSIDE THE CAVES BENEATH BOOTLEGGER'S BLUFF, OUR MISFITS ARE PUSHING INTO UNCHARTED CAVERNS...
ALRIGHT, PIP, NOW'S YOUR TIME TO SHINE. WHICH WAY DO WE GO?
COVE LOVER
?
GUH! WHAT'S THE POINT OF HAVING A DOG IF ITS NOSE DOESN'T WORK?!
SHE'S NOT AN "IT"... AND A NOSE IS A DISTANT SECOND TO HEART ON THE LIST OF MOST VALUABLE ORGANS.
C'MON, LET'S MOVE.
YOU GUYS HEAR THAT?
IT SOUNDS LIKE RUNNING WATER COMING FROM OVER THERE.
IT COULD LEAD OUT TO THE COAST...
FWOOSH
LET'S FOLLOW IT!
BUT WHAT ABOUT FINDING THE TREASURE?
ISN'T THAT WHY WE'RE HERE?

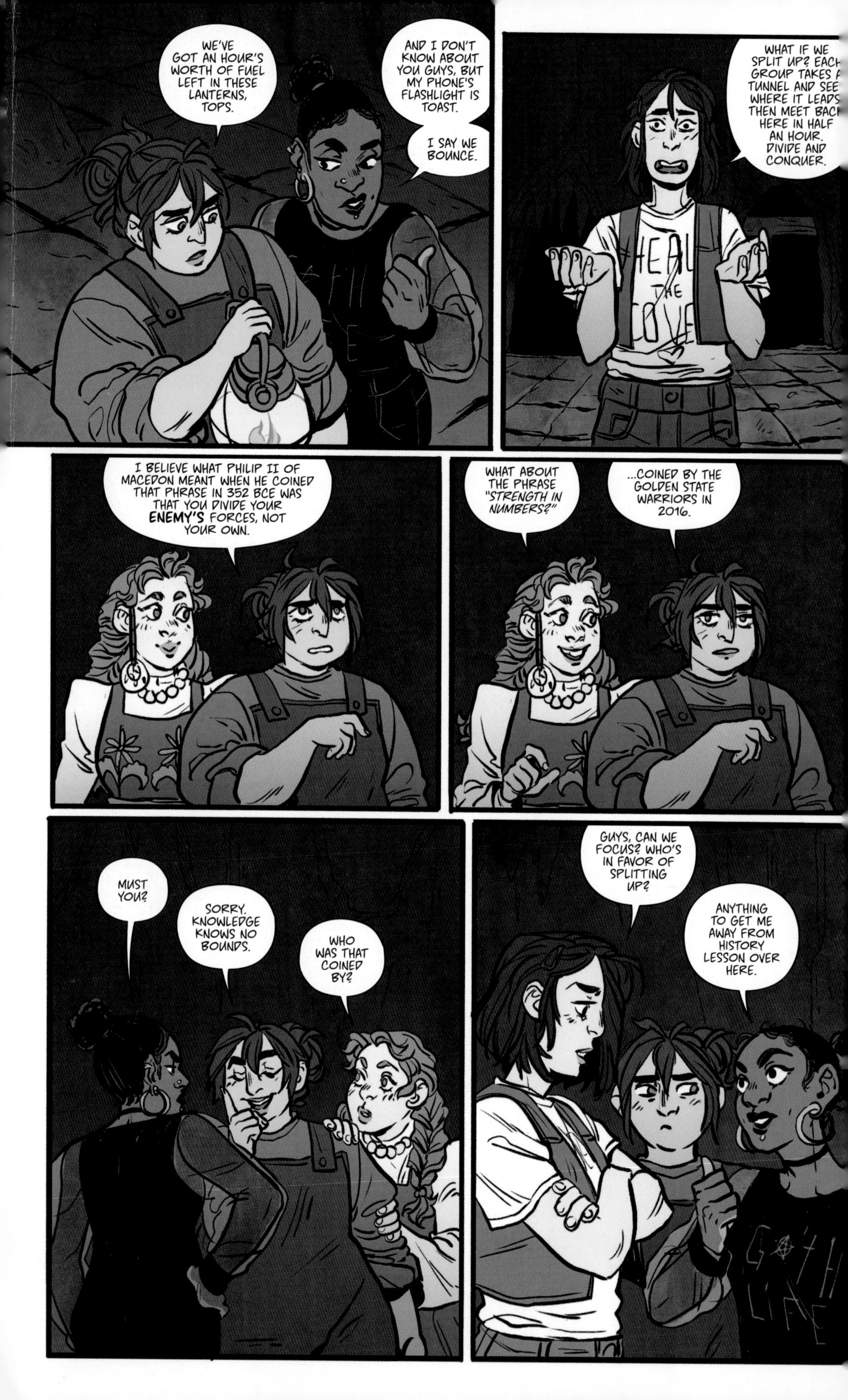
WE'VE GOT AN HOUR'S WORTH OF FUEL LEFT IN THESE LANTERNS, TOPS.
AND I DON'T KNOW ABOUT YOU GUYS, BUT MY PHONE'S FLASHLIGHT IS TOAST.
I SAY WE BOUNCE.
WHAT IF WE SPLIT UP? EACH GROUP TAKES A TUNNEL AND SEES WHERE IT LEADS, THEN MEET BACK HERE IN HALF AN HOUR. DIVIDE AND CONQUER.
I BELIEVE WHAT PHILIP II OF MACEDON MEANT WHEN HE COINED THAT PHRASE IN 352 BCE WAS THAT YOU DIVIDE YOUR **ENEMY'S** FORCES, NOT YOUR OWN.
WHAT ABOUT THE PHRASE *"STRENGTH IN NUMBERS?"*
...COINED BY THE GOLDEN STATE WARRIORS IN 2016.
MUST YOU?
SORRY. KNOWLEDGE KNOWS NO BOUNDS.
WHO WAS THAT COINED BY?
GUYS, CAN WE FOCUS? WHO'S IN FAVOR OF SPLITTING UP?
ANYTHING TO GET ME AWAY FROM HISTORY LESSON OVER HERE.

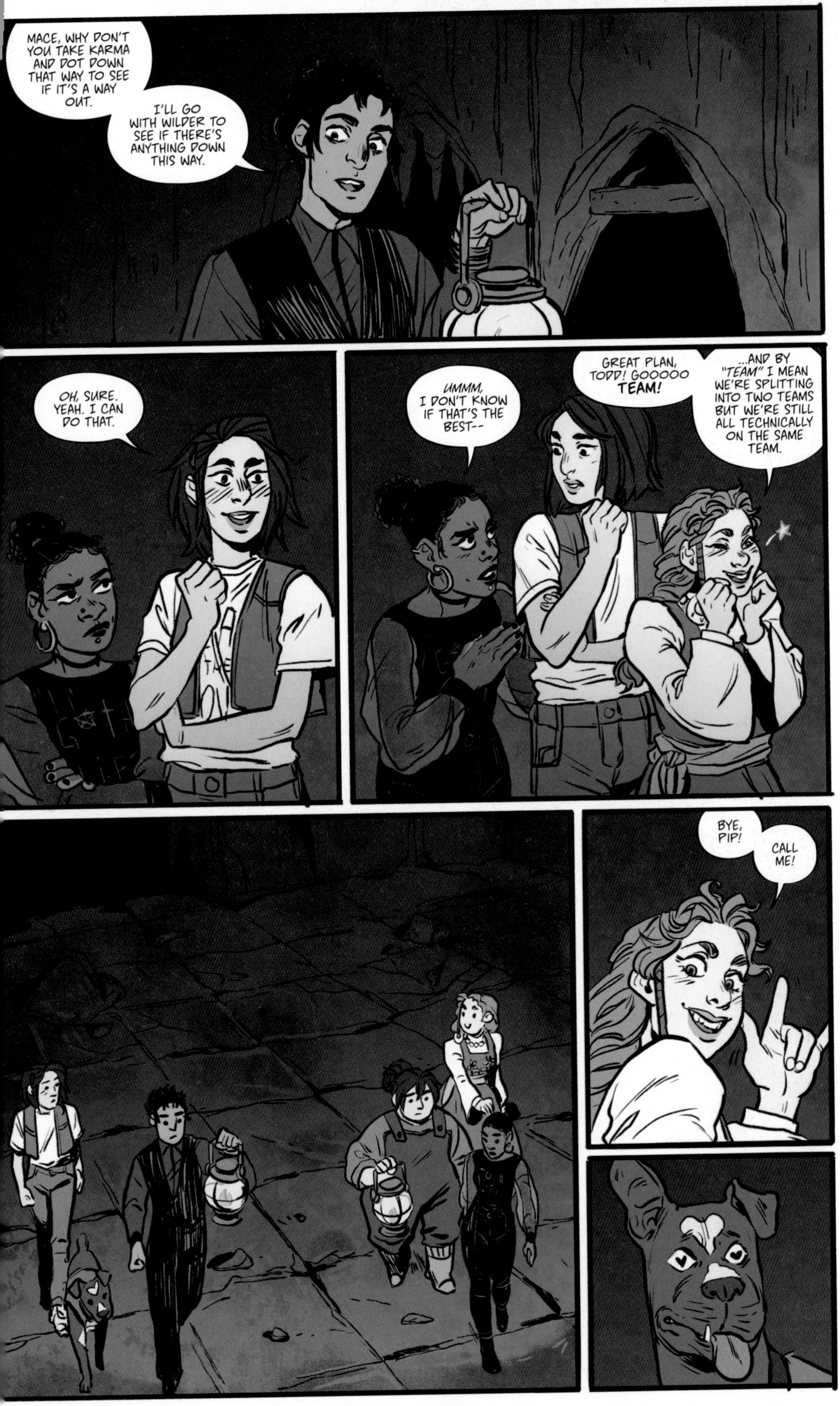
MACE, WHY DON'T YOU TAKE KARMA AND DOT DOWN THAT WAY TO SEE IF IT'S A WAY OUT.
I'LL GO WITH WILDER TO SEE IF THERE'S ANYTHING DOWN THIS WAY.
OH, SURE. YEAH. I CAN DO THAT.
UMMM, I DON'T KNOW IF THAT'S THE BEST--
GREAT PLAN, TODD! GOOOOO TEAM!
...AND BY "TEAM" I MEAN WE'RE SPLITTING INTO TWO TEAMS BUT WE'RE STILL ALL TECHNICALLY ON THE SAME TEAM.
BYE, PIP!
CALL ME!

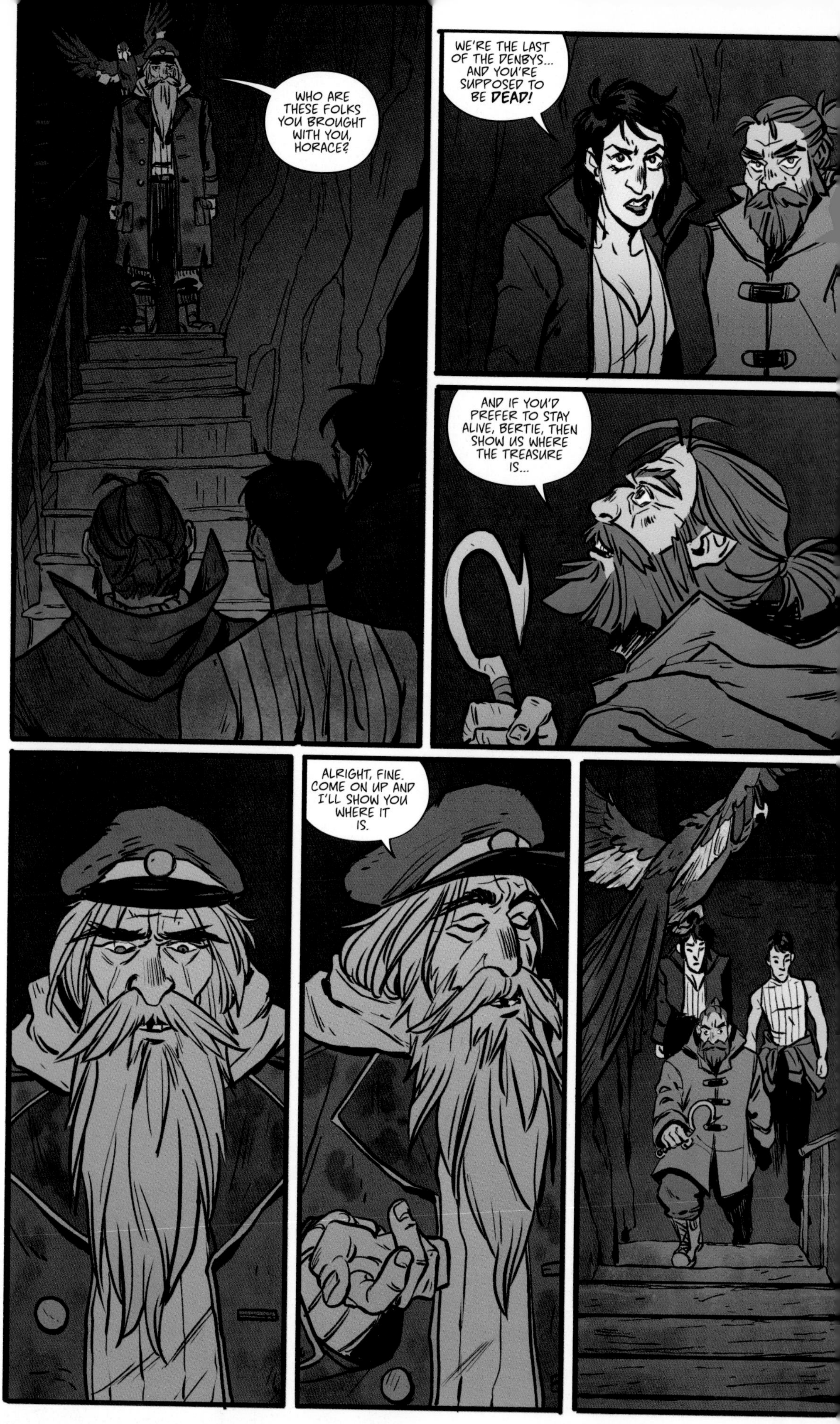
WHO ARE THESE FOLKS YOU BROUGHT WITH YOU, HORACE?
WE'RE THE LAST OF THE DENBYS... AND YOU'RE SUPPOSED TO BE **DEAD!**
AND IF YOU'D PREFER TO STAY ALIVE, BERTIE, THEN SHOW US WHERE THE TREASURE IS...
ALRIGHT, FINE. COME ON UP AND I'LL SHOW YOU WHERE IT IS.

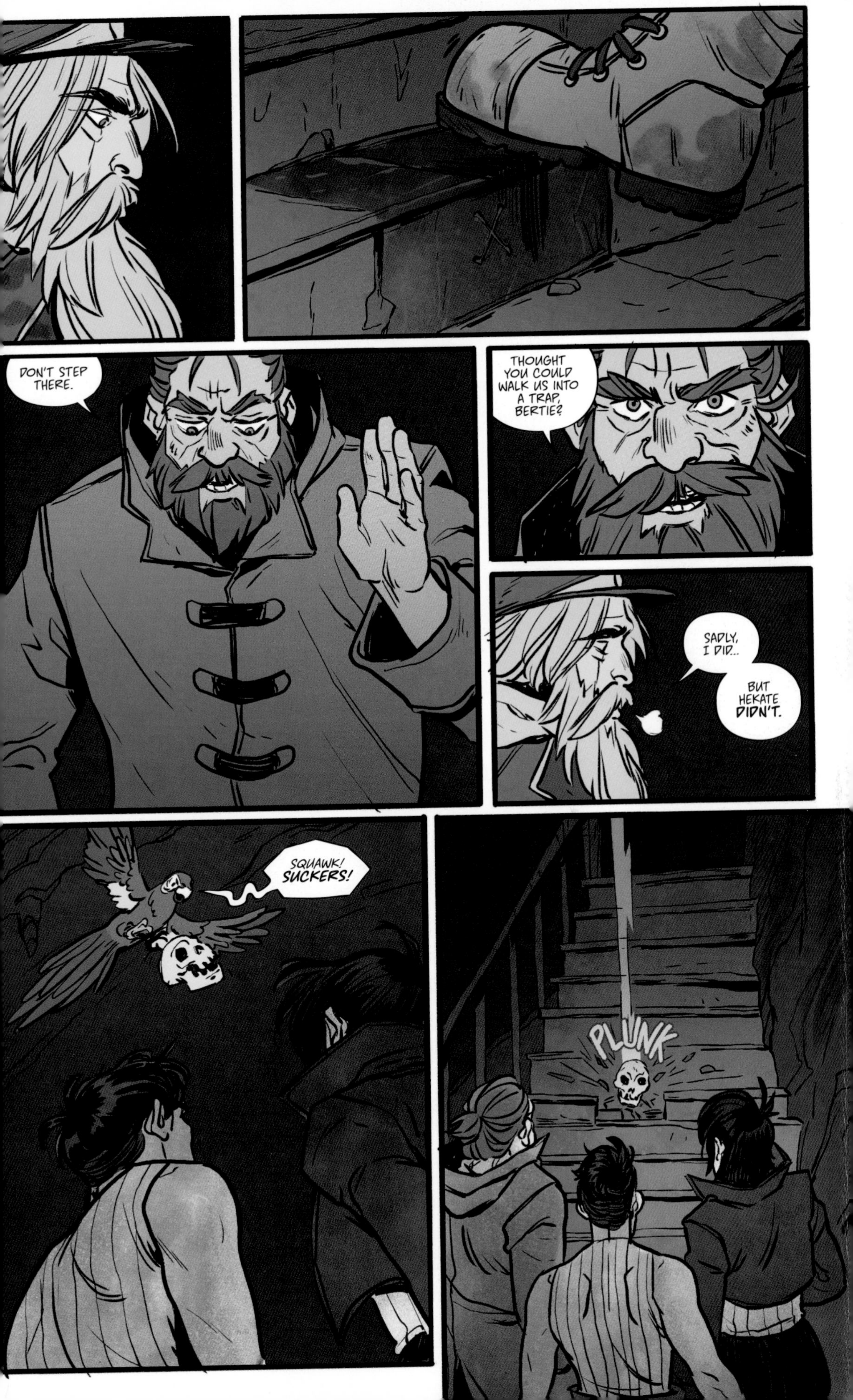
DON'T STEP THERE.
THOUGHT YOU COULD WALK US INTO A TRAP, BERTIE?
SADLY, I DID...
BUT HEKATE DIDN'T.
SQUAWK! SUCKERS!
PLUNK

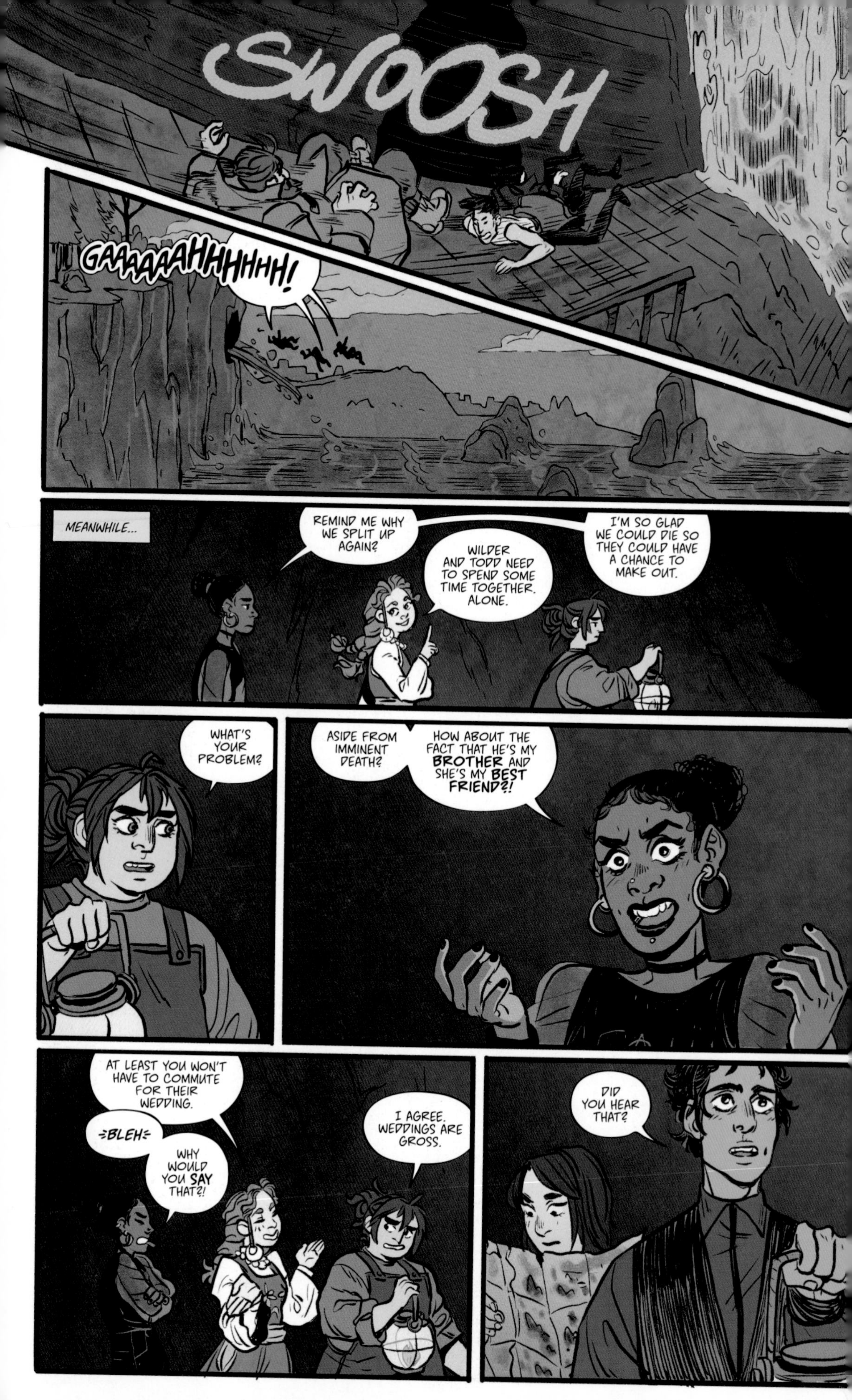
SWOOSH
GAAAAAAHHHHHH!
MEANWHILE...
REMIND ME WHY WE SPLIT UP AGAIN?
WILDER AND TODD NEED TO SPEND SOME TIME TOGETHER. ALONE.
I'M SO GLAD WE COULD DIE SO THEY COULD HAVE A CHANCE TO MAKE OUT.
WHAT'S YOUR PROBLEM?
ASIDE FROM IMMINENT DEATH?
HOW ABOUT THE FACT THAT HE'S MY BROTHER AND SHE'S MY BEST FRIEND?!
AT LEAST YOU WON'T HAVE TO COMMUTE FOR THEIR WEDDING.
BLEH
WHY WOULD YOU SAY THAT?!
I AGREE. WEDDINGS ARE GROSS.
DID YOU HEAR THAT?

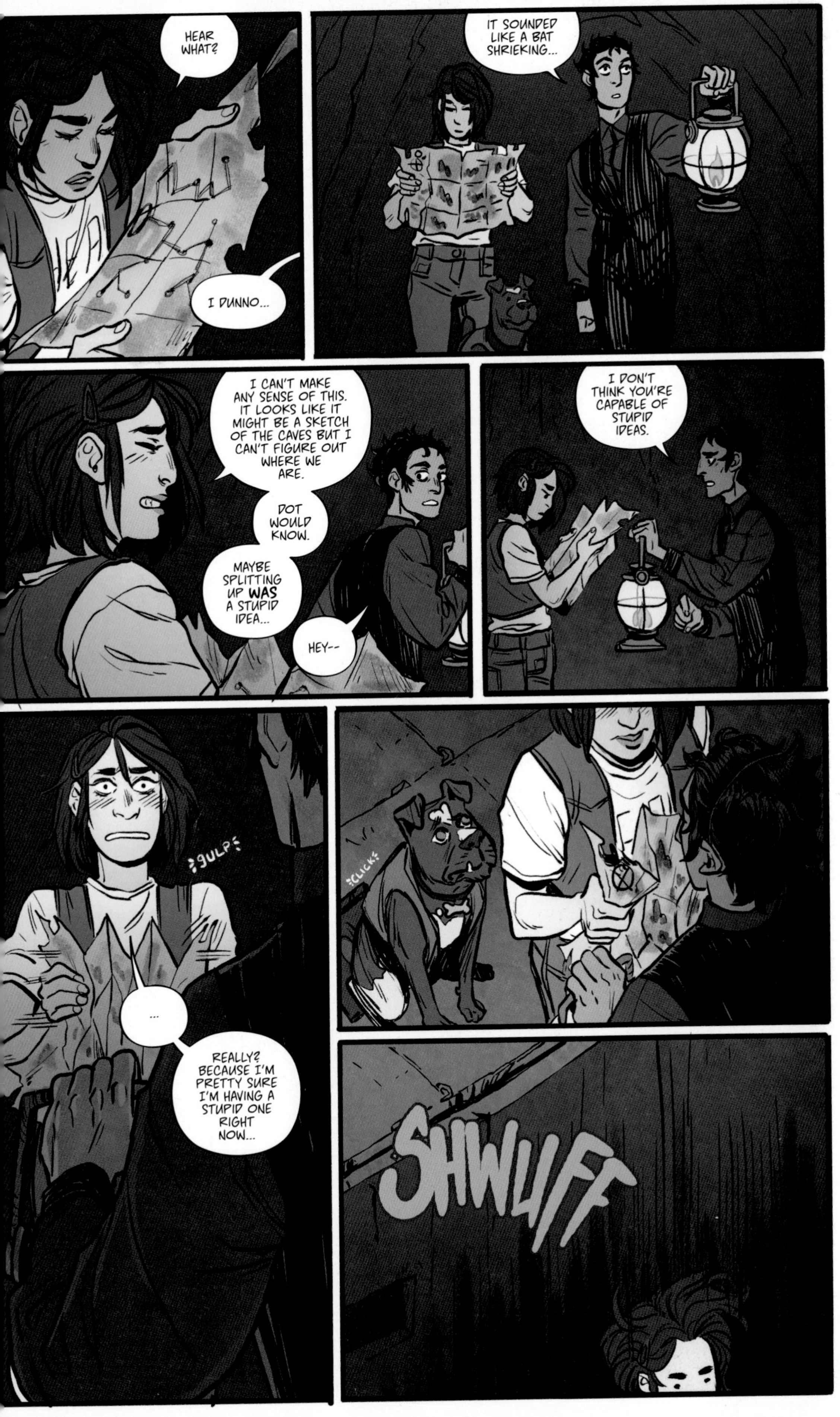
HEAR WHAT?
I DUNNO...
IT SOUNDED LIKE A BAT SHRIEKING...
I CAN'T MAKE ANY SENSE OF THIS. IT LOOKS LIKE IT MIGHT BE A SKETCH OF THE CAVES BUT I CAN'T FIGURE OUT WHERE WE ARE.
DOT WOULD KNOW.
MAYBE SPLITTING UP WAS A STUPID IDEA...
HEY--
I DON'T THINK YOU'RE CAPABLE OF STUPID IDEAS.
GULP
...
REALLY? BECAUSE I'M PRETTY SURE I'M HAVING A STUPID ONE RIGHT NOW...
CLICK
SHWUFF

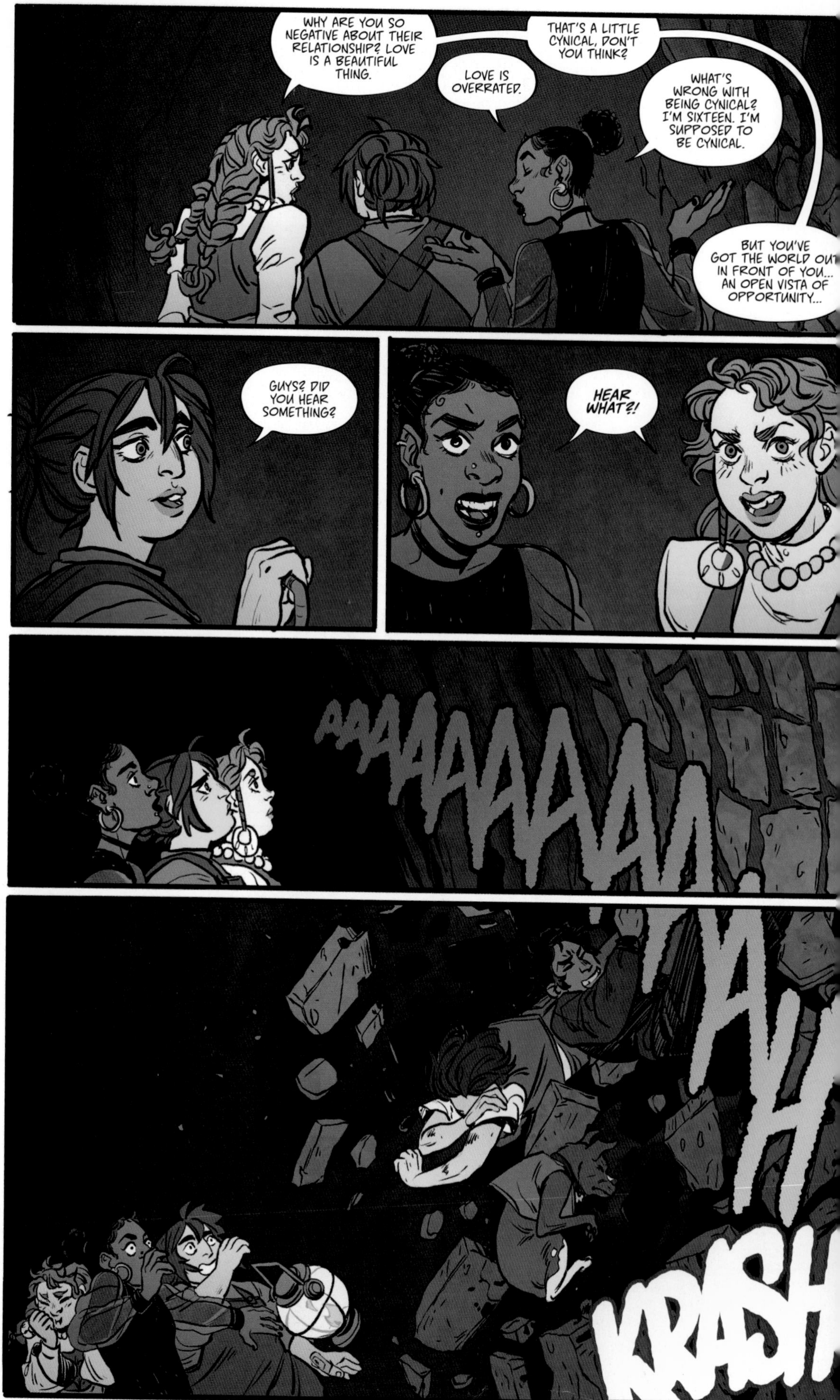

WHY ARE YOU SO NEGATIVE ABOUT THEIR RELATIONSHIP? LOVE IS A BEAUTIFUL THING.
LOVE IS OVERRATED.
THAT'S A LITTLE CYNICAL, DON'T YOU THINK?
WHAT'S WRONG WITH BEING CYNICAL? I'M SIXTEEN. I'M SUPPOSED TO BE CYNICAL.
BUT YOU'VE GOT THE WORLD OUT IN FRONT OF YOU... AN OPEN VISTA OF OPPORTUNITY...
GUYS? DID YOU HEAR SOMETHING?
HEAR WHAT?!
AAAAAAAAAA
AH
KRASH

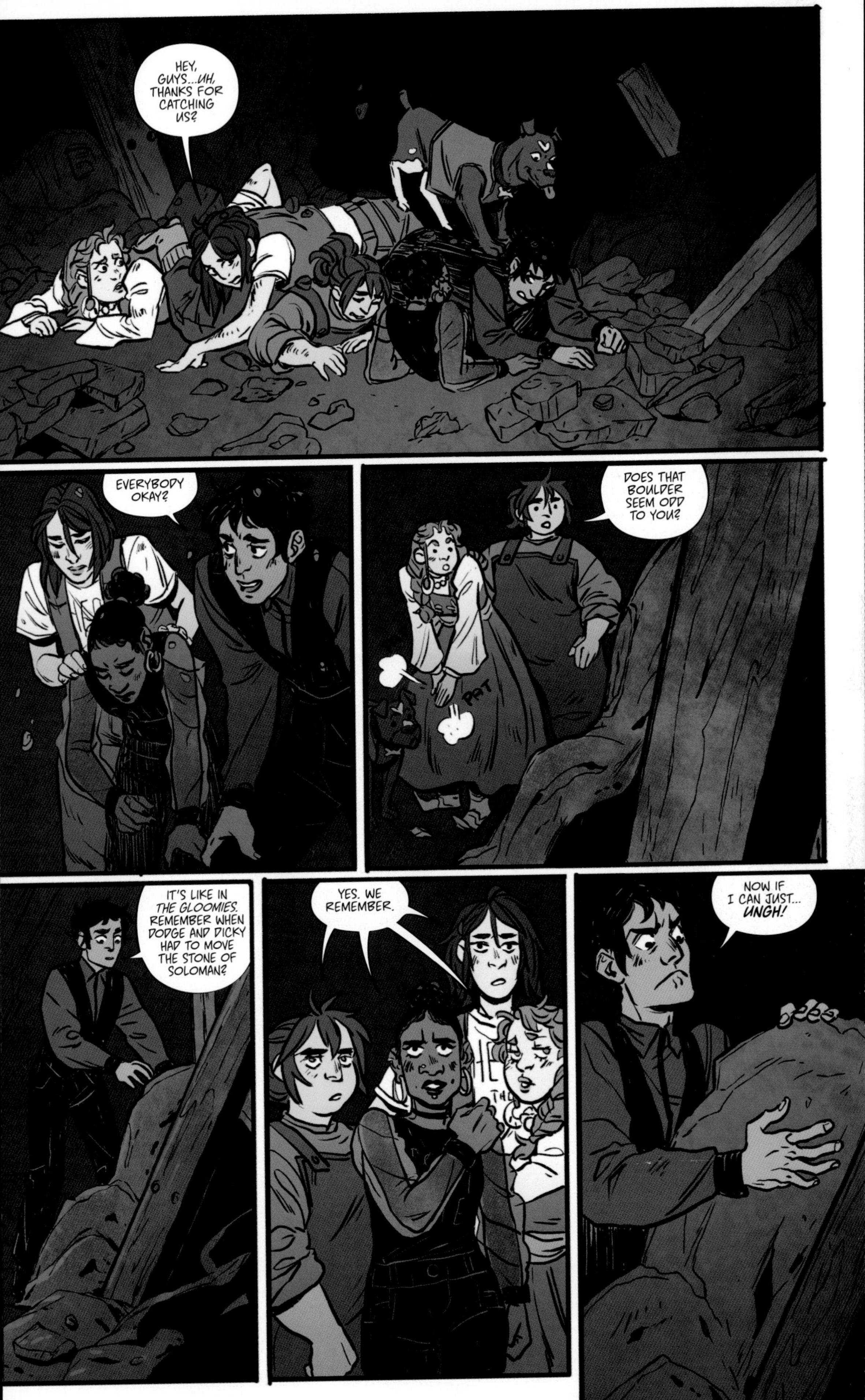
HEY, GUYS...UH, THANKS FOR CATCHING US?
EVERYBODY OKAY?
DOES THAT BOULDER SEEM ODD TO YOU?
PAT
IT'S LIKE IN THE GLOOMIES. REMEMBER WHEN DODGE AND DICKY HAD TO MOVE THE STONE OF SOLOMAN?
YES. WE REMEMBER.
NOW IF I CAN JUST... UNGH!

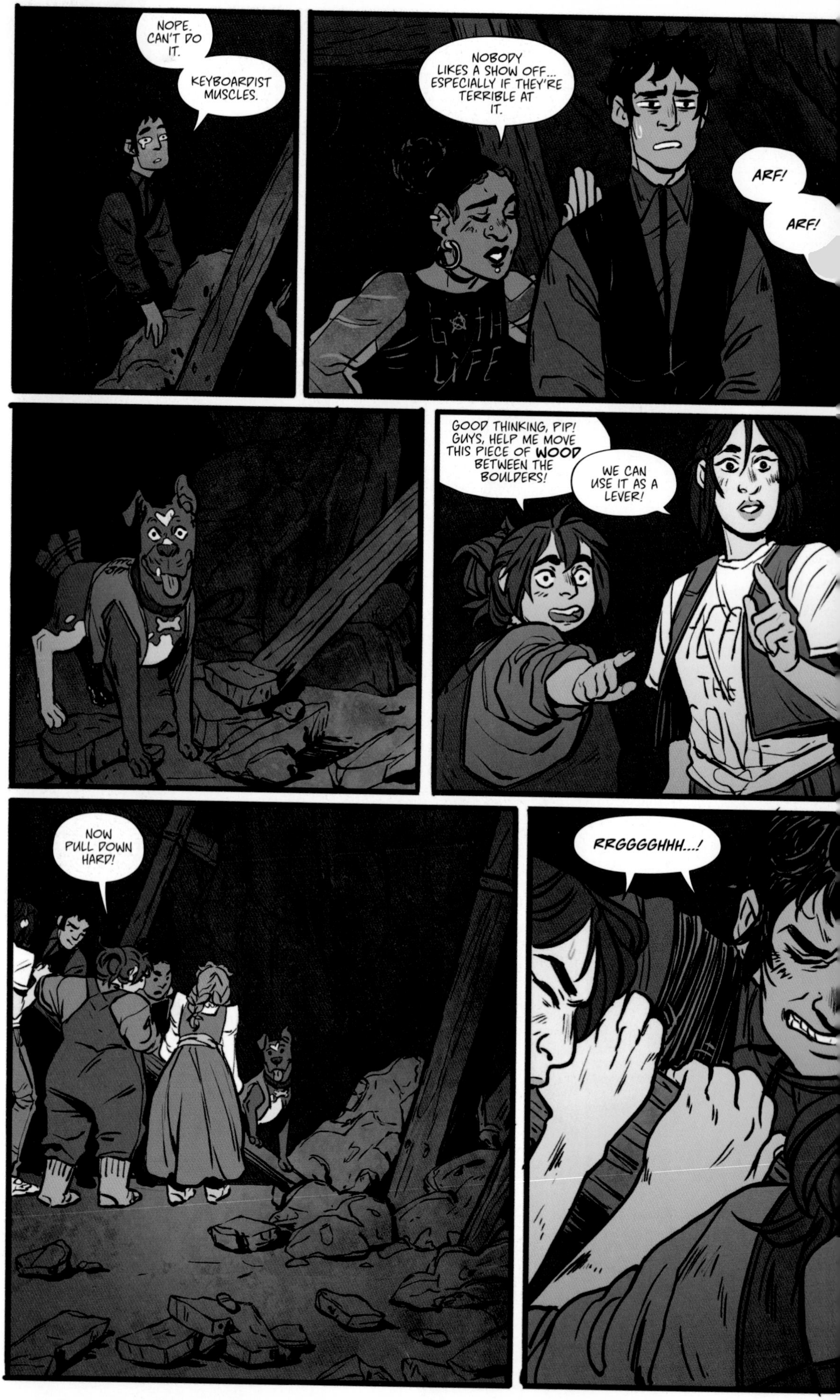
NOPE. CAN'T DO IT.
KEYBOARDIST MUSCLES.
NOBODY LIKES A SHOW OFF... ESPECIALLY IF THEY'RE TERRIBLE AT IT.
ARF!
ARF!
GOOD THINKING, PIP! GUYS, HELP ME MOVE THIS PIECE OF **WOOD** BETWEEN THE BOULDERS!
WE CAN USE IT AS A LEVER!
NOW PULL DOWN HARD!
RRGGGGHHH...!

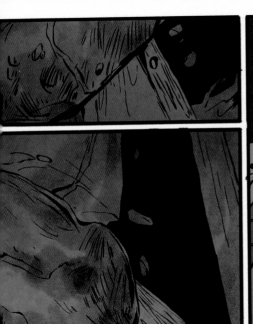

THAT WAS PRETTY FIERCE, D.

THANKS.

I SAW WONDER WOMAN SIX TIMES.

THERE'S SOMETHING HERE...

GAH! WHAT IS THAT?!

I THINK IT'S A CATAMOUNT SKULL.

MACE, BRING THE LIGHT CLOSER...

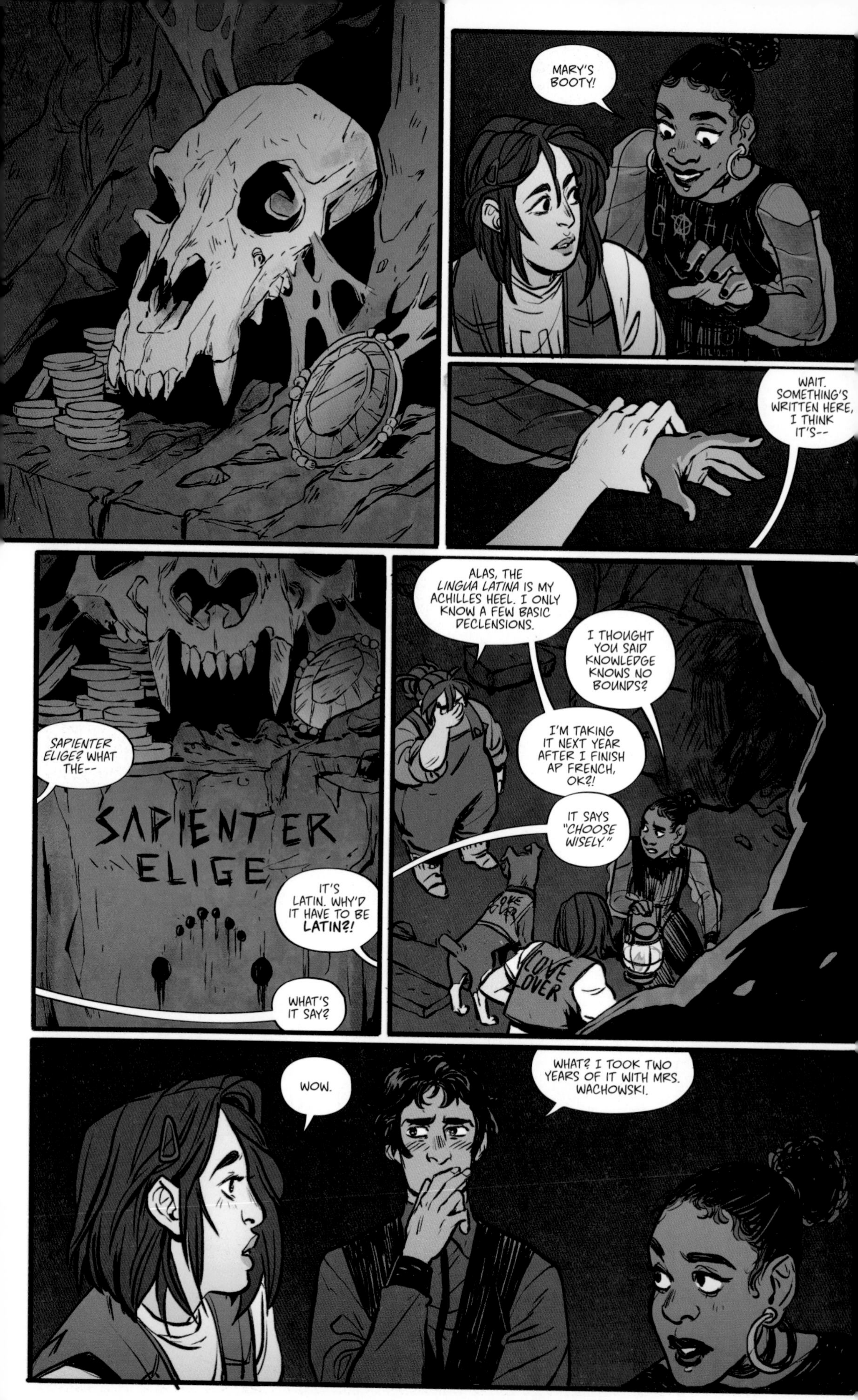
MARY'S BOOTY!
WAIT. SOMETHING'S WRITTEN HERE, I THINK IT'S--
SAPIENTER ELIGE? WHAT THE--
SAPIENTER ELIGE
IT'S LATIN. WHY'D IT HAVE TO BE **LATIN?!**
WHAT'S IT SAY?
ALAS, THE *LINGUA LATINA* IS MY ACHILLES HEEL. I ONLY KNOW A FEW BASIC DECLENSIONS.
I THOUGHT YOU SAID KNOWLEDGE KNOWS NO BOUNDS?
I'M TAKING IT NEXT YEAR AFTER I FINISH AP FRENCH, OK?!
IT SAYS *"CHOOSE WISELY."*
LOVE OVER
WOW.
WHAT? I TOOK TWO YEARS OF IT WITH MRS. WACHOWSKI.

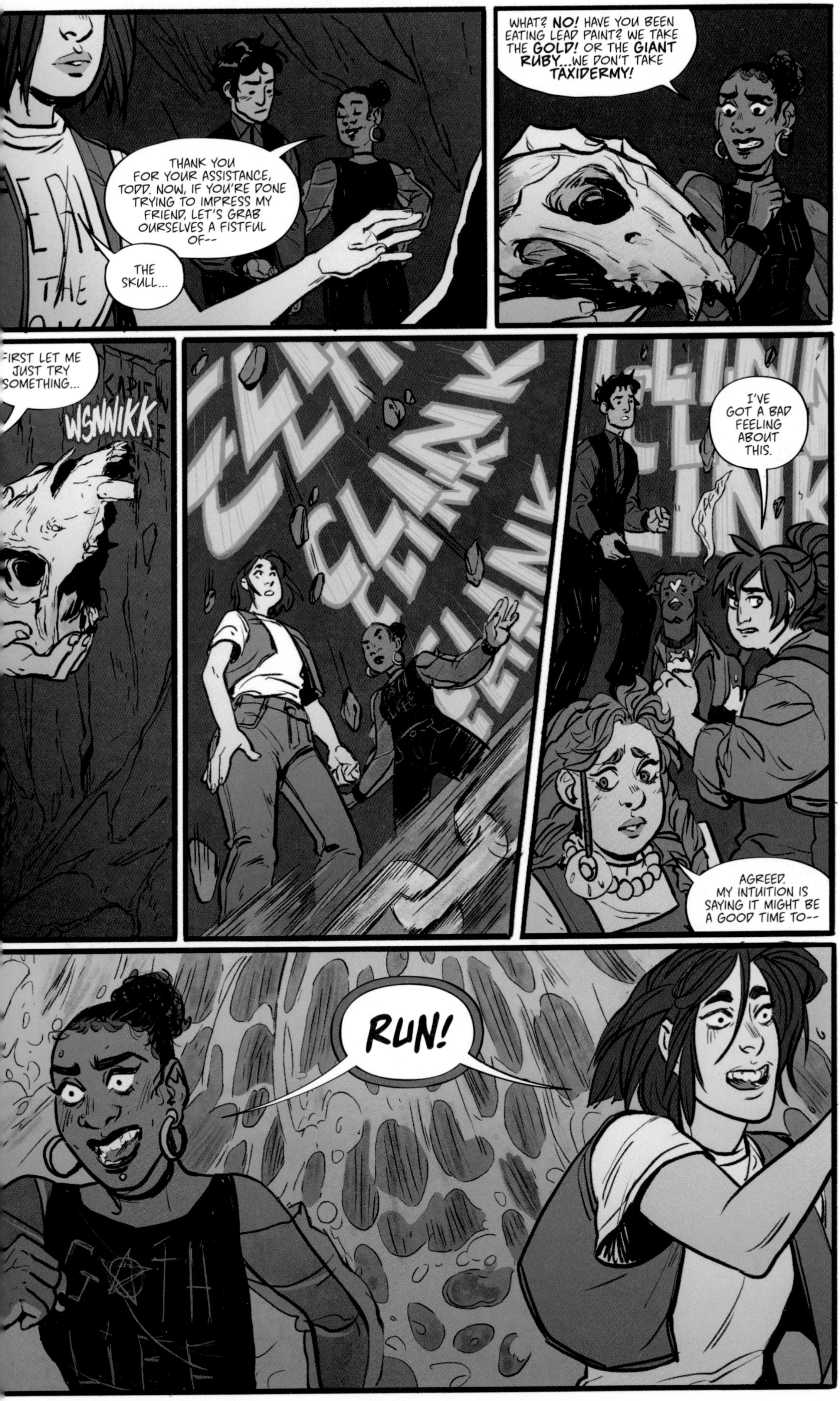
THANK YOU FOR YOUR ASSISTANCE, TODD. NOW, IF YOU'RE DONE TRYING TO IMPRESS MY FRIEND, LET'S GRAB OURSELVES A FISTFUL OF--
THE SKULL...
WHAT? NO! HAVE YOU BEEN EATING LEAD PAINT? WE TAKE THE GOLD! OR THE GIANT RUBY...WE DON'T TAKE TAXIDERMY!
FIRST LET ME JUST TRY SOMETHING...
WSNNIKK
CLINK
I'VE GOT A BAD FEELING ABOUT THIS.
AGREED. MY INTUITION IS SAYING IT MIGHT BE A GOOD TIME TO--
RUN!

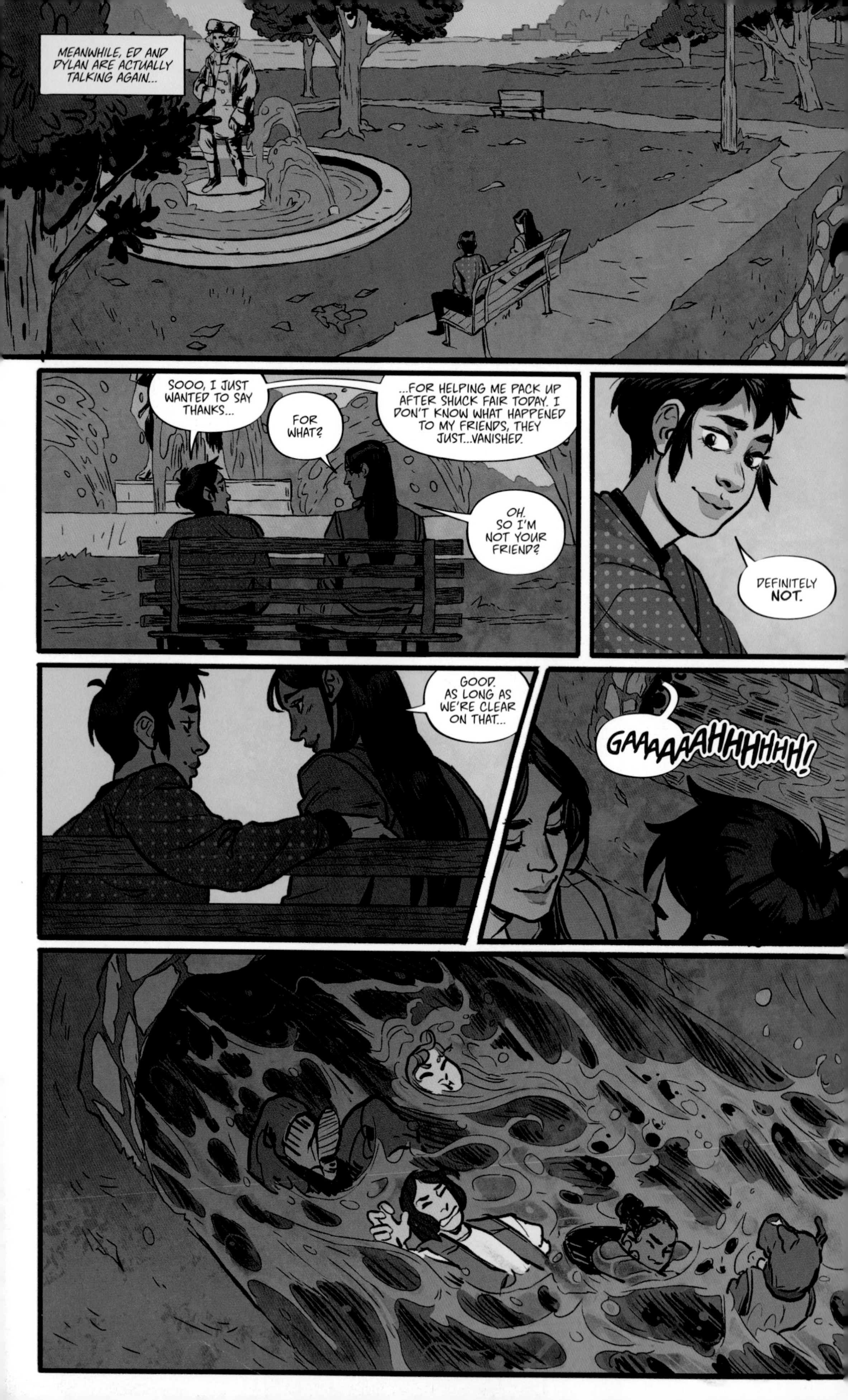
MEANWHILE, ED AND DYLAN ARE ACTUALLY TALKING AGAIN...
SOOO, I JUST WANTED TO SAY THANKS...
FOR WHAT?
...FOR HELPING ME PACK UP AFTER SHUCK FAIR TODAY. I DON'T KNOW WHAT HAPPENED TO MY FRIENDS, THEY JUST...VANISHED.
OH. SO I'M NOT YOUR FRIEND?
DEFINITELY NOT.
GOOD. AS LONG AS WE'RE CLEAR ON THAT...
GAAAAAAHHHHHH!

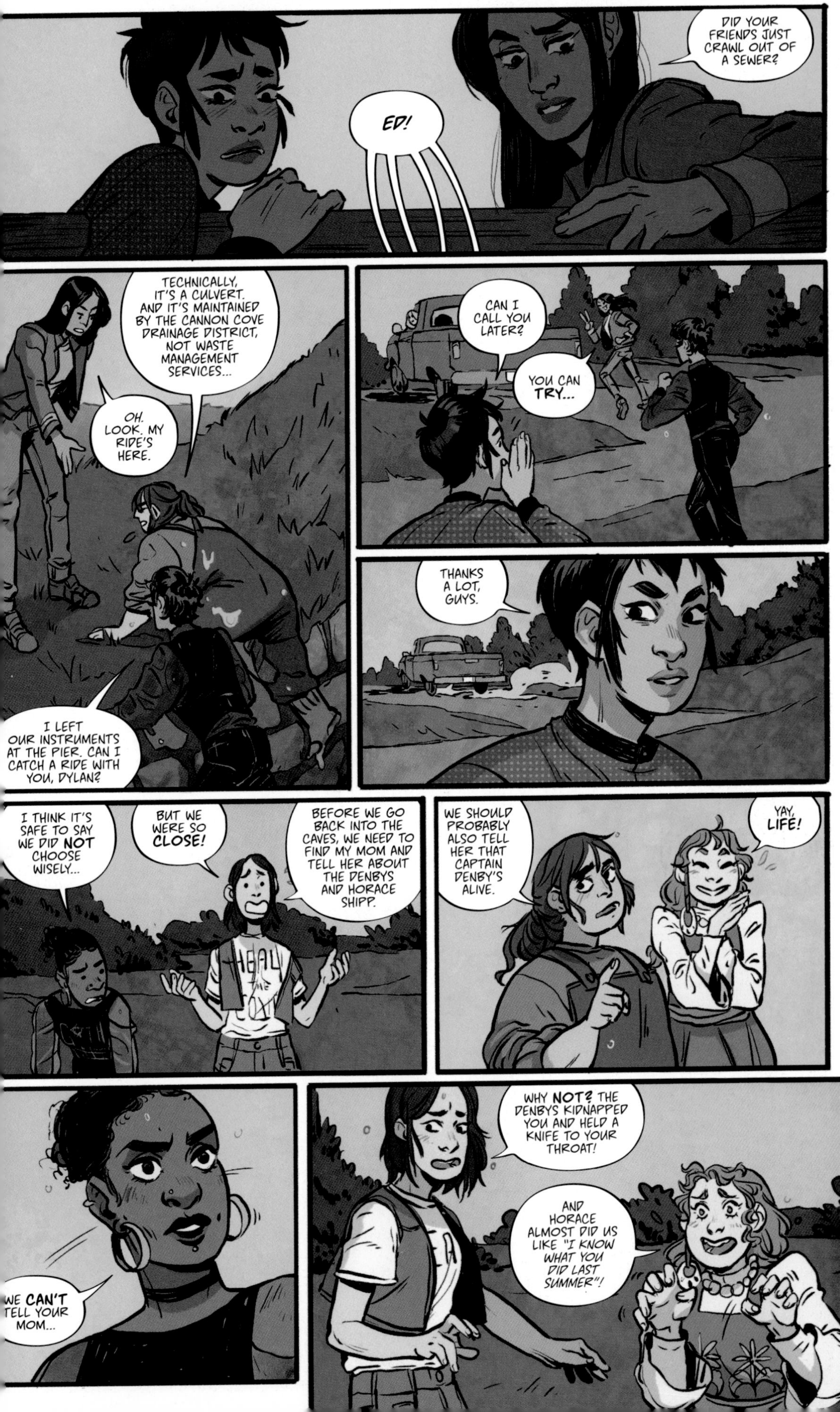
DID YOUR FRIENDS JUST CRAWL OUT OF A SEWER?
ED!
TECHNICALLY, IT'S A CULVERT. AND IT'S MAINTAINED BY THE CANNON COVE DRAINAGE DISTRICT, NOT WASTE MANAGEMENT SERVICES...
OH. LOOK. MY RIDE'S HERE.
I LEFT OUR INSTRUMENTS AT THE PIER. CAN I CATCH A RIDE WITH YOU, DYLAN?
CAN I CALL YOU LATER?
YOU CAN TRY...
THANKS A LOT, GUYS.
I THINK IT'S SAFE TO SAY WE DID NOT CHOOSE WISELY...
BUT WE WERE SO CLOSE!
BEFORE WE GO BACK INTO THE CAVES, WE NEED TO FIND MY MOM AND TELL HER ABOUT THE DENBYS AND HORACE SHIPP.
WE SHOULD PROBABLY ALSO TELL HER THAT CAPTAIN DENBY'S ALIVE.
YAY, LIFE!
WE CAN'T TELL YOUR MOM...
WHY NOT? THE DENBYS KIDNAPPED YOU AND HELD A KNIFE TO YOUR THROAT!
AND HORACE ALMOST DID US LIKE "I KNOW WHAT YOU DID LAST SUMMER"!

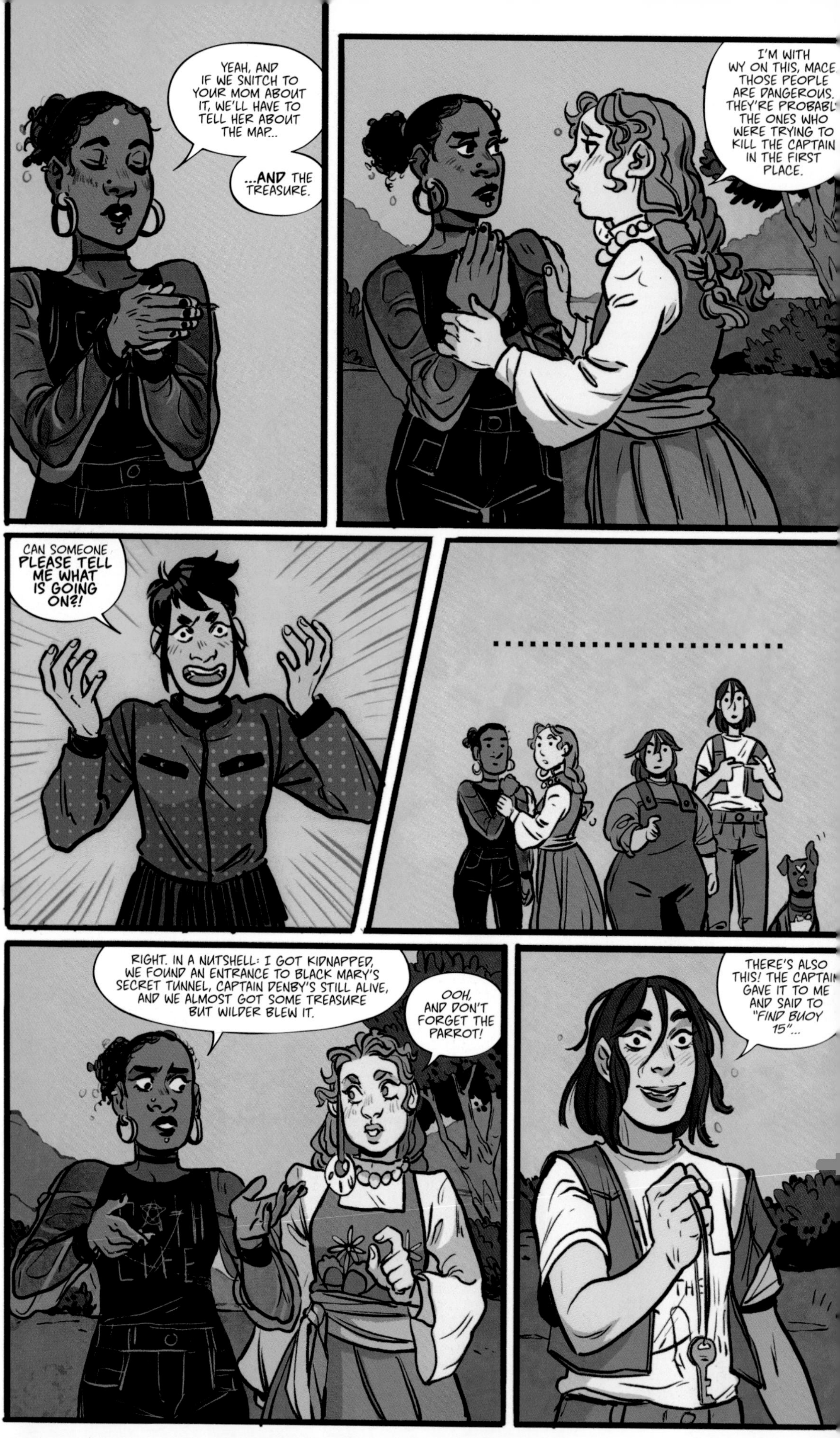
YEAH, AND IF WE SNITCH TO YOUR MOM ABOUT IT, WE'LL HAVE TO TELL HER ABOUT THE MAP...
...AND THE TREASURE.
I'M WITH WY ON THIS, MACE. THOSE PEOPLE ARE DANGEROUS. THEY'RE PROBABLY THE ONES WHO WERE TRYING TO KILL THE CAPTAIN IN THE FIRST PLACE.
CAN SOMEONE PLEASE TELL ME WHAT IS GOING ON?!
....
RIGHT. IN A NUTSHELL: I GOT KIDNAPPED, WE FOUND AN ENTRANCE TO BLACK MARY'S SECRET TUNNEL, CAPTAIN DENBY'S STILL ALIVE, AND WE ALMOST GOT SOME TREASURE BUT WILDER BLEW IT.
OOH, AND DON'T FORGET THE PARROT!
THERE'S ALSO THIS! THE CAPTAIN GAVE IT TO ME AND SAID TO "FIND BUOY 15"...

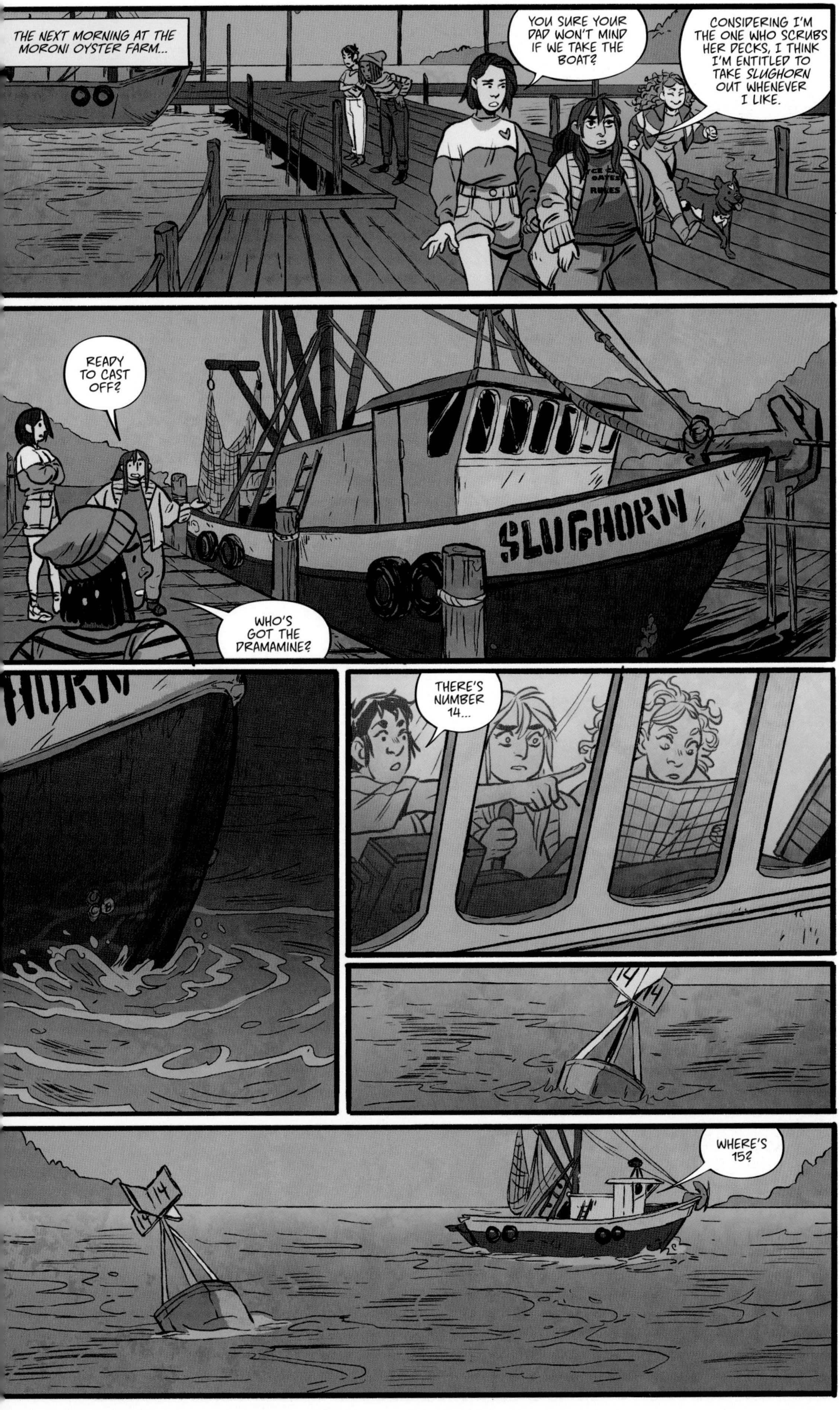
THE NEXT MORNING AT THE MORONI OYSTER FARM...
YOU SURE YOUR DAD WON'T MIND IF WE TAKE THE BOAT?
CONSIDERING I'M THE ONE WHO SCRUBS HER DECKS, I THINK I'M ENTITLED TO TAKE SLUGHORN OUT WHENEVER I LIKE.
READY TO CAST OFF?
SLUGHORN
WHO'S GOT THE DRAMAMINE?
THERE'S NUMBER 14...
14
WHERE'S 15?

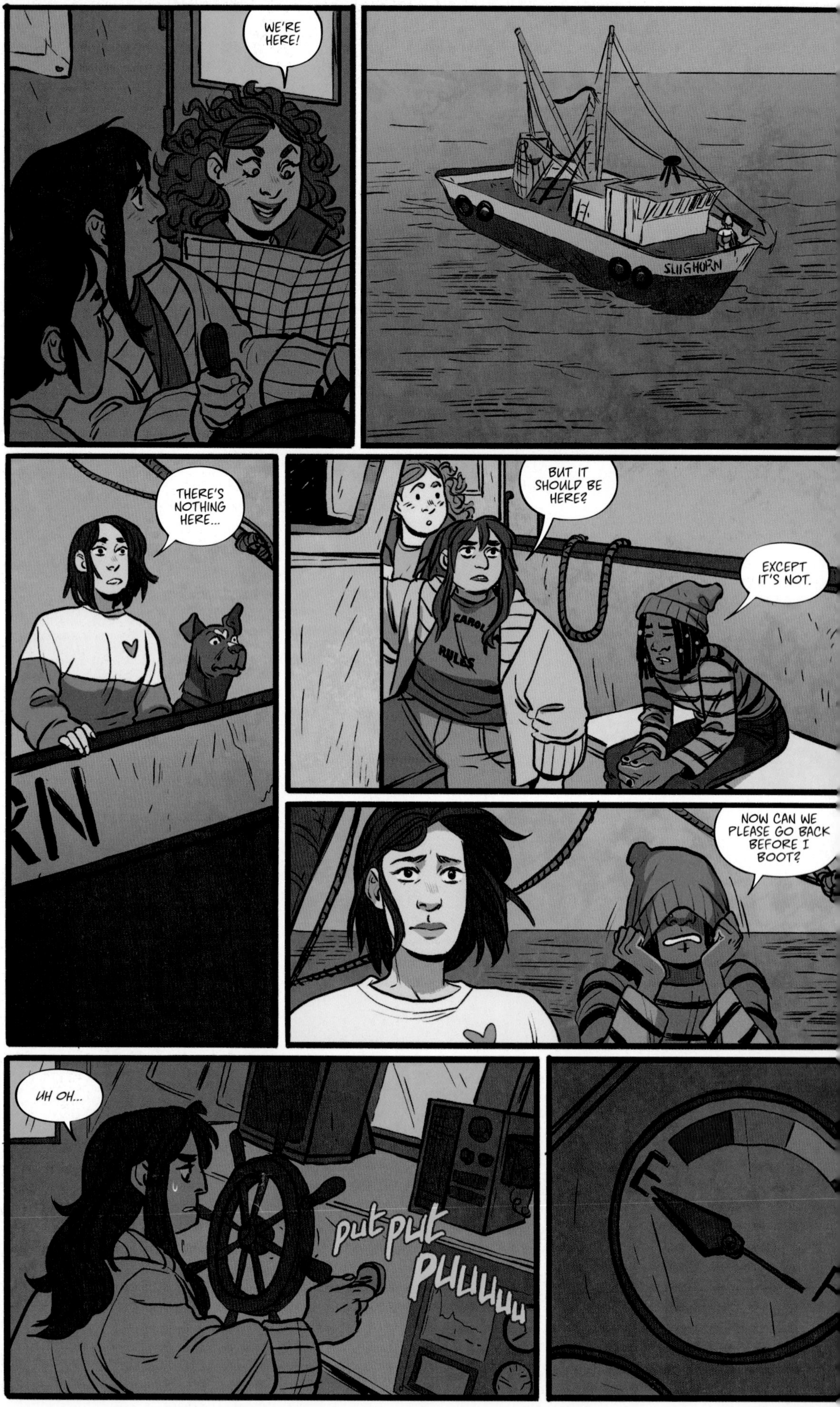
WE'RE HERE!
SLIGHORN
THERE'S NOTHING HERE...
BUT IT SHOULD BE HERE?
EXCEPT IT'S NOT.
NOW CAN WE PLEASE GO BACK BEFORE I BOOT?
UH OH...
put put puuuuu

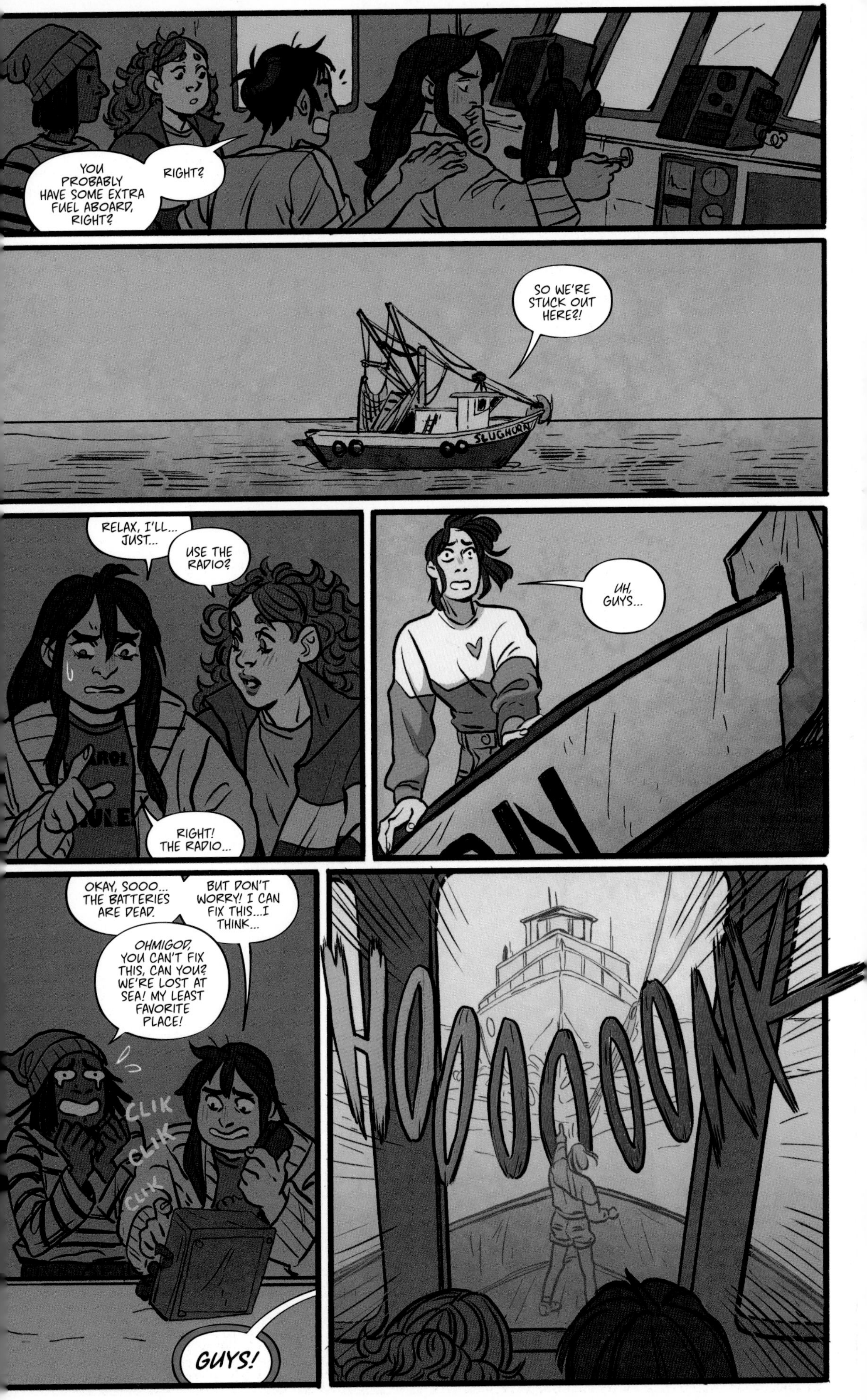

YOU PROBABLY HAVE SOME EXTRA FUEL ABOARD, RIGHT?
RIGHT?
SO WE'RE STUCK OUT HERE?!
SLUGHORN
RELAX, I'LL... JUST...
USE THE RADIO?
RIGHT! THE RADIO...
UH, GUYS...
OKAY, SOOO... THE BATTERIES ARE DEAD.
BUT DON'T WORRY! I CAN FIX THIS...I THINK...
OHMIGOD, YOU CAN'T FIX THIS, CAN YOU? WE'RE LOST AT SEA! MY LEAST FAVORITE PLACE!
CLIK
CLIK
CLIK
GUYS!
HOOOOONK

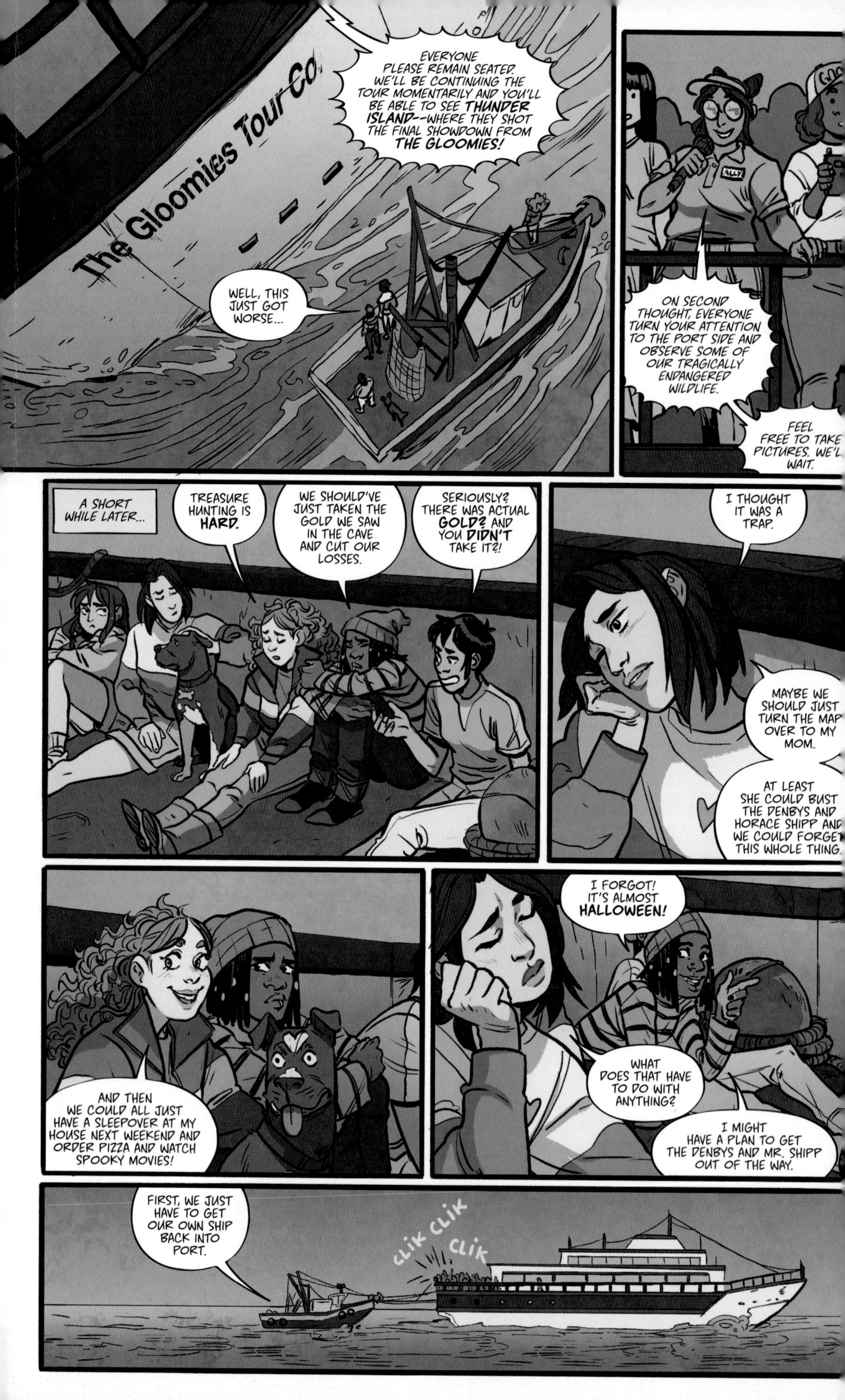

EVERYONE PLEASE REMAIN SEATED. WE'LL BE CONTINUING THE TOUR MOMENTARILY AND YOU'LL BE ABLE TO SEE THUNDER ISLAND--WHERE THEY SHOT THE FINAL SHOWDOWN FROM THE GLOOMIES!
The Gloomies Tour Co.
WELL, THIS JUST GOT WORSE...
ALLY
ON SECOND THOUGHT, EVERYONE TURN YOUR ATTENTION TO THE PORT SIDE AND OBSERVE SOME OF OUR TRAGICALLY ENDANGERED WILDLIFE.
FEEL FREE TO TAKE PICTURES. WE'LL WAIT.
A SHORT WHILE LATER...
TREASURE HUNTING IS HARD.
WE SHOULD'VE JUST TAKEN THE GOLD WE SAW IN THE CAVE AND CUT OUR LOSSES.
SERIOUSLY? THERE WAS ACTUAL GOLD? AND YOU DIDN'T TAKE IT?!
I THOUGHT IT WAS A TRAP.
MAYBE WE SHOULD JUST TURN THE MAP OVER TO MY MOM.
AT LEAST SHE COULD BUST THE DENBYS AND HORACE SHIPP AND WE COULD FORGET THIS WHOLE THING.
AND THEN WE COULD ALL JUST HAVE A SLEEPOVER AT MY HOUSE NEXT WEEKEND AND ORDER PIZZA AND WATCH SPOOKY MOVIES!
I FORGOT! IT'S ALMOST HALLOWEEN!
WHAT DOES THAT HAVE TO DO WITH ANYTHING?
I MIGHT HAVE A PLAN TO GET THE DENBYS AND MR. SHIPP OUT OF THE WAY.
FIRST, WE JUST HAVE TO GET OUR OWN SHIP BACK INTO PORT.
CLIK CLIK CLIK

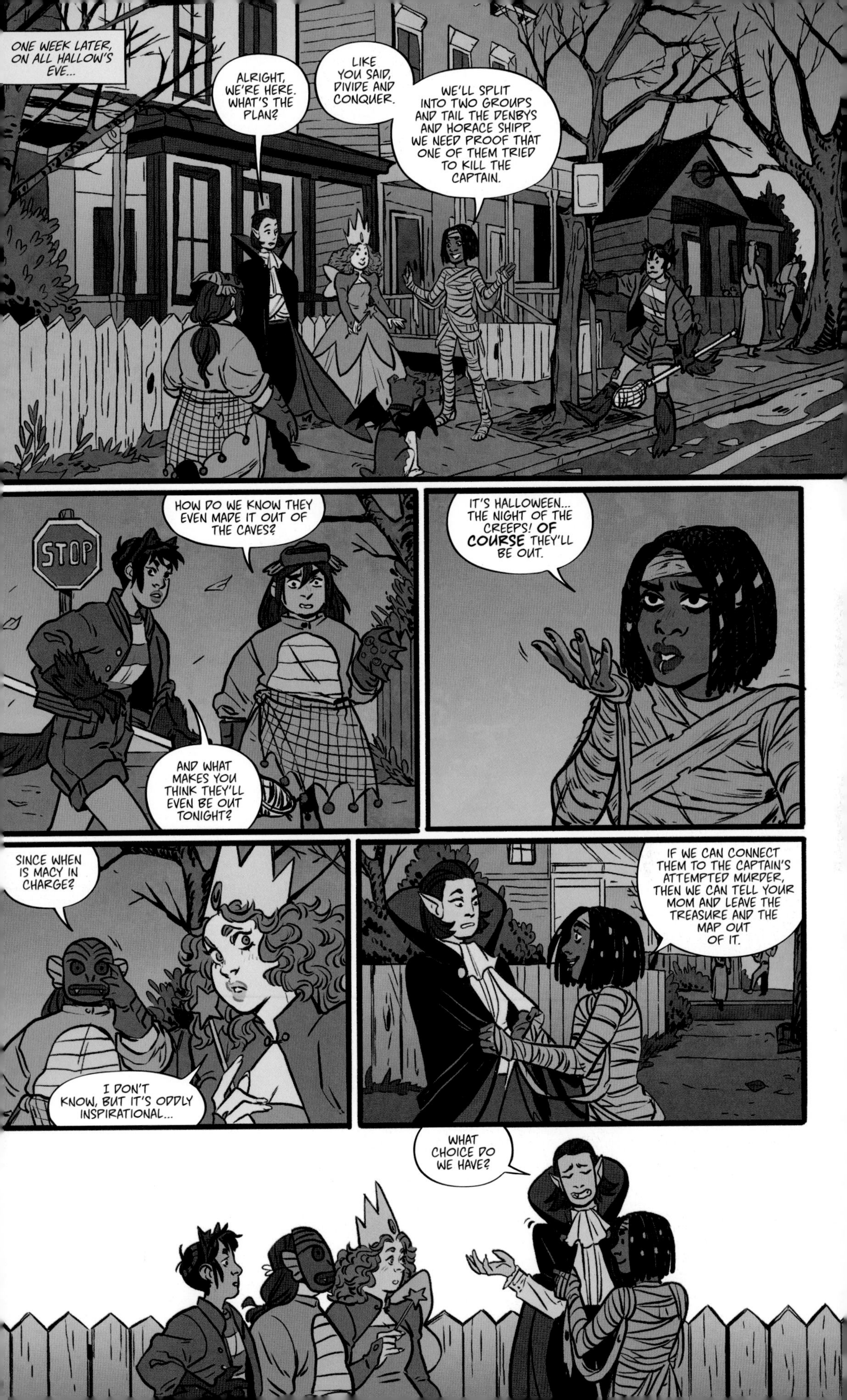
ONE WEEK LATER, ON ALL HALLOW'S EVE...
ALRIGHT, WE'RE HERE. WHAT'S THE PLAN?
LIKE YOU SAID, DIVIDE AND CONQUER.
WE'LL SPLIT INTO TWO GROUPS AND TAIL THE DENBYS AND HORACE SHIPP. WE NEED PROOF THAT ONE OF THEM TRIED TO KILL THE CAPTAIN.
STOP
HOW DO WE KNOW THEY EVEN MADE IT OUT OF THE CAVES?
AND WHAT MAKES YOU THINK THEY'LL EVEN BE OUT TONIGHT?
IT'S HALLOWEEN... THE NIGHT OF THE CREEPS! OF COURSE THEY'LL BE OUT.
SINCE WHEN IS MACY IN CHARGE?
I DON'T KNOW, BUT IT'S ODDLY INSPIRATIONAL...
IF WE CAN CONNECT THEM TO THE CAPTAIN'S ATTEMPTED MURDER, THEN WE CAN TELL YOUR MOM AND LEAVE THE TREASURE AND THE MAP OUT OF IT.
WHAT CHOICE DO WE HAVE?

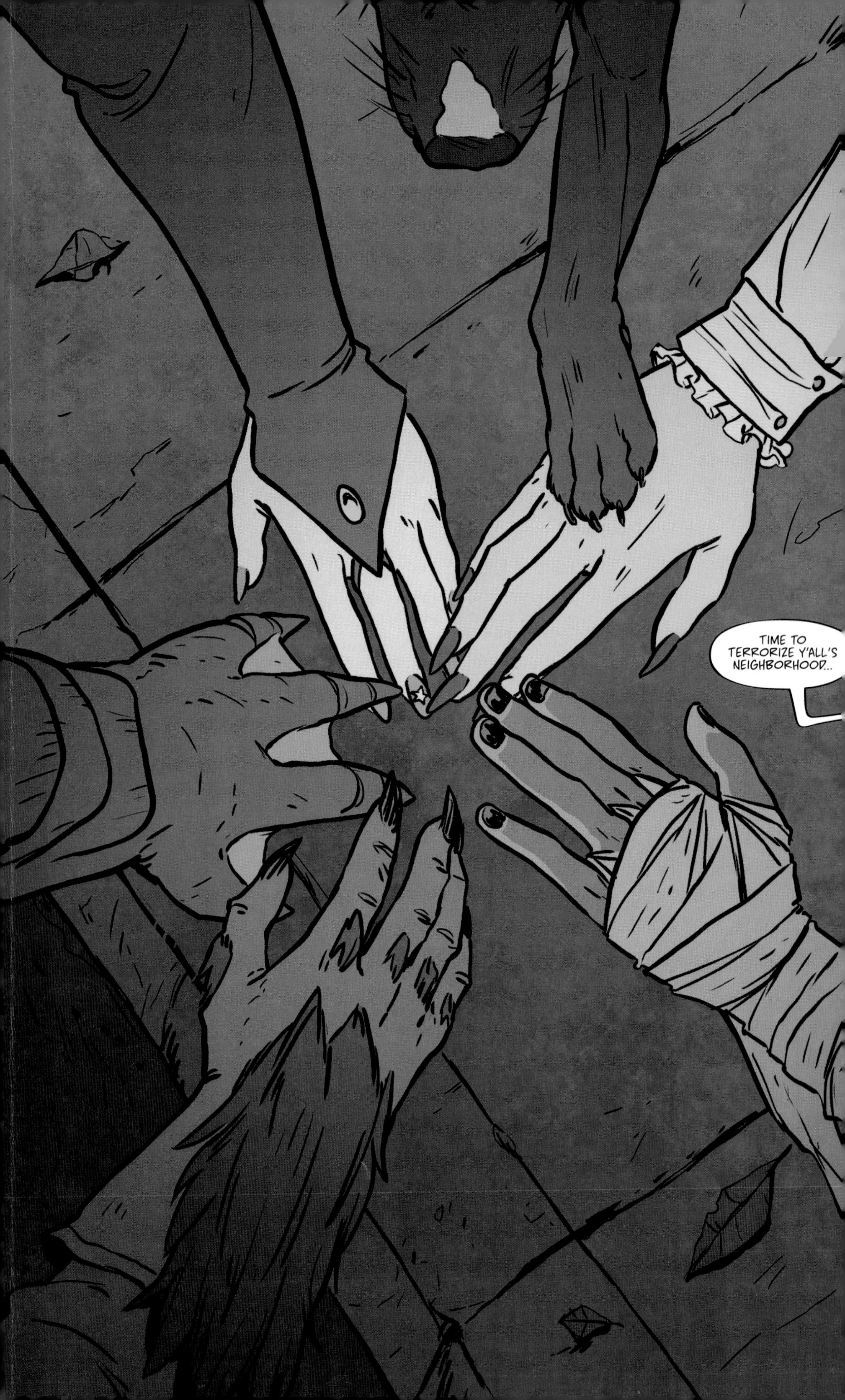
TIME TO
TERRORIZE Y'ALL'S
NEIGHBORHOOD...

CHAPTER
VII

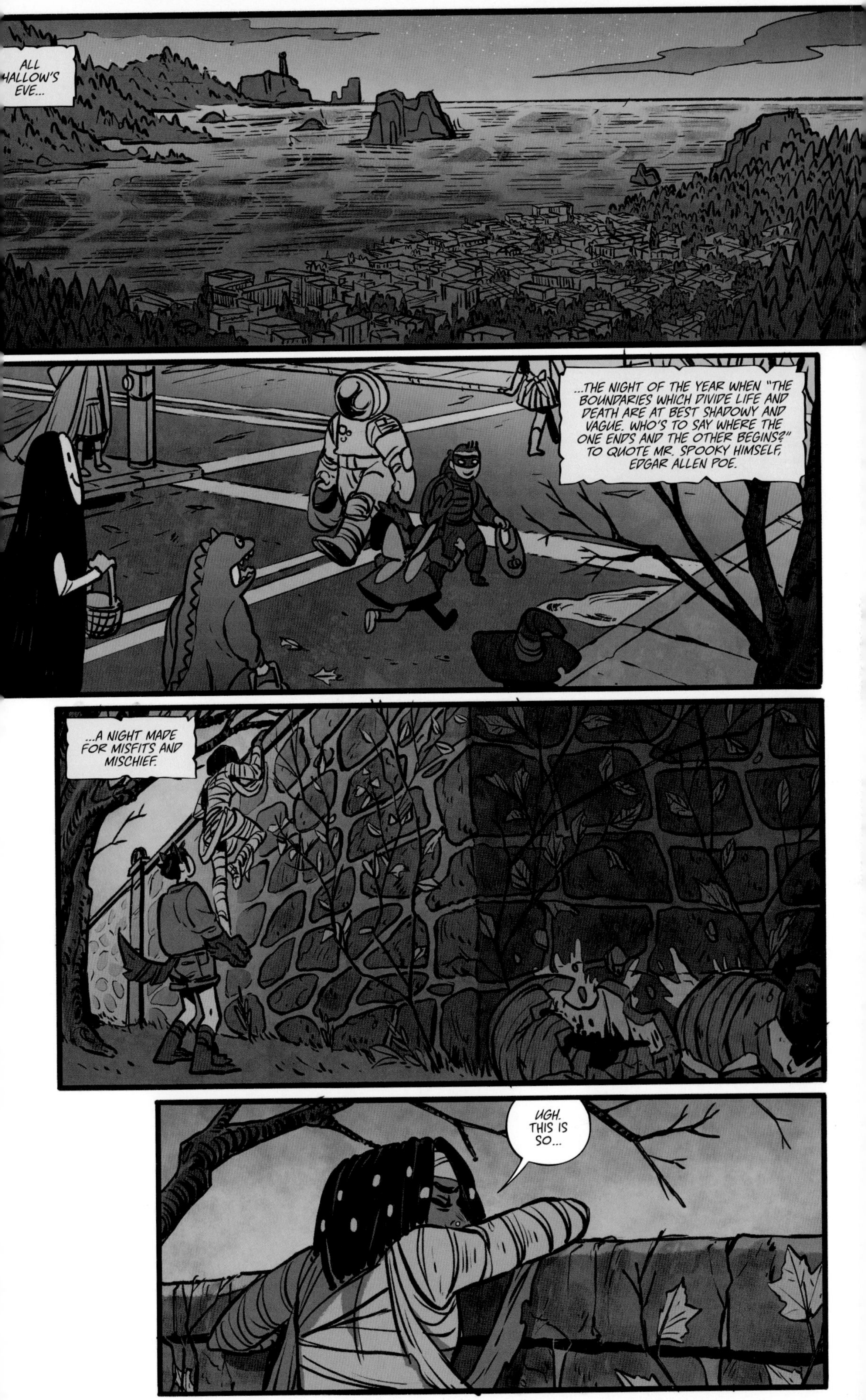
ALL HALLOW'S EVE...
...THE NIGHT OF THE YEAR WHEN "THE BOUNDARIES WHICH DIVIDE LIFE AND DEATH ARE AT BEST SHADOWY AND VAGUE. WHO'S TO SAY WHERE THE ONE ENDS AND THE OTHER BEGINS?" TO QUOTE MR. SPOOKY HIMSELF, EDGAR ALLEN POE.
...A NIGHT MADE FOR MISFITS AND MISCHIEF.
UGH. THIS IS SO...

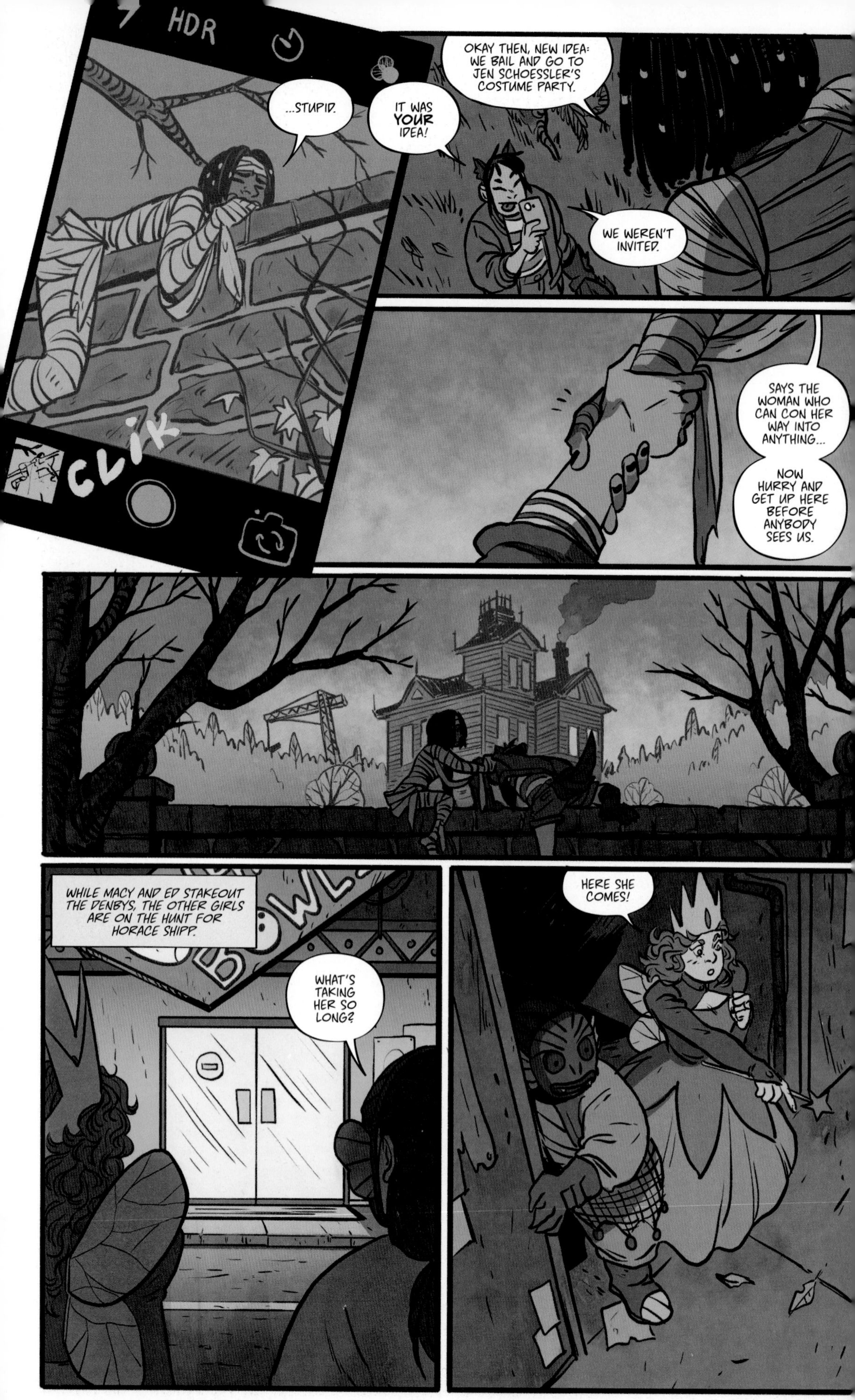
HDR
...STUPID.
CLIK
IT WAS YOUR IDEA!
OKAY THEN, NEW IDEA: WE BAIL AND GO TO JEN SCHOESSLER'S COSTUME PARTY.
WE WEREN'T INVITED.
SAYS THE WOMAN WHO CAN CON HER WAY INTO ANYTHING...
NOW HURRY AND GET UP HERE BEFORE ANYBODY SEES US.
WHILE MACY AND ED STAKEOUT THE DENBYS, THE OTHER GIRLS ARE ON THE HUNT FOR HORACE SHIPP.
WHAT'S TAKING HER SO LONG?
HERE SHE COMES!

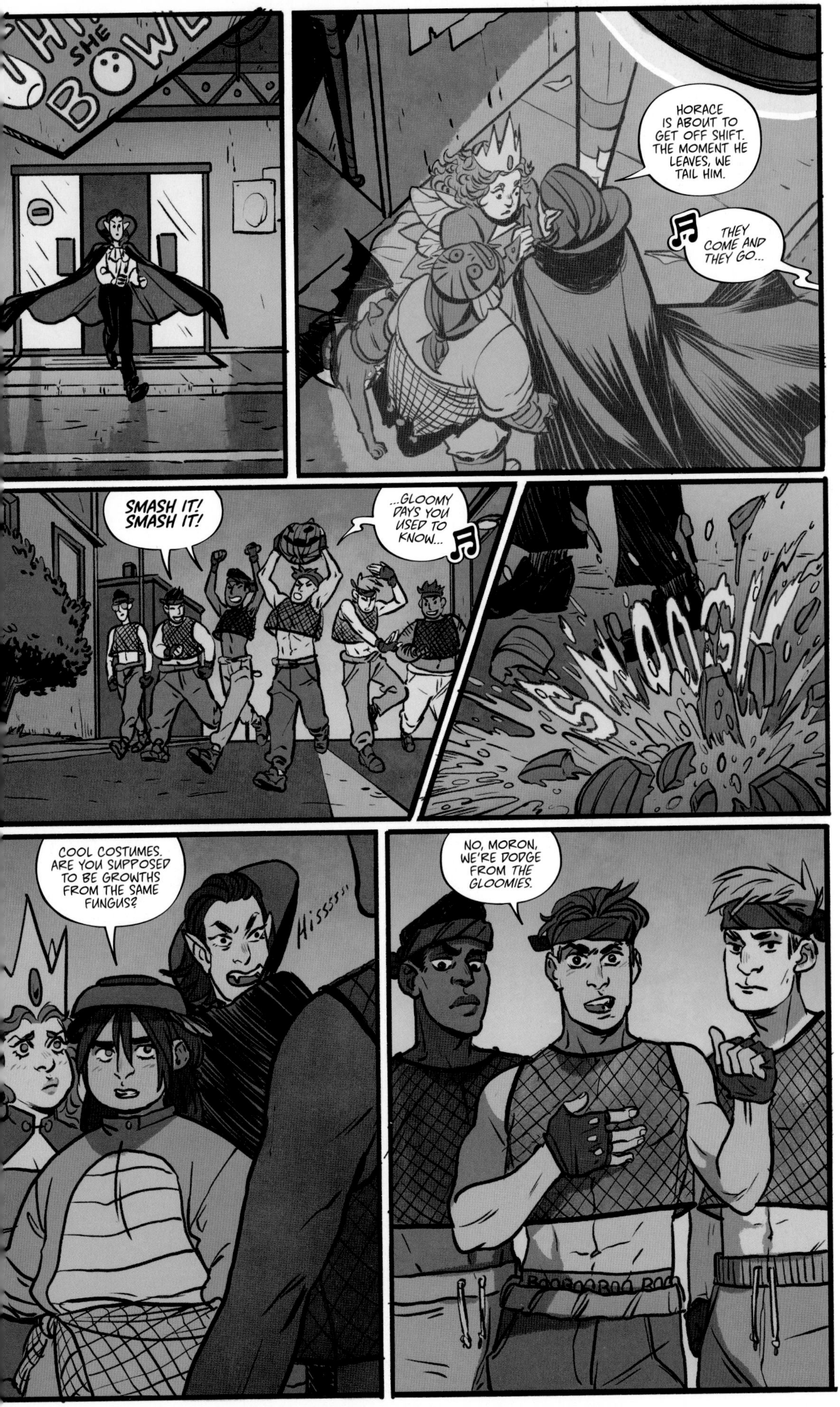
SHE
BOWL
HORACE IS ABOUT TO GET OFF SHIFT. THE MOMENT HE LEAVES, WE TAIL HIM.
THEY COME AND THEY GO...
SMASH IT! SMASH IT!
...GLOOMY DAYS YOU USED TO KNOW...
SMOOSH
COOL COSTUMES. ARE YOU SUPPOSED TO BE GROWTHS FROM THE SAME FUNGUS?
Hissss
NO, MORON, WE'RE DODGE FROM THE GLOOMIES.

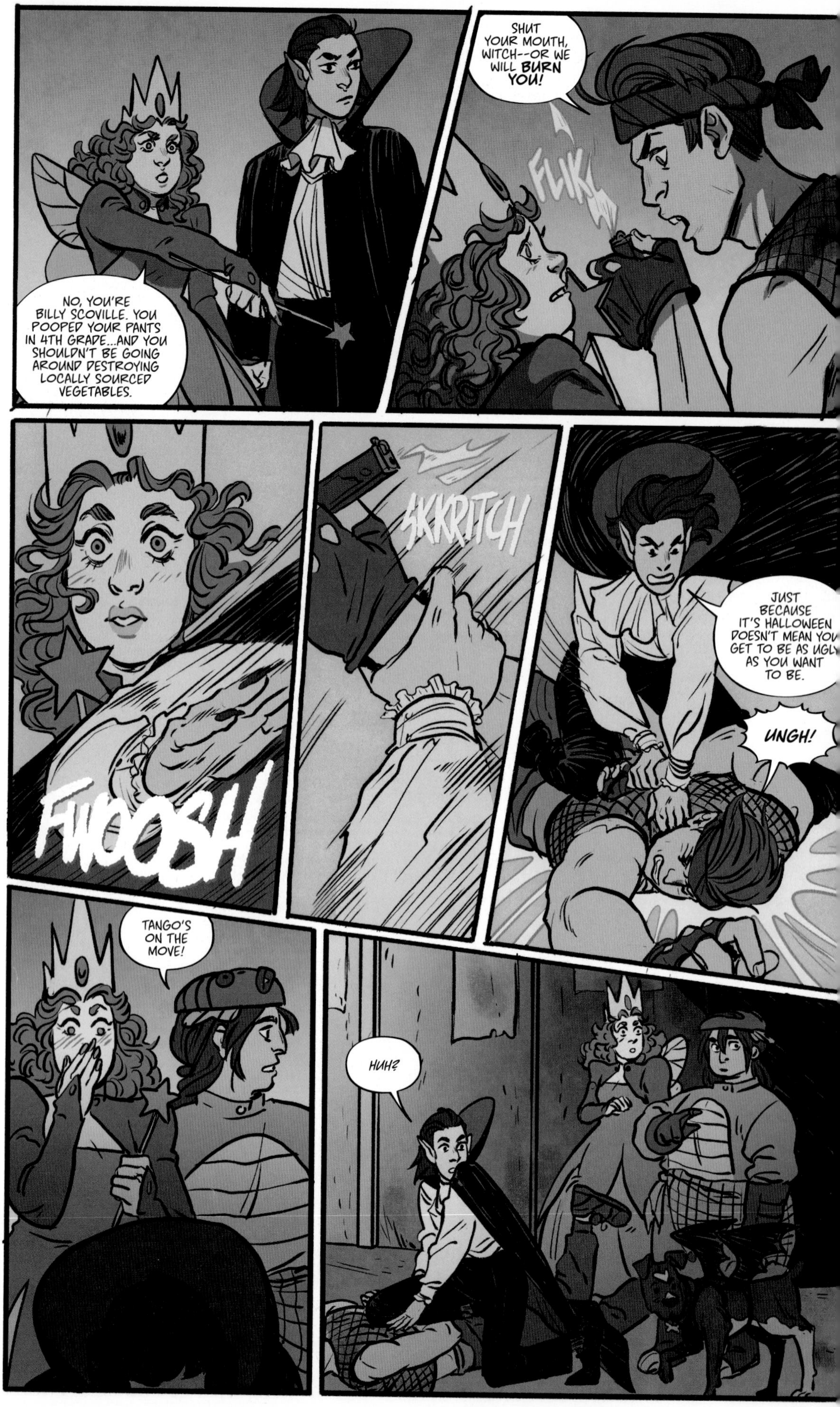
NO, YOU'RE BILLY SCOVILLE. YOU POOPED YOUR PANTS IN 4TH GRADE...AND YOU SHOULDN'T BE GOING AROUND DESTROYING LOCALLY SOURCED VEGETABLES.
SHUT YOUR MOUTH, WITCH--OR WE WILL **BURN YOU!**
FLIK
FWOOSH
SKKRITCH
JUST BECAUSE IT'S HALLOWEEN DOESN'T MEAN YOU GET TO BE AS UGLY AS YOU WANT TO BE.
UNGH!
TANGO'S ON THE MOVE!
HUH?

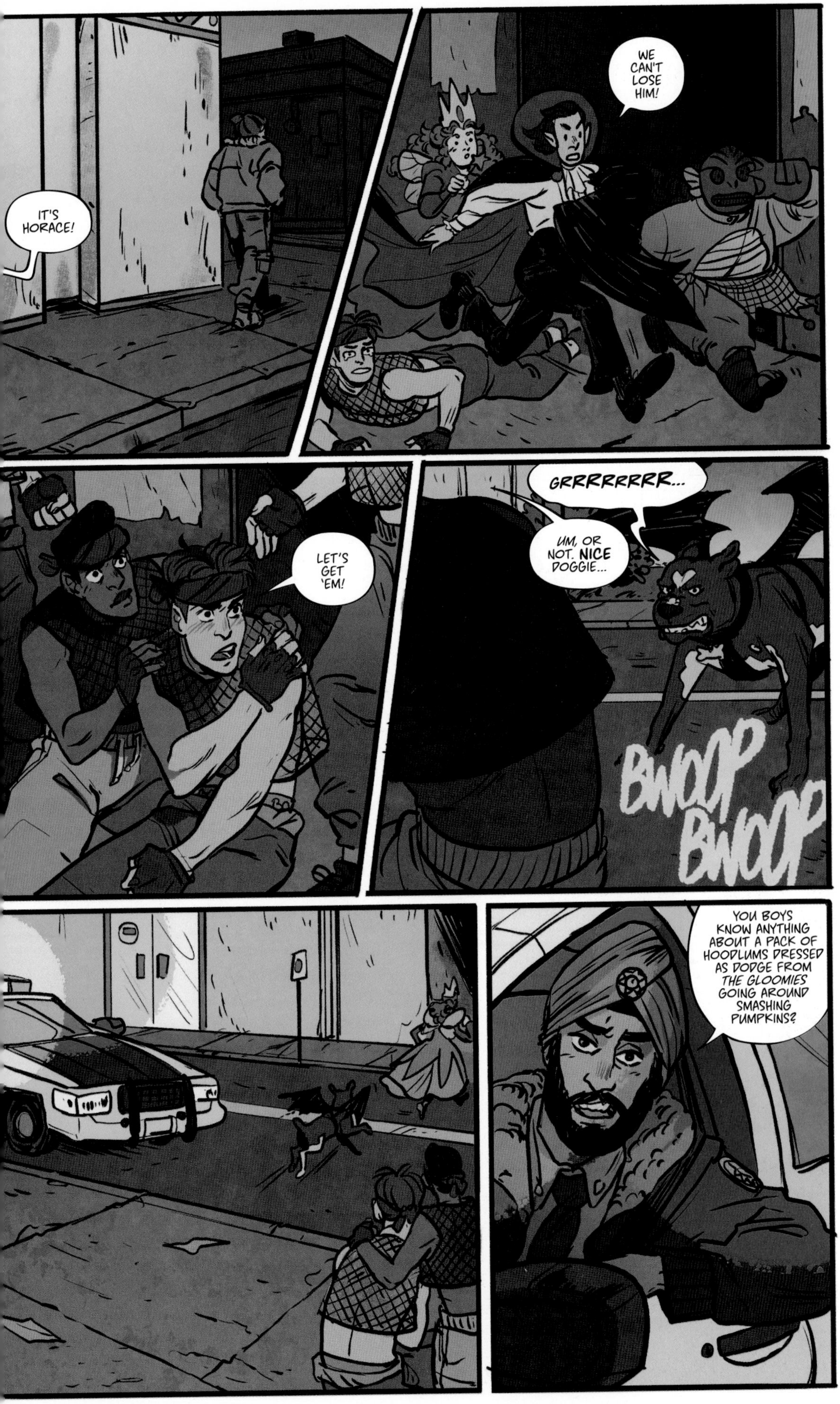
IT'S HORACE!
WE CAN'T LOSE HIM!
LET'S GET 'EM!
GRRRRRRRR...
UM, OR NOT. NICE DOGGIE...
BWOOP BWOOP
YOU BOYS KNOW ANYTHING ABOUT A PACK OF HOODLUMS DRESSED AS DODGE FROM THE GLOOMIES GOING AROUND SMASHING PUMPKINS?

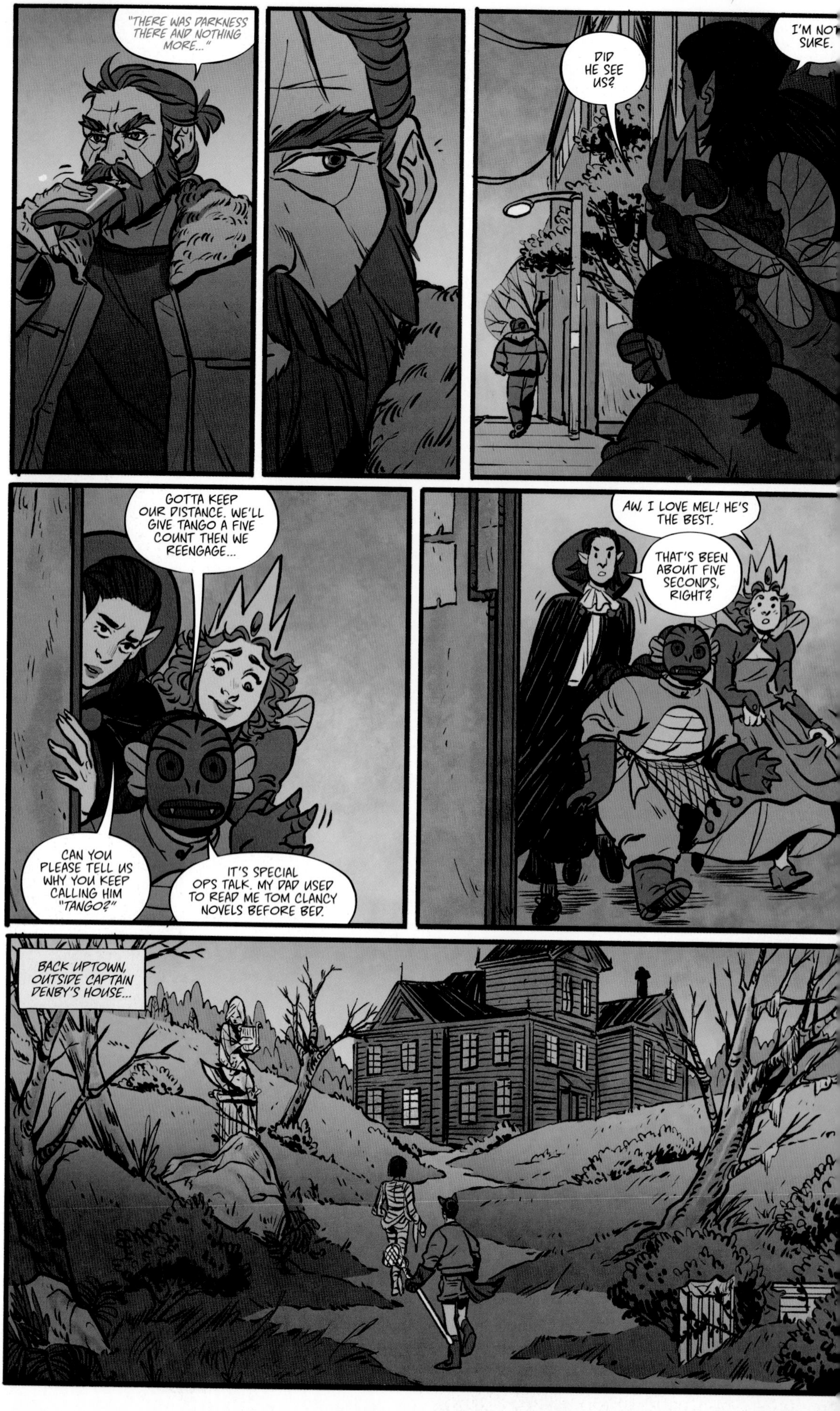
"THERE WAS DARKNESS THERE AND NOTHING MORE..."
DID HE SEE US?
I'M NOT SURE.
GOTTA KEEP OUR DISTANCE. WE'LL GIVE TANGO A FIVE COUNT THEN WE REENGAGE...
CAN YOU PLEASE TELL US WHY YOU KEEP CALLING HIM "TANGO?"
IT'S SPECIAL OPS TALK. MY DAD USED TO READ ME TOM CLANCY NOVELS BEFORE BED.
AW, I LOVE MEL! HE'S THE BEST.
THAT'S BEEN ABOUT FIVE SECONDS, RIGHT?
BACK UPTOWN, OUTSIDE CAPTAIN DENBY'S HOUSE...

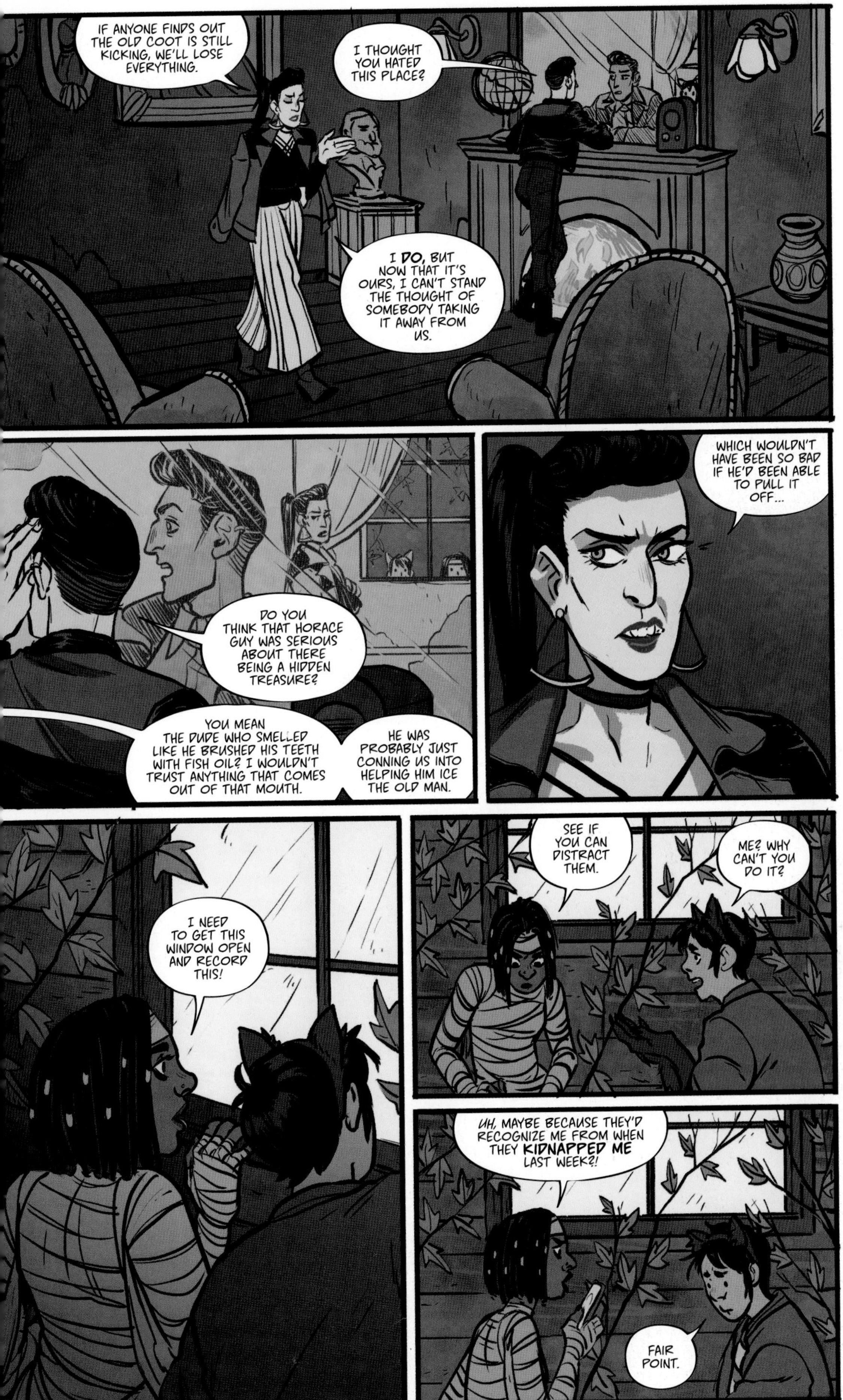
IF ANYONE FINDS OUT THE OLD COOT IS STILL KICKING, WE'LL LOSE EVERYTHING.
I THOUGHT YOU HATED THIS PLACE?
I **DO**, BUT NOW THAT IT'S OURS, I CAN'T STAND THE THOUGHT OF SOMEBODY TAKING IT AWAY FROM US.
DO YOU THINK THAT HORACE GUY WAS SERIOUS ABOUT THERE BEING A HIDDEN TREASURE?
YOU MEAN THE DUDE WHO SMELLED LIKE HE BRUSHED HIS TEETH WITH FISH OIL? I WOULDN'T TRUST ANYTHING THAT COMES OUT OF THAT MOUTH.
HE WAS PROBABLY JUST CONNING US INTO HELPING HIM ICE THE OLD MAN.
WHICH WOULDN'T HAVE BEEN SO BAD IF HE'D BEEN ABLE TO PULL IT OFF...
I NEED TO GET THIS WINDOW OPEN AND RECORD THIS!
SEE IF YOU CAN DISTRACT THEM.
ME? WHY CAN'T YOU DO IT?
UH, MAYBE BECAUSE THEY'D RECOGNIZE ME FROM WHEN THEY **KIDNAPPED ME** LAST WEEK?!
FAIR POINT.

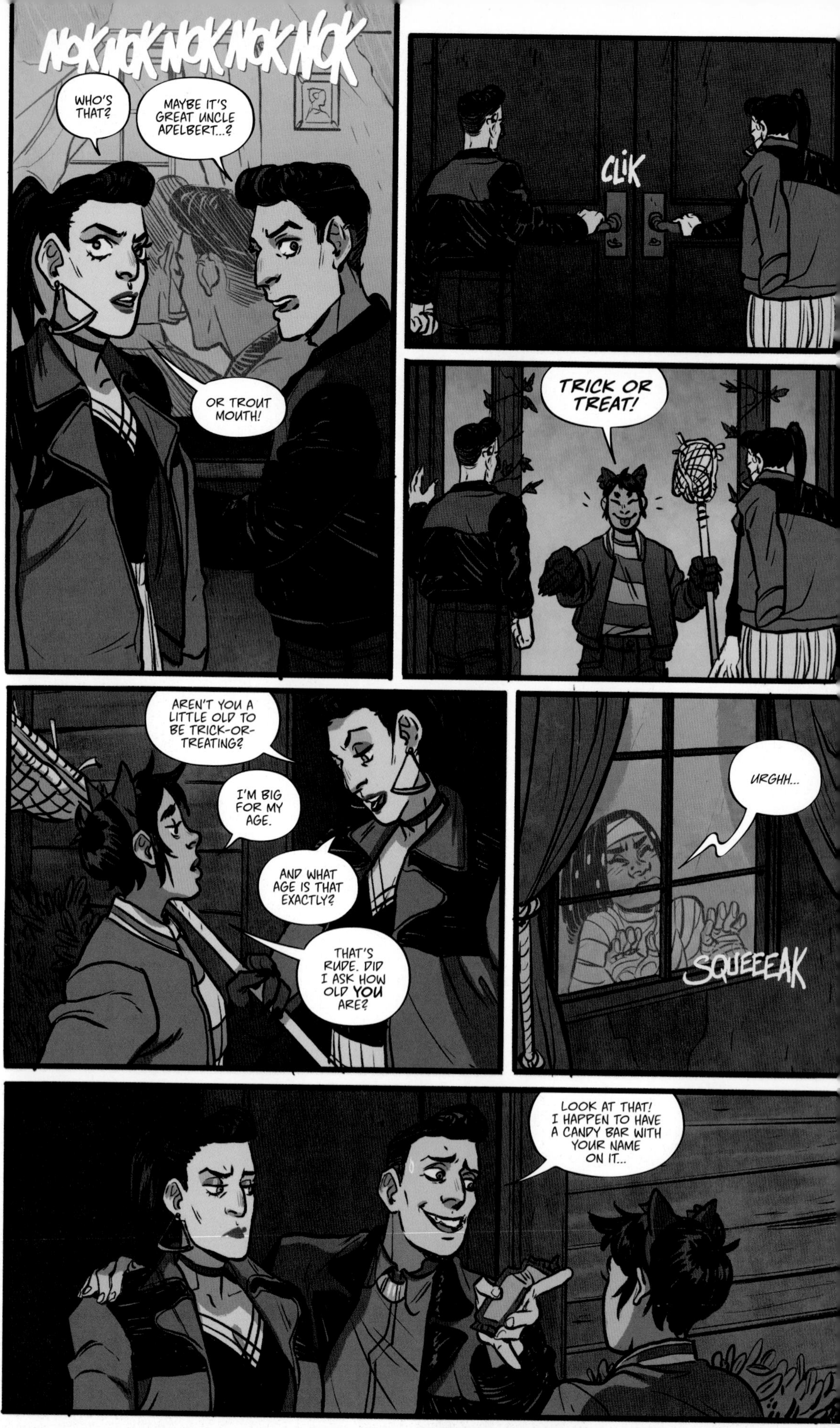
NOK NOK NOK NOK NOK
WHO'S THAT?
MAYBE IT'S GREAT UNCLE ADELBERT...?
OR TROUT MOUTH!
CLIK
TRICK OR TREAT!
AREN'T YOU A LITTLE OLD TO BE TRICK-OR-TREATING?
I'M BIG FOR MY AGE.
AND WHAT AGE IS THAT EXACTLY?
THAT'S RUDE. DID I ASK HOW OLD YOU ARE?
URGHH...
SQUEEEAK
LOOK AT THAT! I HAPPEN TO HAVE A CANDY BAR WITH YOUR NAME ON IT...

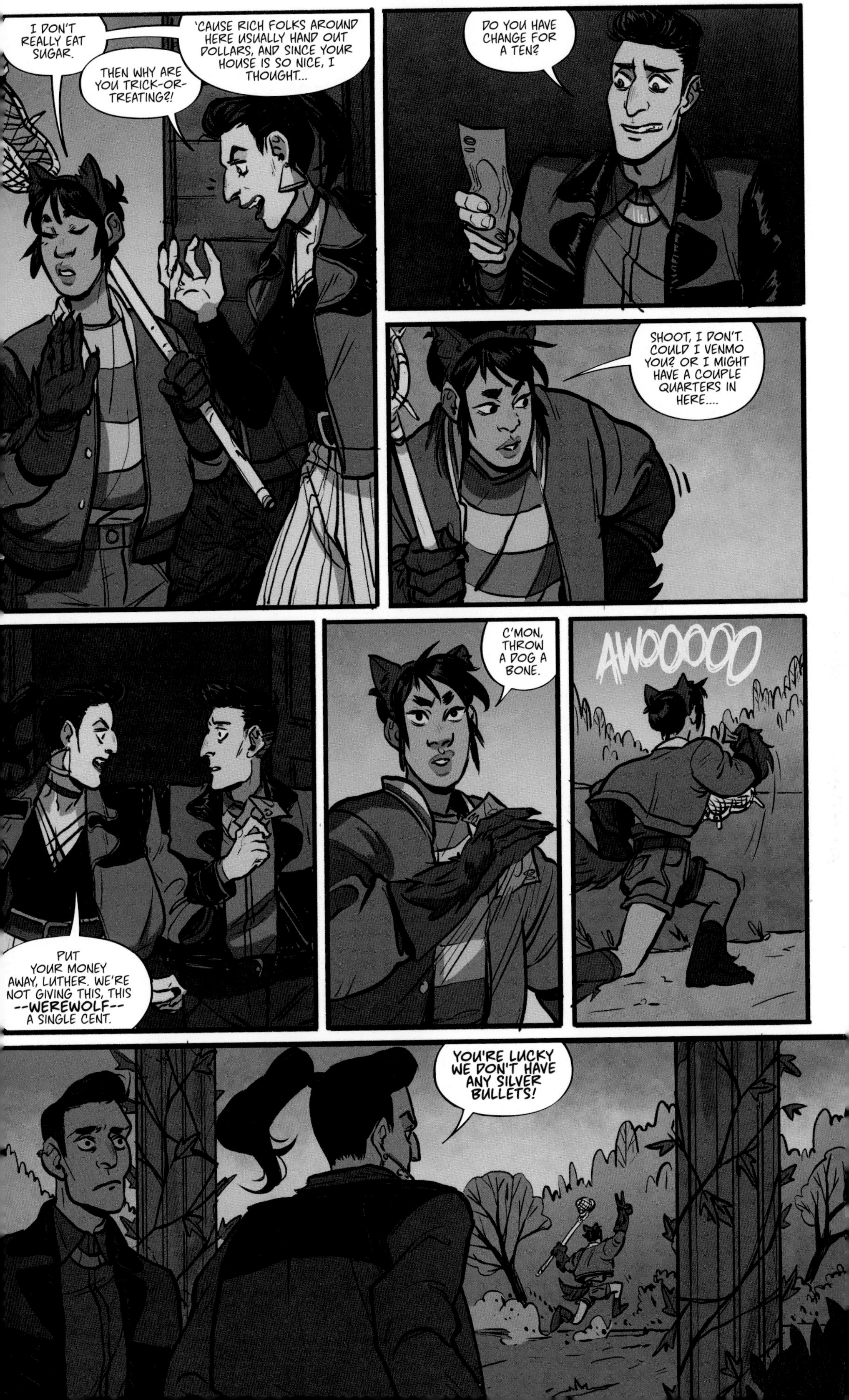

I DON'T REALLY EAT SUGAR.
THEN WHY ARE YOU TRICK-OR-TREATING?!
'CAUSE RICH FOLKS AROUND HERE USUALLY HAND OUT DOLLARS, AND SINCE YOUR HOUSE IS SO NICE, I THOUGHT...
DO YOU HAVE CHANGE FOR A TEN?
SHOOT, I DON'T. COULD I VENMO YOU? OR I MIGHT HAVE A COUPLE QUARTERS IN HERE....
PUT YOUR MONEY AWAY, LUTHER. WE'RE NOT GIVING THIS, THIS --**WEREWOLF**-- A SINGLE CENT.
C'MON, THROW A DOG A BONE.
AWOOOOOO
YOU'RE LUCKY WE DON'T HAVE ANY SILVER BULLETS!

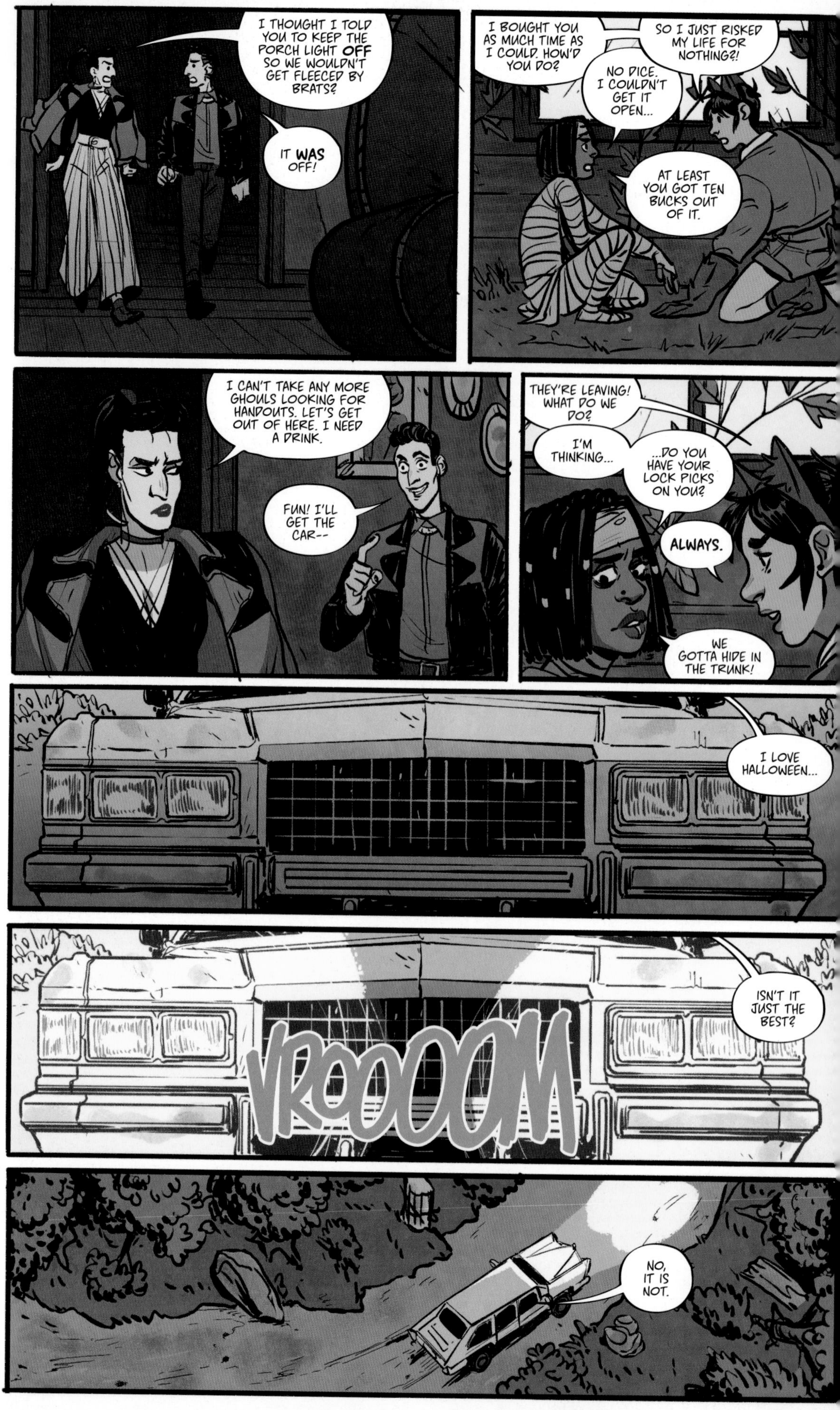

I THOUGHT I TOLD YOU TO KEEP THE PORCH LIGHT **OFF** SO WE WOULDN'T GET FLEECED BY BRATS?
IT **WAS** OFF!
I BOUGHT YOU AS MUCH TIME AS I COULD. HOW'D YOU DO?
NO DICE. I COULDN'T GET IT OPEN...
SO I JUST RISKED MY LIFE FOR NOTHING?!
AT LEAST YOU GOT TEN BUCKS OUT OF IT.
I CAN'T TAKE ANY MORE GHOULS LOOKING FOR HANDOUTS. LET'S GET OUT OF HERE. I NEED A DRINK.
FUN! I'LL GET THE CAR--
THEY'RE LEAVING! WHAT DO WE DO?
I'M THINKING...
...DO YOU HAVE YOUR LOCK PICKS ON YOU?
ALWAYS.
WE GOTTA HIDE IN THE TRUNK!
I LOVE HALLOWEEN...
ISN'T IT JUST THE BEST?
VROOOOM
NO, IT IS NOT.

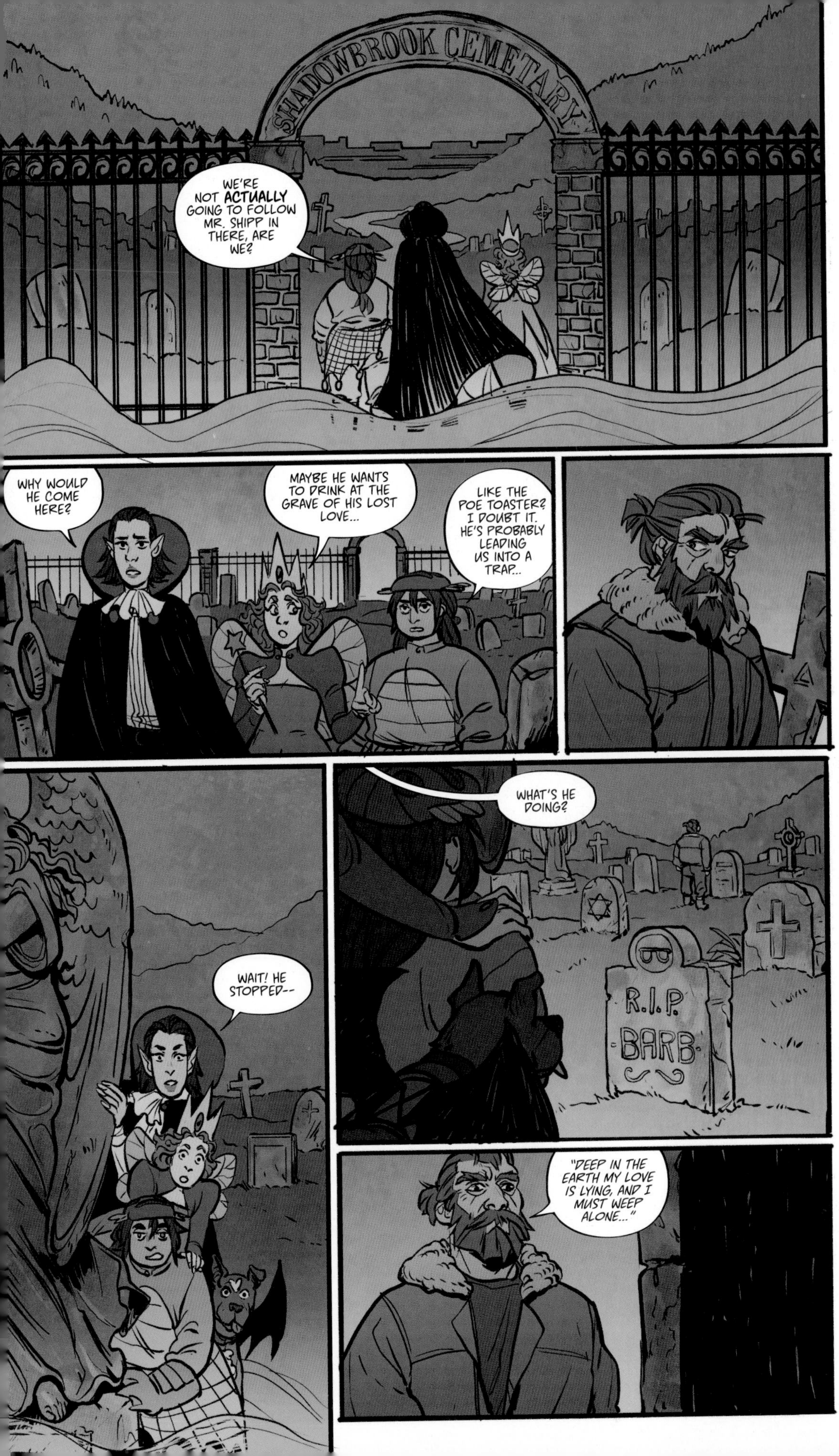
SHADOWBROOK CEMETARY
WE'RE NOT **ACTUALLY** GOING TO FOLLOW MR. SHIPP IN THERE, ARE WE?
WHY WOULD HE COME HERE?
MAYBE HE WANTS TO DRINK AT THE GRAVE OF HIS LOST LOVE...
LIKE THE POE TOASTER? I DOUBT IT. HE'S PROBABLY LEADING US INTO A TRAP...
WAIT! HE STOPPED--
WHAT'S HE DOING?
R.I.P. BARB
"DEEP IN THE EARTH MY LOVE IS LYING, AND I MUST WEEP ALONE..."

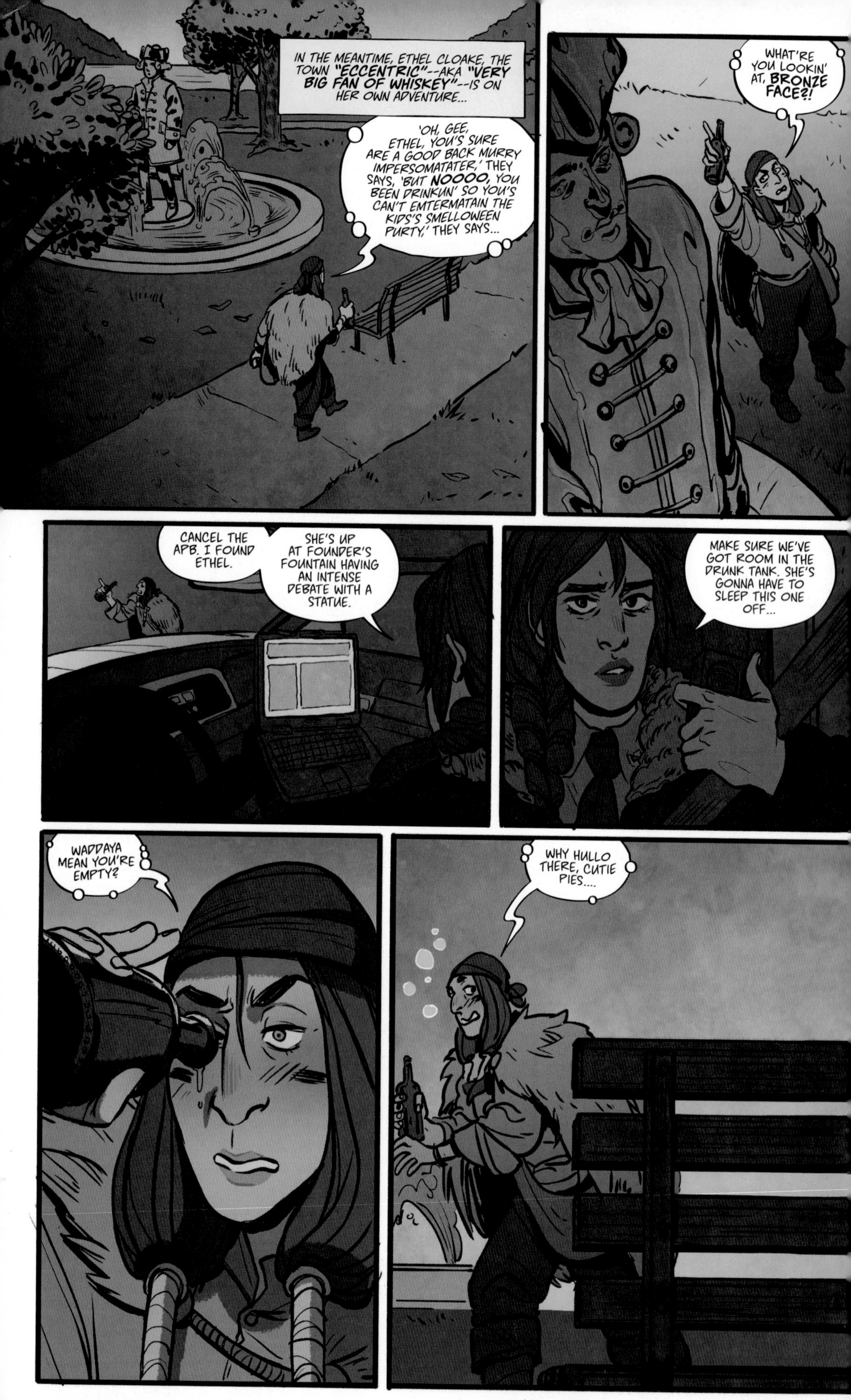
IN THE MEANTIME, ETHEL CLOAKE, THE TOWN "ECCENTRIC"--AKA "VERY BIG FAN OF WHISKEY"--IS ON HER OWN ADVENTURE...
'OH, GEE, ETHEL, YOU'S SURE ARE A GOOD BACK MURRY IMPERSOMATATER,' THEY SAYS, 'BUT NOOOO, YOU BEEN DRINKUN' SO YOU'S CAN'T EMTERMATAIN THE KIDS'S SMELLOWEEN PURTY,' THEY SAYS...
WHAT'RE YOU LOOKIN' AT, BRONZE FACE?!
CANCEL THE APB. I FOUND ETHEL.
SHE'S UP AT FOUNDER'S FOUNTAIN HAVING AN INTENSE DEBATE WITH A STATUE.
MAKE SURE WE'VE GOT ROOM IN THE DRUNK TANK. SHE'S GONNA HAVE TO SLEEP THIS ONE OFF...
WADDAYA MEAN YOU'RE EMPTY?
WHY HULLO THERE, CUTIE PIES....

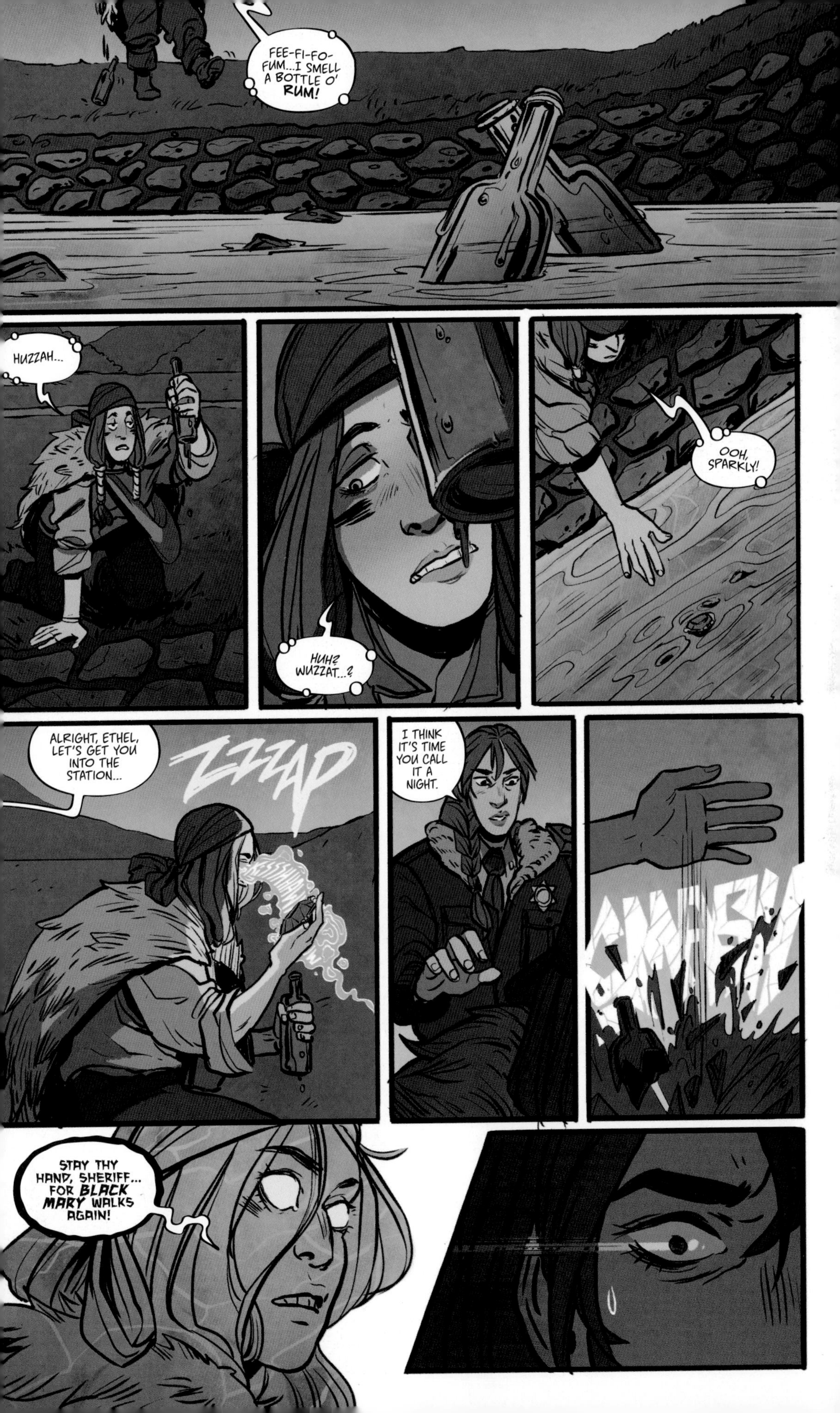
FEE-FI-FO-FUM...I SMELL A BOTTLE O' RUM!
HUZZAH...
HUH? WUZZAT...?
OOH, SPARKLY!
ALRIGHT, ETHEL, LET'S GET YOU INTO THE STATION...
ZZZAP
I THINK IT'S TIME YOU CALL IT A NIGHT.
STAY THY HAND, SHERIFF... FOR BLACK MARY WALKS AGAIN!

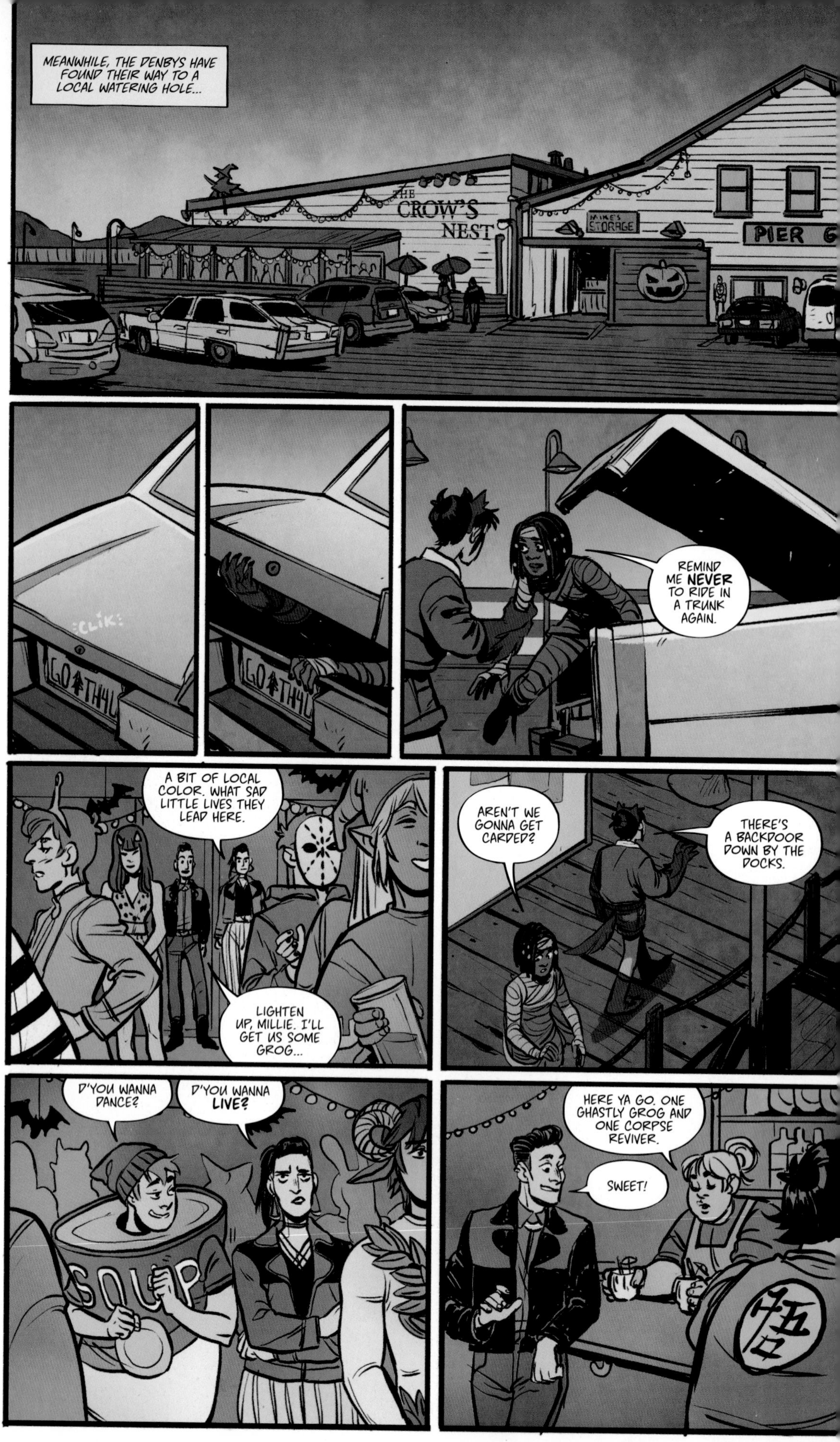
MEANWHILE, THE DENBYS HAVE FOUND THEIR WAY TO A LOCAL WATERING HOLE...
THE CROW'S NEST
MIKE'S STORAGE
PIER G
CLIK
GO TH4U
GO TH4U
REMIND ME NEVER TO RIDE IN A TRUNK AGAIN.
A BIT OF LOCAL COLOR. WHAT SAD LITTLE LIVES THEY LEAD HERE.
LIGHTEN UP, MILLIE. I'LL GET US SOME GROG...
AREN'T WE GONNA GET CARDED?
THERE'S A BACKDOOR DOWN BY THE DOCKS.
D'YOU WANNA DANCE?
D'YOU WANNA LIVE?
SOUP
HERE YA GO. ONE GHASTLY GROG AND ONE CORPSE REVIVER.
SWEET!

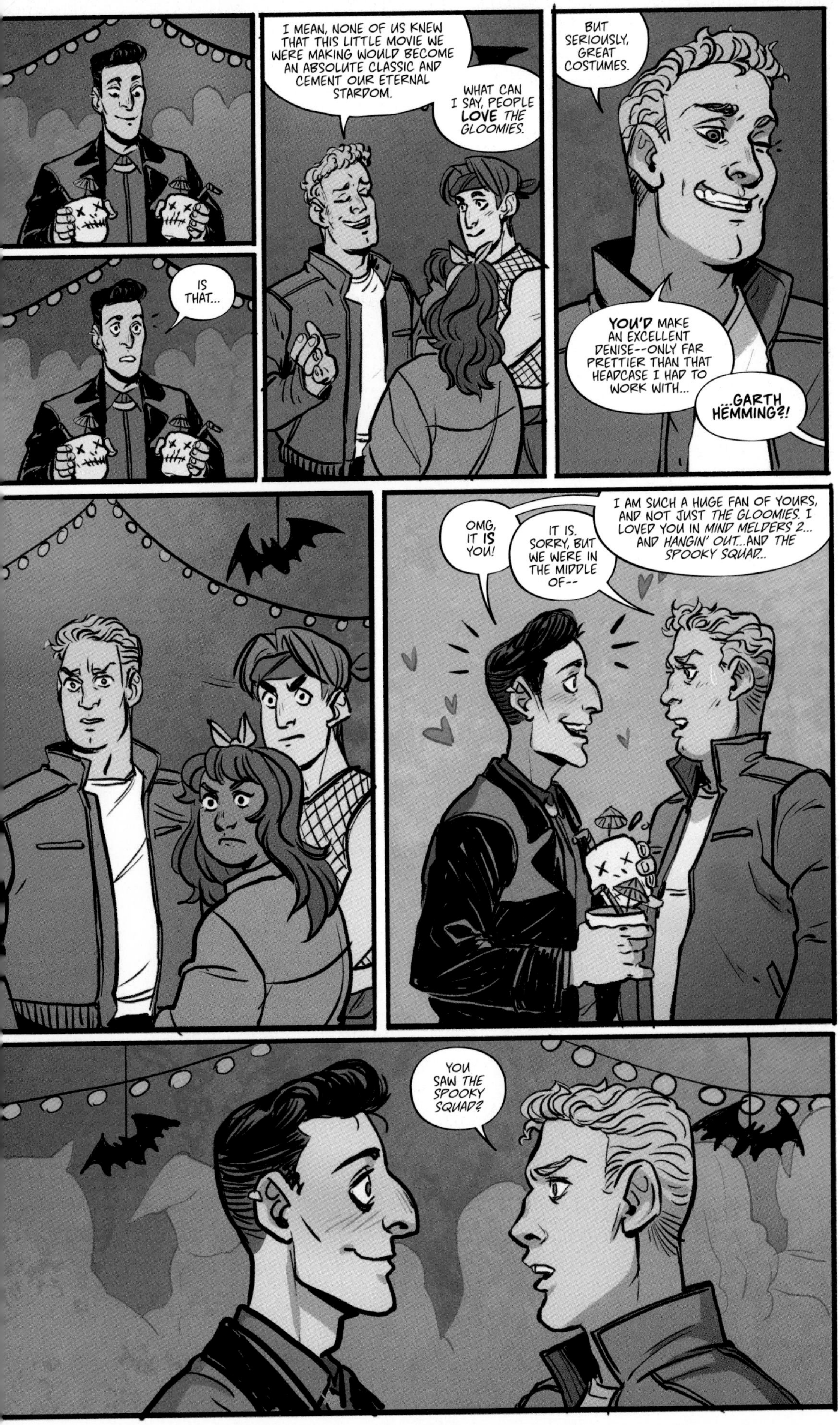

IS THAT...
I MEAN, NONE OF US KNEW THAT THIS LITTLE MOVIE WE WERE MAKING WOULD BECOME AN ABSOLUTE CLASSIC AND CEMENT OUR ETERNAL STARDOM.
WHAT CAN I SAY, PEOPLE **LOVE** *THE GLOOMIES.*
BUT SERIOUSLY, GREAT COSTUMES.
YOU'D MAKE AN EXCELLENT DENISE--ONLY FAR PRETTIER THAN THAT HEADCASE I HAD TO WORK WITH...
...GARTH HEMMING?!
OMG, IT **IS** YOU!
IT IS. SORRY, BUT WE WERE IN THE MIDDLE OF--
I AM SUCH A HUGE FAN OF YOURS, AND NOT JUST *THE GLOOMIES.* I LOVED YOU IN *MIND MELDERS 2*... AND *HANGIN' OUT*...AND *THE SPOOKY SQUAD*...
YOU SAW *THE SPOOKY SQUAD?*

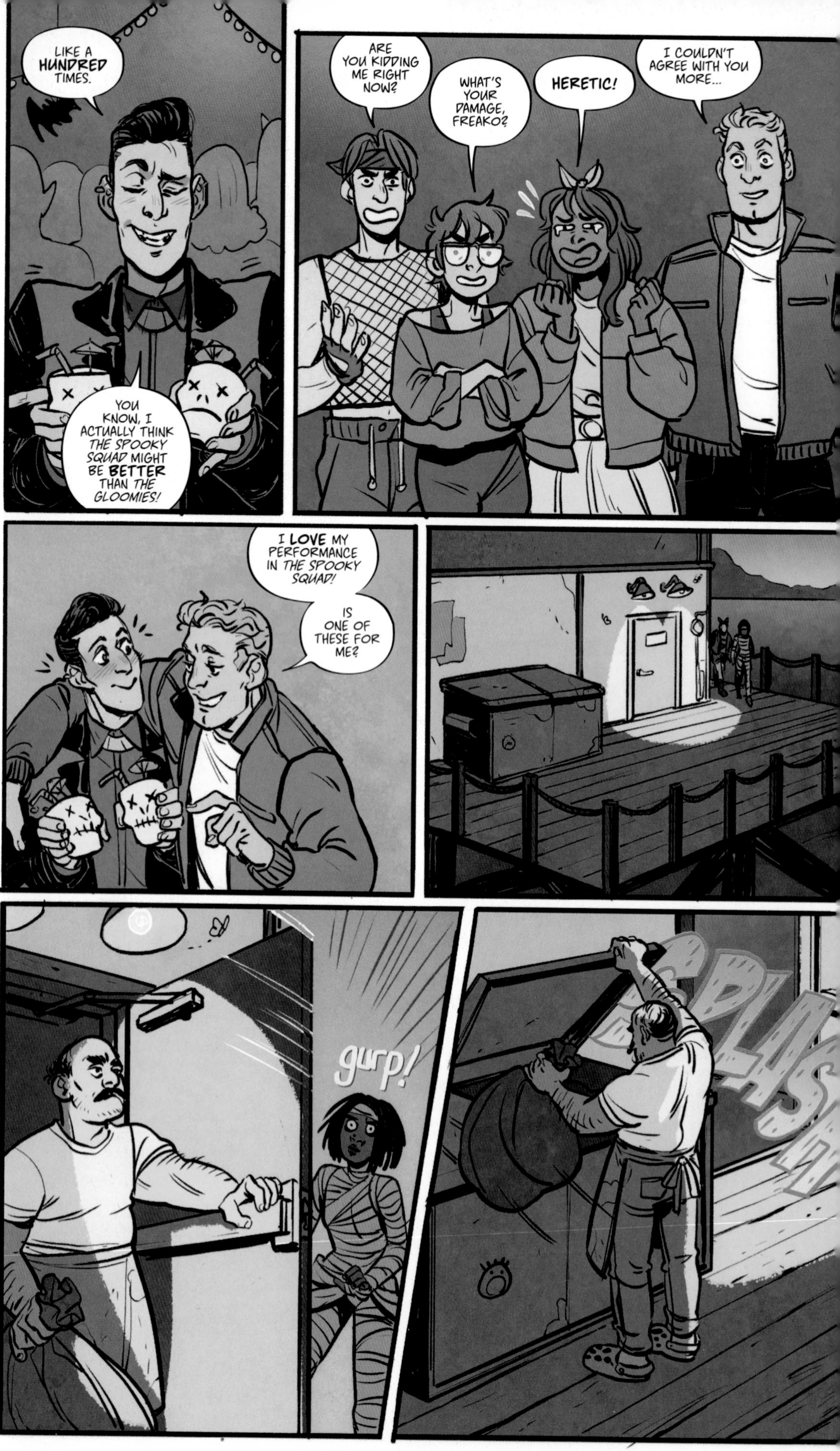

LIKE A **HUNDRED** TIMES.
YOU KNOW, I ACTUALLY THINK *THE SPOOKY SQUAD* MIGHT BE **BETTER** THAN *THE GLOOMIES!*
ARE YOU KIDDING ME RIGHT NOW?
WHAT'S YOUR DAMAGE, FREAKO?
HERETIC!
I COULDN'T AGREE WITH YOU MORE...
I **LOVE** MY PERFORMANCE IN *THE SPOOKY SQUAD!*
IS ONE OF THESE FOR ME?
gurp!

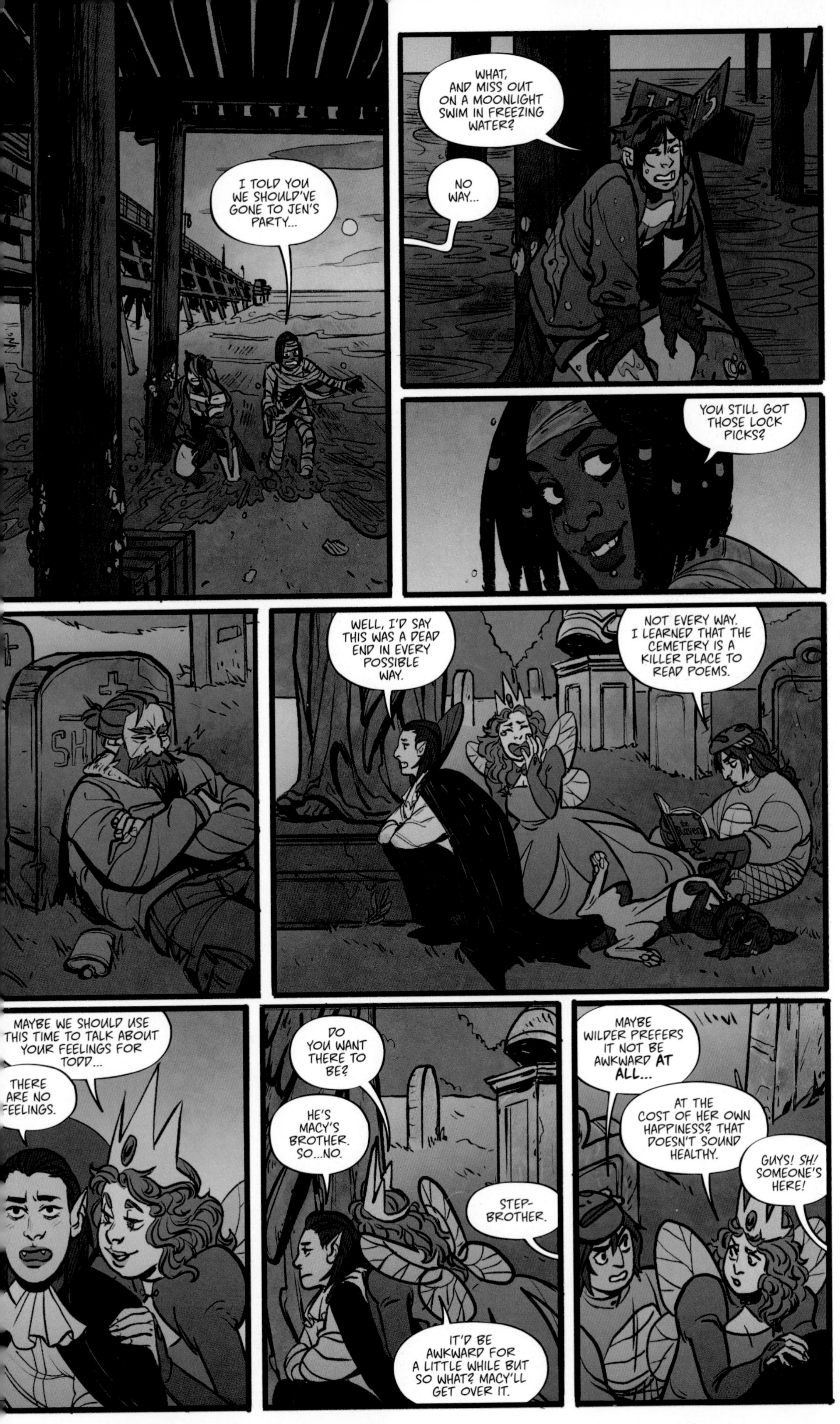
I TOLD YOU WE SHOULD'VE GONE TO JEN'S PARTY...
WHAT, AND MISS OUT ON A MOONLIGHT SWIM IN FREEZING WATER?
NO WAY...
YOU STILL GOT THOSE LOCK PICKS?
WELL, I'D SAY THIS WAS A DEAD END IN EVERY POSSIBLE WAY.
NOT EVERY WAY. I LEARNED THAT THE CEMETERY IS A KILLER PLACE TO READ POEMS.
MAYBE WE SHOULD USE THIS TIME TO TALK ABOUT YOUR FEELINGS FOR TODD...
THERE ARE NO FEELINGS.
DO YOU WANT THERE TO BE?
HE'S MACY'S BROTHER. SO...NO.
STEP-BROTHER.
IT'D BE AWKWARD FOR A LITTLE WHILE BUT SO WHAT? MACY'LL GET OVER IT.
MAYBE WILDER PREFERS IT NOT BE AWKWARD **AT ALL...**
AT THE COST OF HER OWN HAPPINESS? THAT DOESN'T SOUND HEALTHY.
GUYS! *SH!* SOMEONE'S HERE!

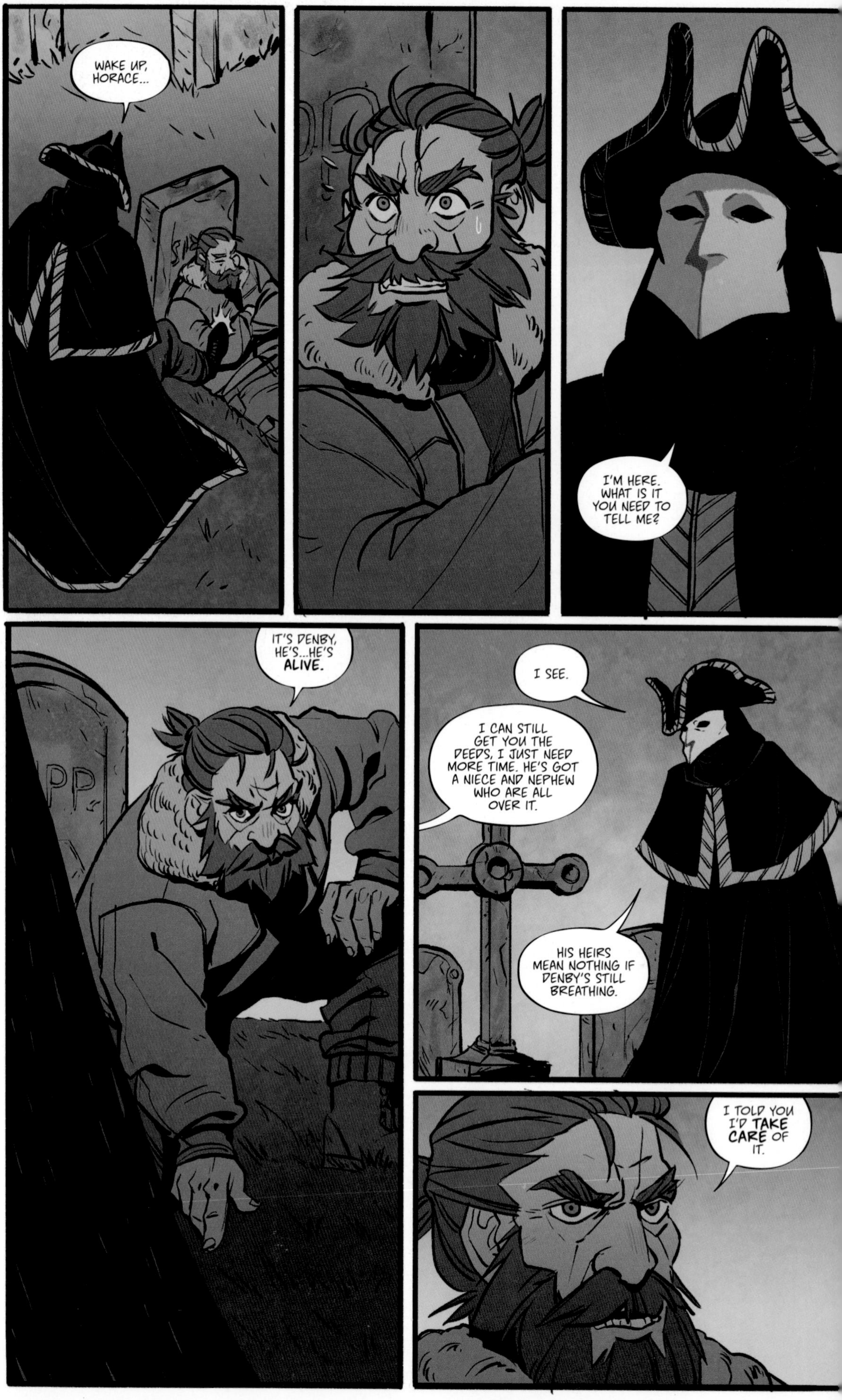
WAKE UP, HORACE...
I'M HERE. WHAT IS IT YOU NEED TO TELL ME?
IT'S DENBY, HE'S...HE'S ALIVE.
I SEE.
I CAN STILL GET YOU THE DEEDS, I JUST NEED MORE TIME. HE'S GOT A NIECE AND NEPHEW WHO ARE ALL OVER IT.
HIS HEIRS MEAN NOTHING IF DENBY'S STILL BREATHING.
I TOLD YOU I'D TAKE CARE OF IT.

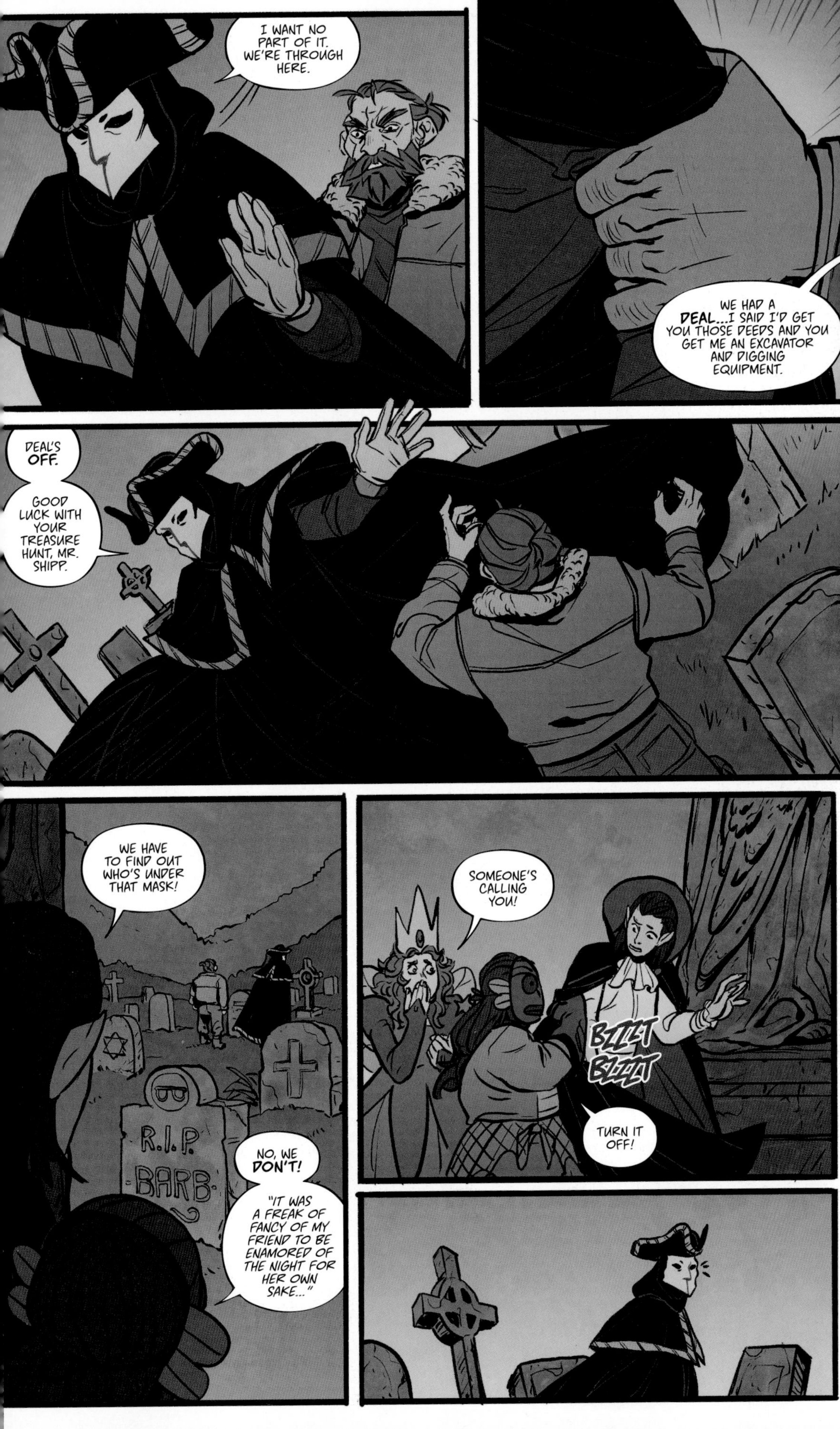
I WANT NO PART OF IT. WE'RE THROUGH HERE.
WE HAD A DEAL...I SAID I'D GET YOU THOSE DEEDS AND YOU GET ME AN EXCAVATOR AND DIGGING EQUIPMENT.
DEAL'S OFF.
GOOD LUCK WITH YOUR TREASURE HUNT, MR. SHIPP.
WE HAVE TO FIND OUT WHO'S UNDER THAT MASK!
R.I.P. BARB
NO, WE DON'T!
"IT WAS A FREAK OF FANCY OF MY FRIEND TO BE ENAMORED OF THE NIGHT FOR HER OWN SAKE..."
SOMEONE'S CALLING YOU!
BZZZT BZZZT
TURN IT OFF!

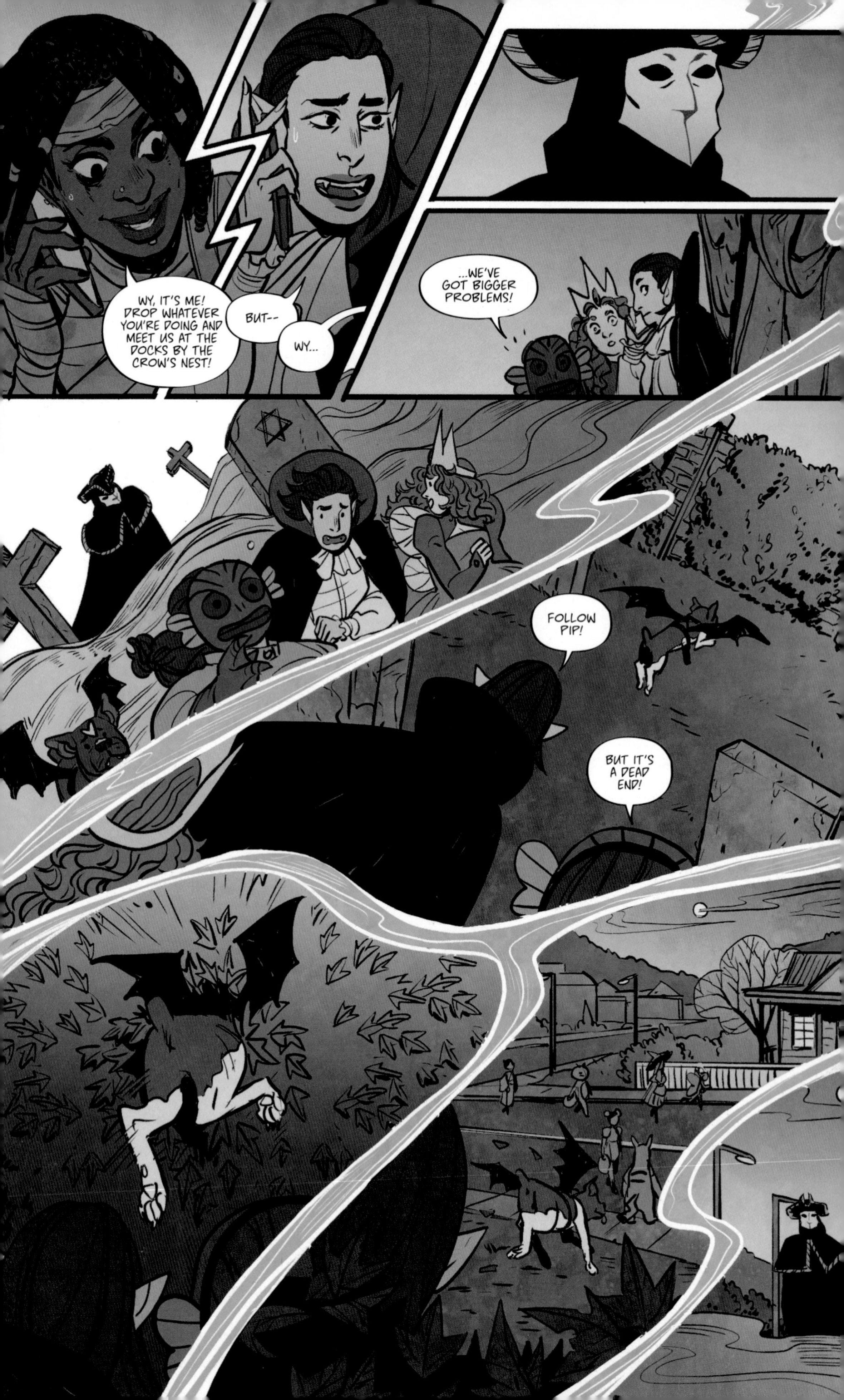
WY, IT'S ME! DROP WHATEVER YOU'RE DOING AND MEET US AT THE DOCKS BY THE CROW'S NEST!
BUT--
WY...
...WE'VE GOT BIGGER PROBLEMS!
FOLLOW PIP!
BUT IT'S A DEAD END!

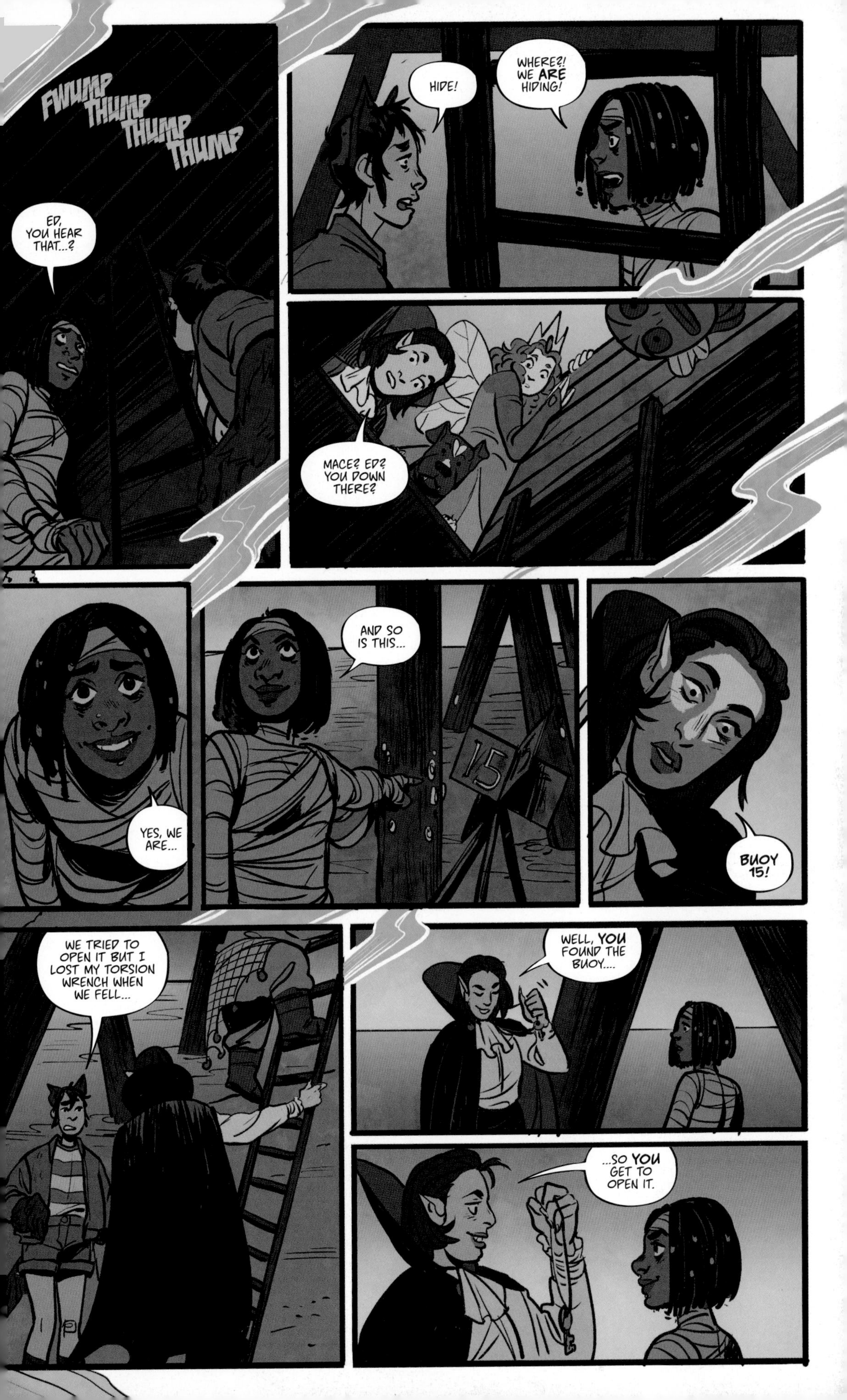
FWUMP THUMP THUMP THUMP
ED, YOU HEAR THAT...?
HIDE!
WHERE?! WE **ARE** HIDING!
MACE? ED? YOU DOWN THERE?
YES, WE ARE...
AND SO IS THIS...
15
BUOY 15!
WE TRIED TO OPEN IT BUT I LOST MY TORSION WRENCH WHEN WE FELL...
WELL, **YOU** FOUND THE BUOY....
...SO **YOU** GET TO OPEN IT.

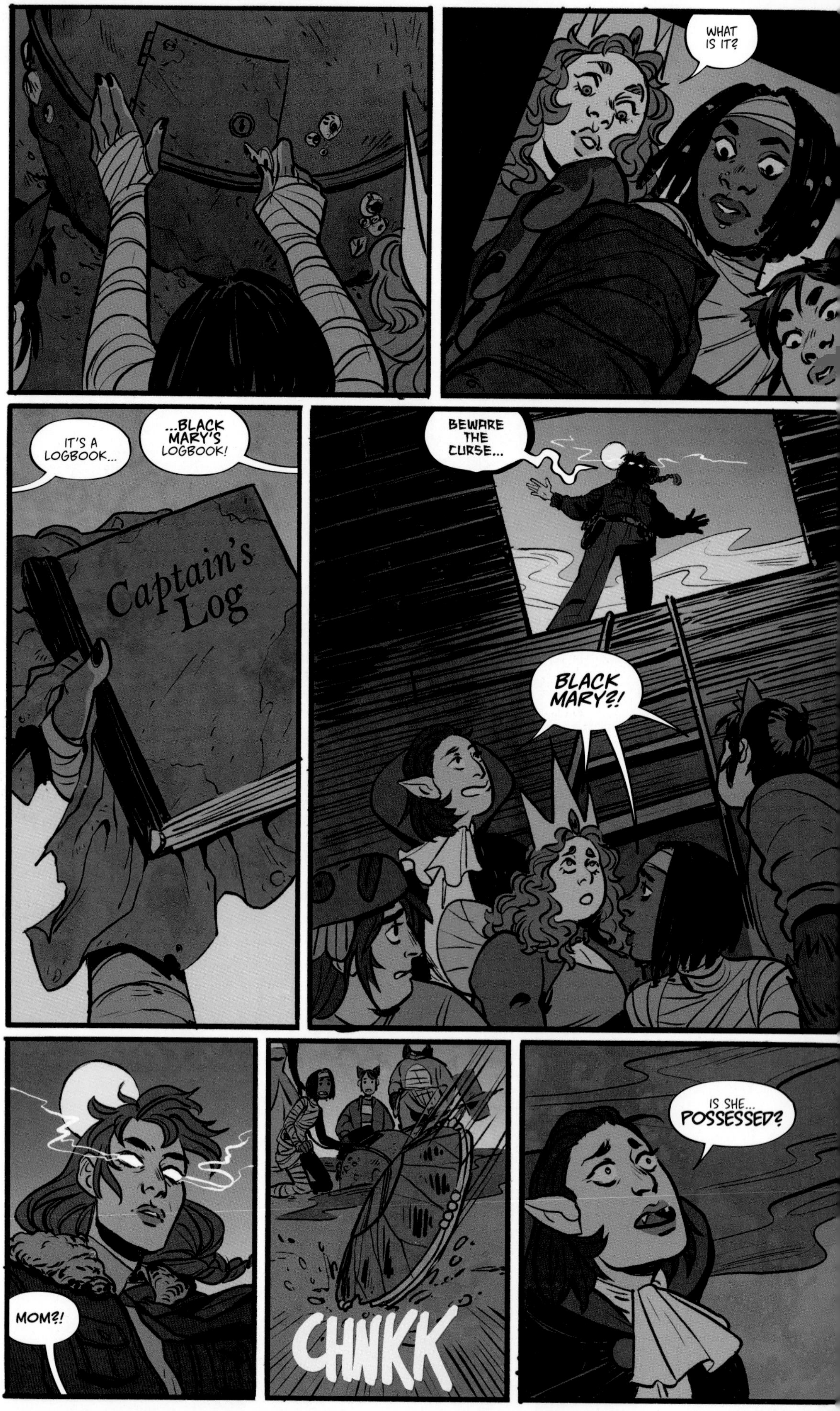
WHAT IS IT?
IT'S A LOGBOOK...
...BLACK MARY'S LOGBOOK!
Captain's Log
BEWARE THE CURSE...
BLACK MARY?!
MOM?!
CHNKK
IS SHE... POSSESSED?

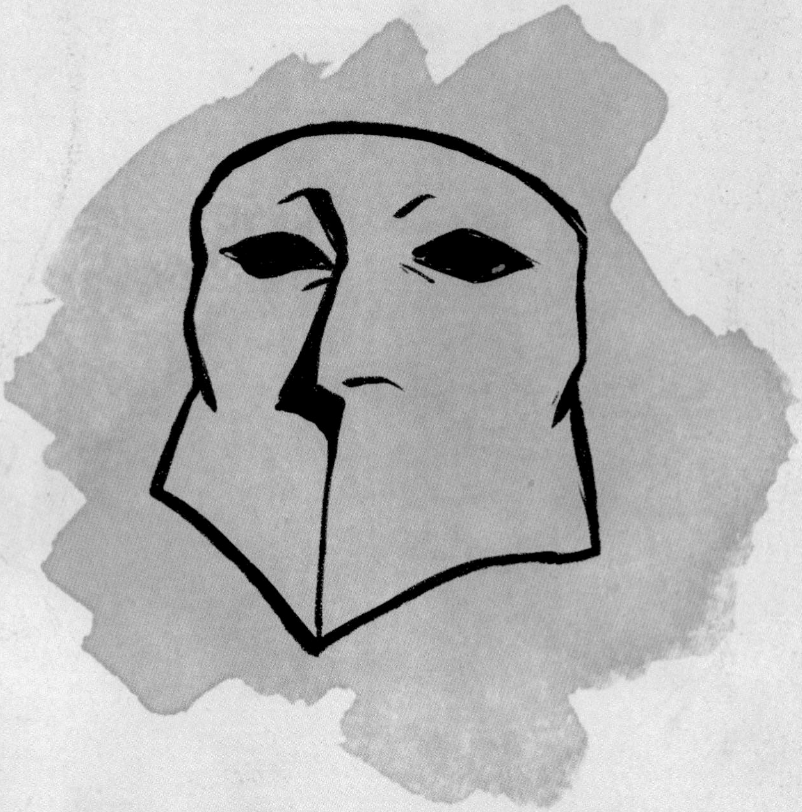

CHAPTER
VIII

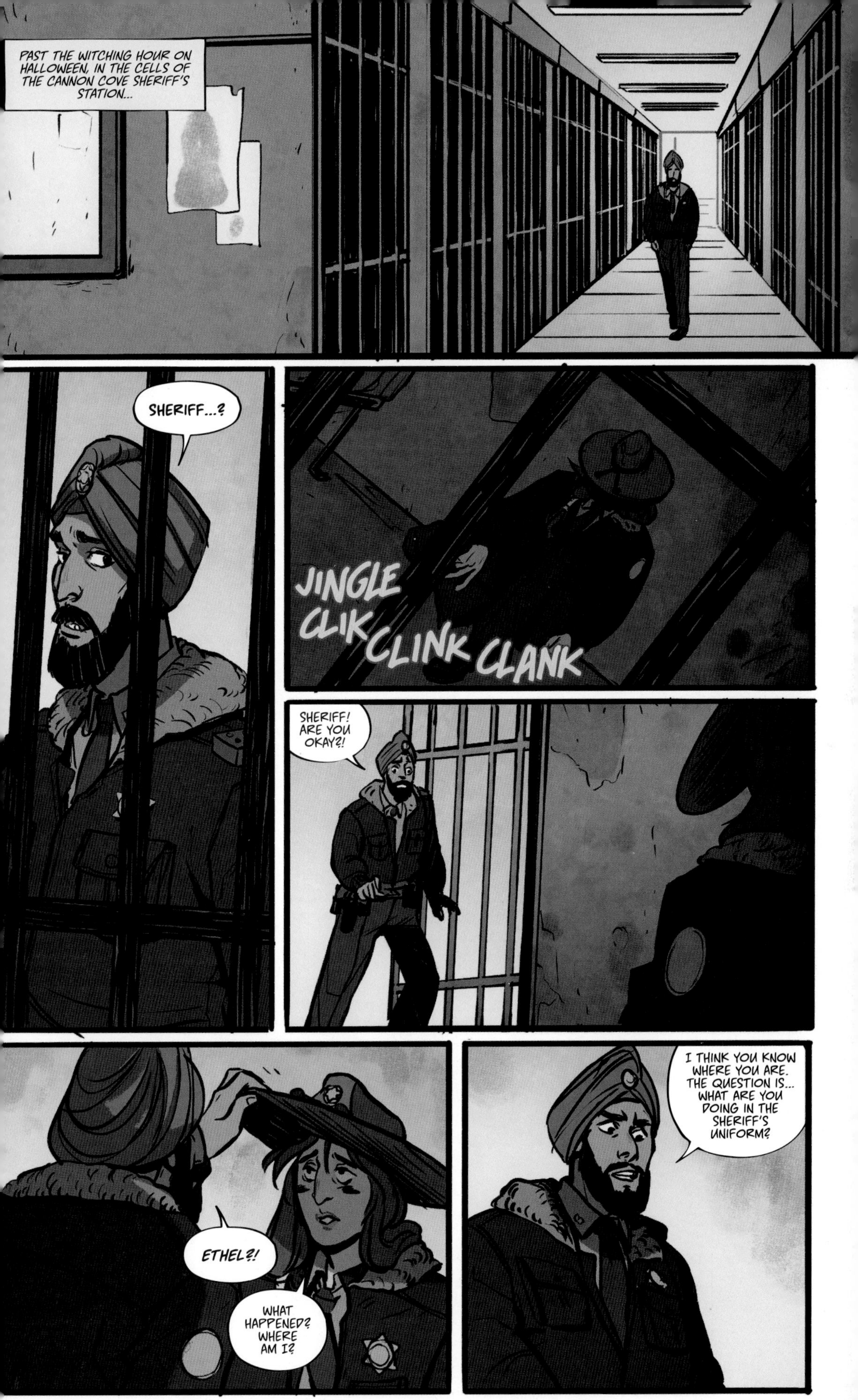

PAST THE WITCHING HOUR ON HALLOWEEN, IN THE CELLS OF THE CANNON COVE SHERIFF'S STATION...
SHERIFF...?
JINGLE
CLIK
CLINK
CLANK
SHERIFF! ARE YOU OKAY?!
ETHEL?!
WHAT HAPPENED? WHERE AM I?
I THINK YOU KNOW WHERE YOU ARE. THE QUESTION IS... WHAT ARE YOU DOING IN THE SHERIFF'S UNIFORM?

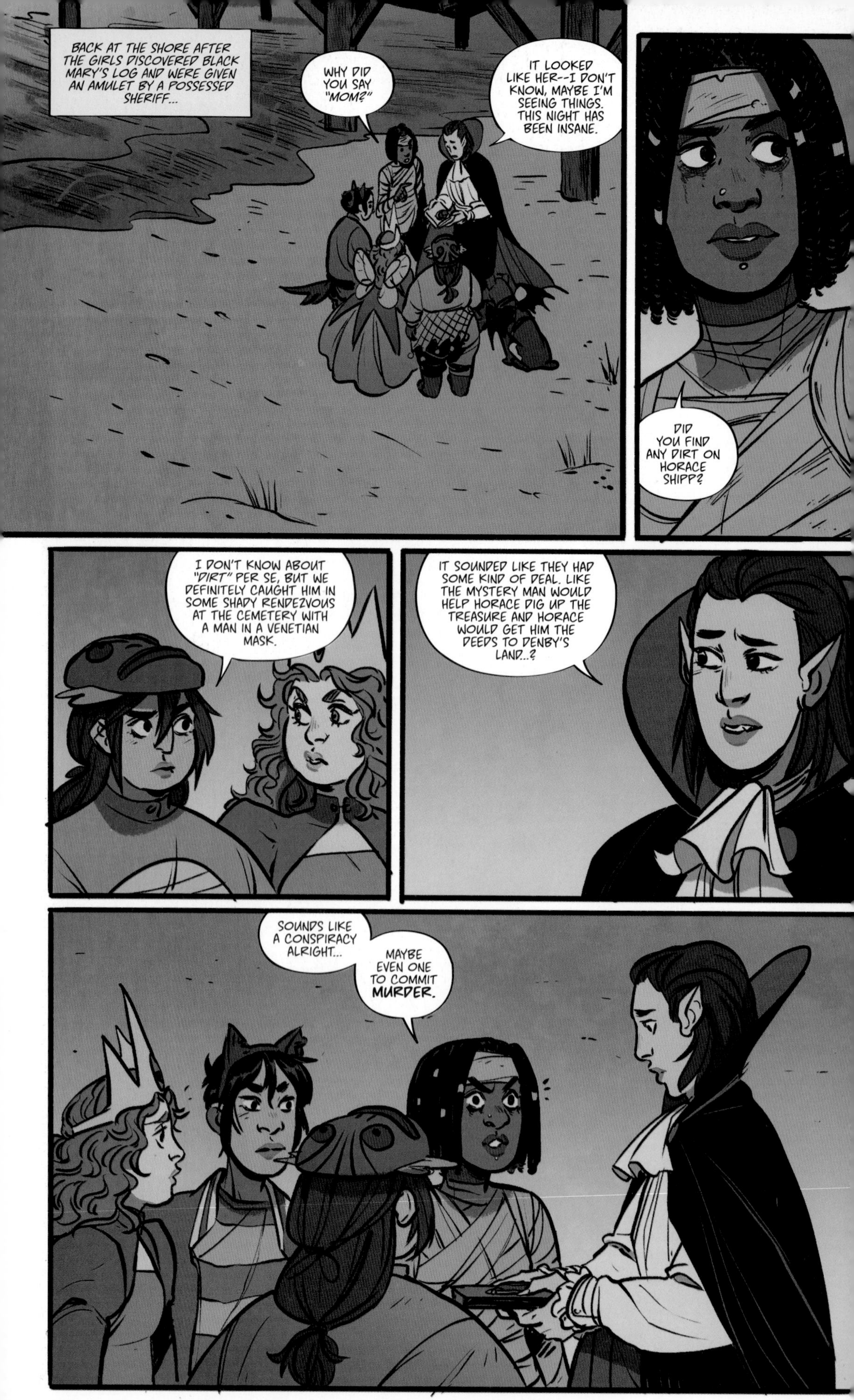
BACK AT THE SHORE AFTER THE GIRLS DISCOVERED BLACK MARY'S LOG AND WERE GIVEN AN AMULET BY A POSSESSED SHERIFF...
WHY DID YOU SAY "MOM?"
IT LOOKED LIKE HER--I DON'T KNOW, MAYBE I'M SEEING THINGS. THIS NIGHT HAS BEEN INSANE.
DID YOU FIND ANY DIRT ON HORACE SHIPP?
I DON'T KNOW ABOUT "DIRT" PER SE, BUT WE DEFINITELY CAUGHT HIM IN SOME SHADY RENDEZVOUS AT THE CEMETERY WITH A MAN IN A VENETIAN MASK.
IT SOUNDED LIKE THEY HAD SOME KIND OF DEAL. LIKE THE MYSTERY MAN WOULD HELP HORACE DIG UP THE TREASURE AND HORACE WOULD GET HIM THE DEEDS TO DENBY'S LAND...?
SOUNDS LIKE A CONSPIRACY ALRIGHT...
MAYBE EVEN ONE TO COMMIT **MURDER.**

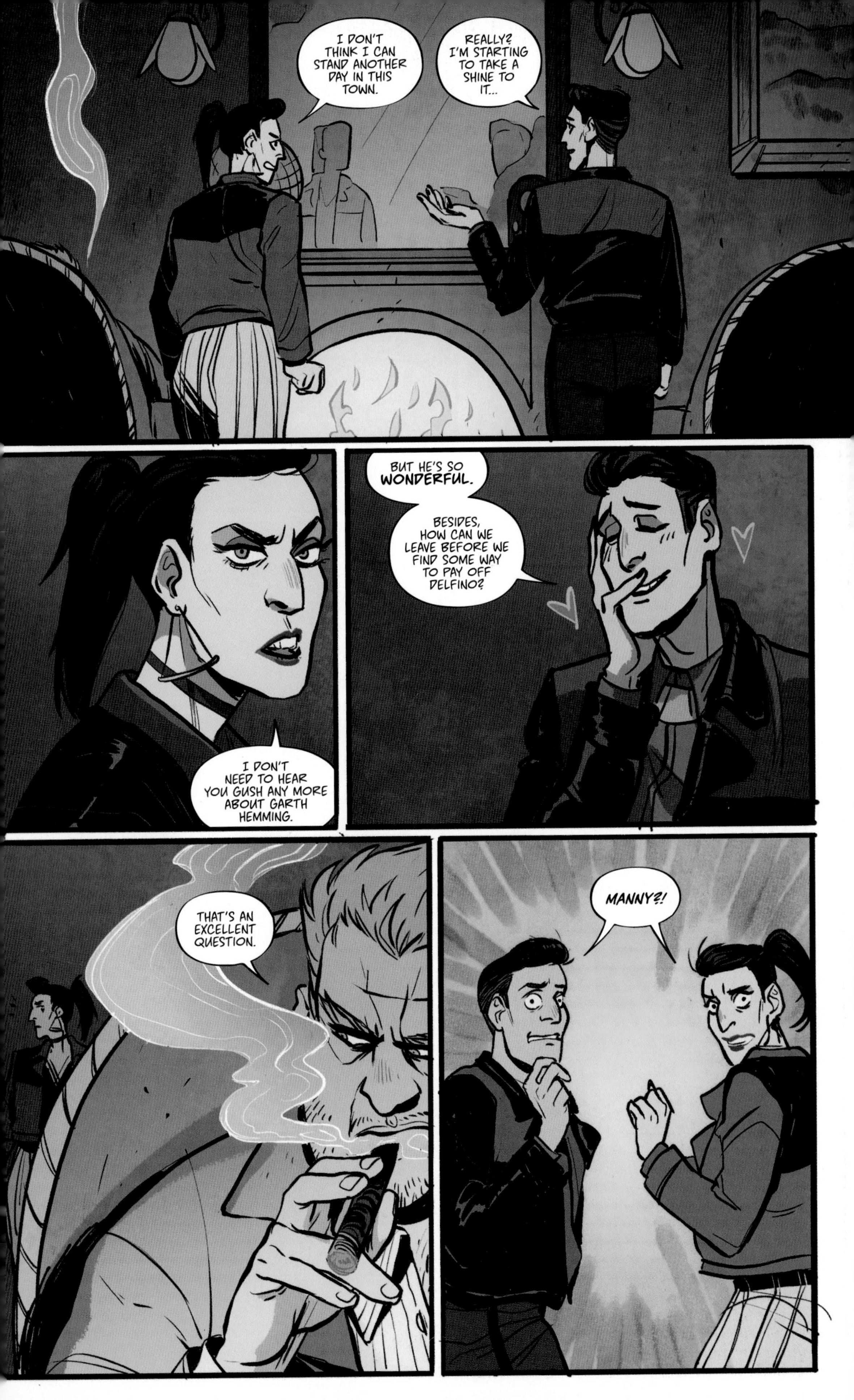
I DON'T THINK I CAN STAND ANOTHER DAY IN THIS TOWN.
REALLY? I'M STARTING TO TAKE A SHINE TO IT...
I DON'T NEED TO HEAR YOU GUSH ANY MORE ABOUT GARTH HEMMING.
BUT HE'S SO WONDERFUL.
BESIDES, HOW CAN WE LEAVE BEFORE WE FIND SOME WAY TO PAY OFF DELFINO?
THAT'S AN EXCELLENT QUESTION.
MANNY?!

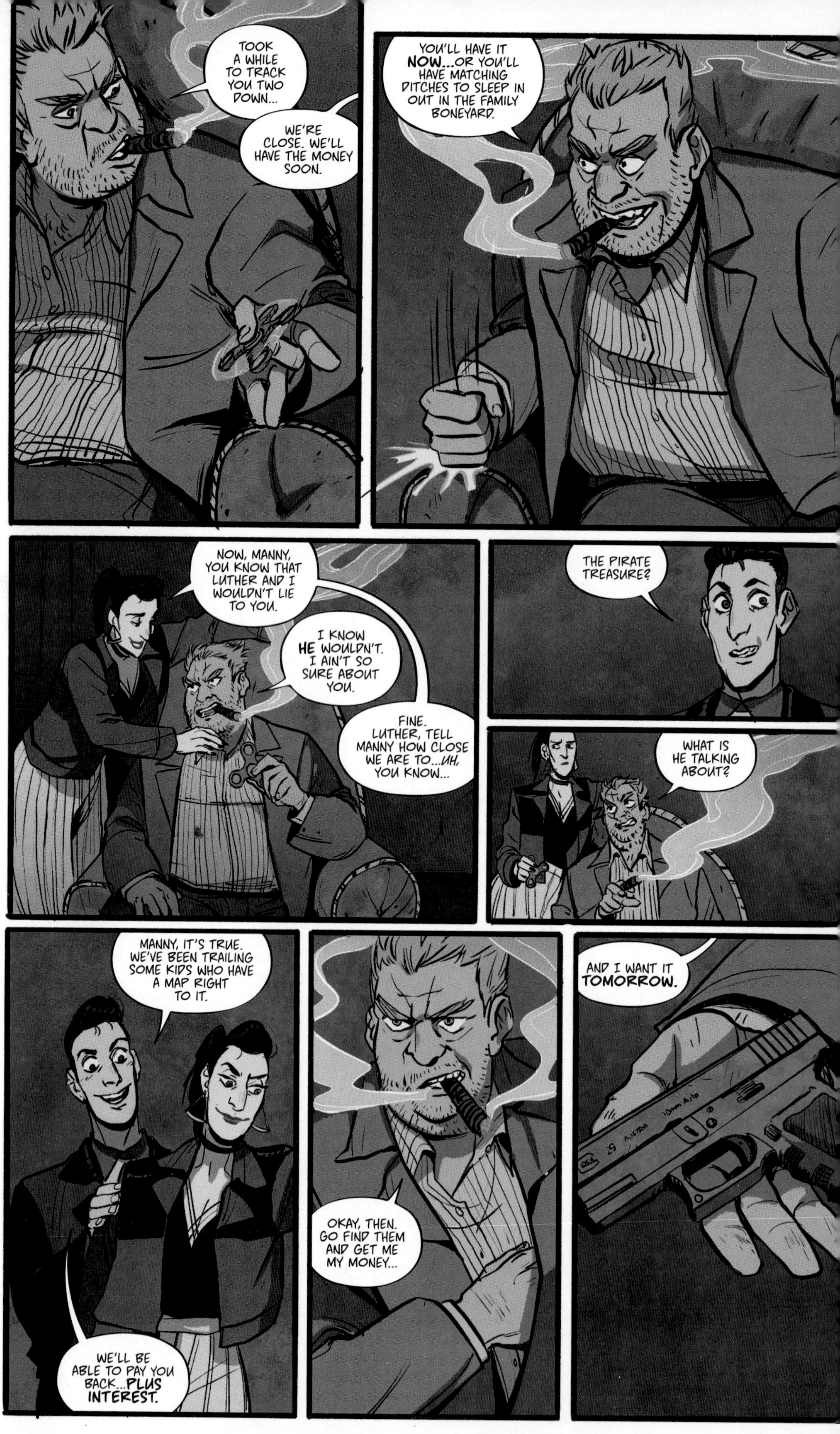
TOOK A WHILE TO TRACK YOU TWO DOWN...
WE'RE CLOSE. WE'LL HAVE THE MONEY SOON.
YOU'LL HAVE IT NOW...OR YOU'LL HAVE MATCHING DITCHES TO SLEEP IN OUT IN THE FAMILY BONEYARD.
NOW, MANNY, YOU KNOW THAT LUTHER AND I WOULDN'T LIE TO YOU.
I KNOW HE WOULDN'T. I AIN'T SO SURE ABOUT YOU.
FINE. LUTHER, TELL MANNY HOW CLOSE WE ARE TO...UH, YOU KNOW...
THE PIRATE TREASURE?
WHAT IS HE TALKING ABOUT?
MANNY, IT'S TRUE. WE'VE BEEN TRAILING SOME KIDS WHO HAVE A MAP RIGHT TO IT.
WE'LL BE ABLE TO PAY YOU BACK...PLUS INTEREST.
OKAY, THEN. GO FIND THEM AND GET ME MY MONEY...
AND I WANT IT TOMORROW.

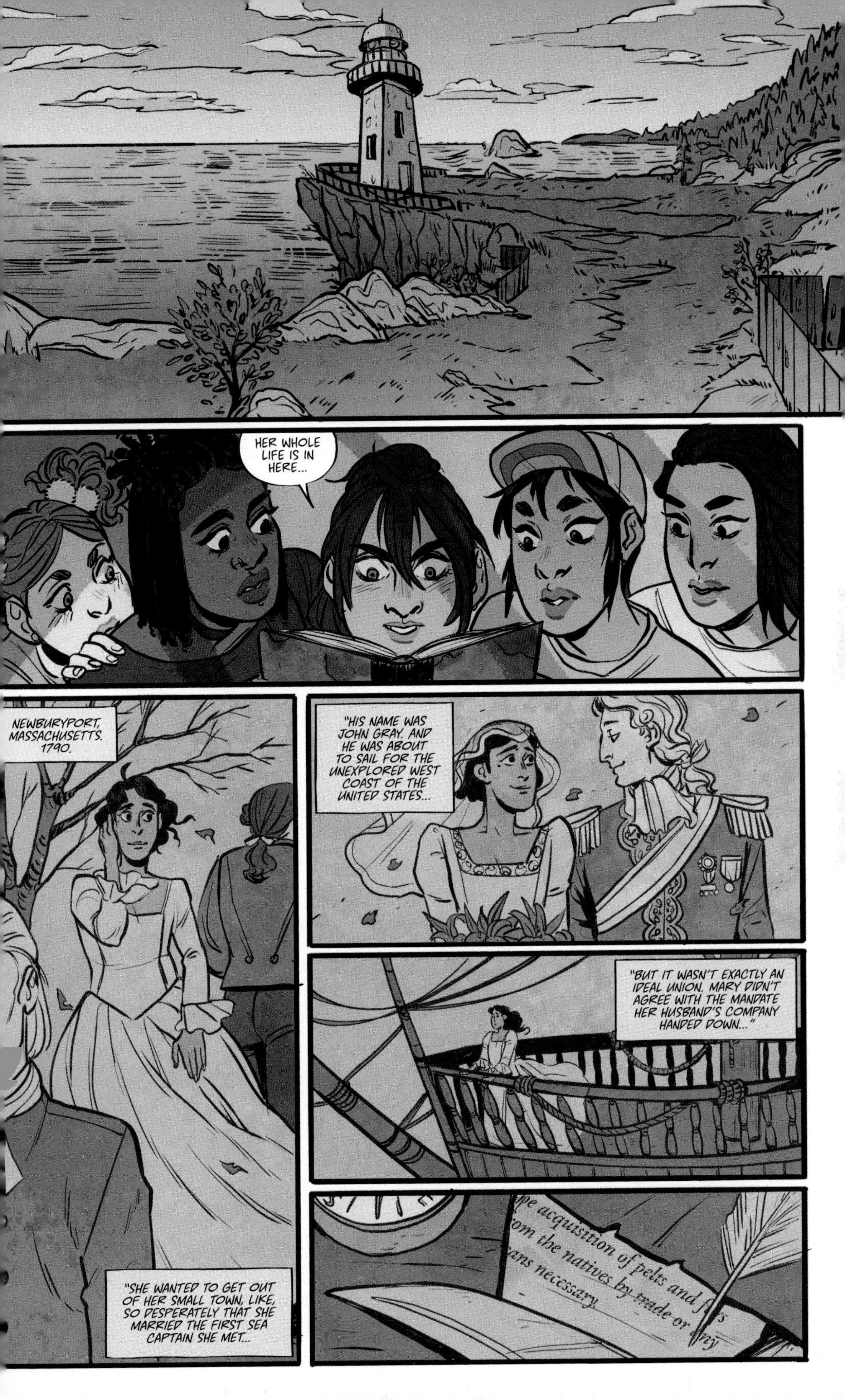

HER WHOLE LIFE IS IN HERE...
NEWBURYPORT, MASSACHUSETTS. 1790.
"SHE WANTED TO GET OUT OF HER SMALL TOWN, LIKE, SO DESPERATELY THAT SHE MARRIED THE FIRST SEA CAPTAIN SHE MET...
"HIS NAME WAS JOHN GRAY. AND HE WAS ABOUT TO SAIL FOR THE UNEXPLORED WEST COAST OF THE UNITED STATES...
"BUT IT WASN'T EXACTLY AN IDEAL UNION. MARY DIDN'T AGREE WITH THE MANDATE HER HUSBAND'S COMPANY HANDED DOWN..."
acquisition of pelts and
the natives by trade or
necessary

IT'S A FINE HAUL, BUT IF WE PURSUE **OTHER** MEASURES WE COULD PRESERVE OUR TRADE STOCK FOR THE HAWAIIAN ISLANDS EN ROUTE TO CHINA.

"AND WHEN SHE REALIZED WHAT WAS ABOUT TO HAPPEN, SHE CHOSE TO RESIST."

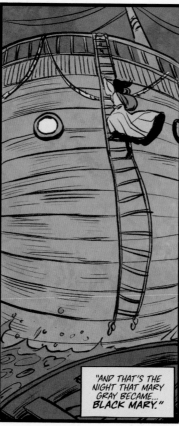

"AND THAT'S THE NIGHT THAT MARY GRAY BECAME... **BLACK MARY.**"

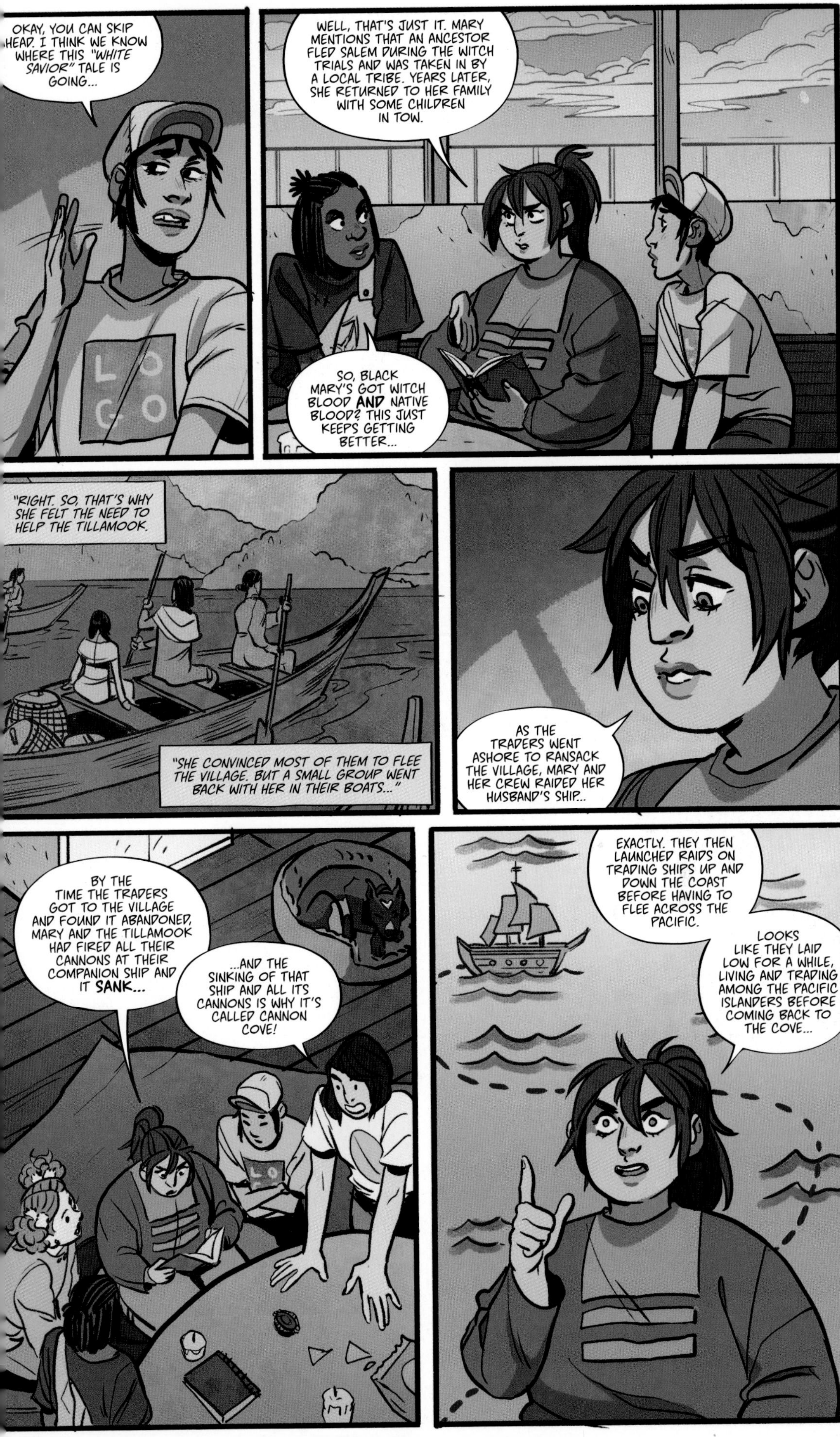

OKAY, YOU CAN SKIP AHEAD. I THINK WE KNOW WHERE THIS "WHITE SAVIOR" TALE IS GOING...
WELL, THAT'S JUST IT. MARY MENTIONS THAT AN ANCESTOR FLED SALEM DURING THE WITCH TRIALS AND WAS TAKEN IN BY A LOCAL TRIBE. YEARS LATER, SHE RETURNED TO HER FAMILY WITH SOME CHILDREN IN TOW.
SO, BLACK MARY'S GOT WITCH BLOOD AND NATIVE BLOOD? THIS JUST KEEPS GETTING BETTER...
"RIGHT. SO, THAT'S WHY SHE FELT THE NEED TO HELP THE TILLAMOOK.
"SHE CONVINCED MOST OF THEM TO FLEE THE VILLAGE. BUT A SMALL GROUP WENT BACK WITH HER IN THEIR BOATS..."
AS THE TRADERS WENT ASHORE TO RANSACK THE VILLAGE, MARY AND HER CREW RAIDED HER HUSBAND'S SHIP...
BY THE TIME THE TRADERS GOT TO THE VILLAGE AND FOUND IT ABANDONED, MARY AND THE TILLAMOOK HAD FIRED ALL THEIR CANNONS AT THEIR COMPANION SHIP AND IT SANK...
...AND THE SINKING OF THAT SHIP AND ALL ITS CANNONS IS WHY IT'S CALLED CANNON COVE!
EXACTLY. THEY THEN LAUNCHED RAIDS ON TRADING SHIPS UP AND DOWN THE COAST BEFORE HAVING TO FLEE ACROSS THE PACIFIC.
LOOKS LIKE THEY LAID LOW FOR A WHILE, LIVING AND TRADING AMONG THE PACIFIC ISLANDERS BEFORE COMING BACK TO THE COVE...

WHAT'S ALL THAT STUFF WRITTEN THERE?

SOMETHING ABOUT THEIR TREASURE GETTING TOO BIG...AND IT WAS GETTING HARDER FOR THEM TO SNEAK INTO PORT, SO THEY BUILT A VAULT ON AN ISLAND OFF THE COAST.

WAIT...THE TREASURE IS ON AN ISLAND SOMEWHERE?

WOW. EVEN PIRATES KNEW TO USE OFFSHORE BANKS. BALLER.

SO WHY DID THE MAP LEAD US OUT TO BOOTLEGGER'S BLUFF?

THAT'S WHERE THEY KEPT IT UNTIL IT GOT TOO HOT. THEY LEFT A KEY THERE THAT WOULD LEAD TO THE LARGER TREASURE...

THE AMULET! THE JEWELS IN IT LINE UP WITH THE GRAY ISLANDS-- THIS EMERALD MUST MARK THE ISLAND WHERE THE TREASURE'S HIDDEN!

HOLD UP. THERE'S SOMETHING ELSE WRITTEN HERE...

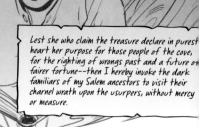

Lest she who claim the treasure declare in purest heart her purpose for those people of the cove, for the righting of wrongs past and a future of fairer fortune--then I hereby invoke the dark familiars of my Salem ancestors to visit their charnel wrath upon the usurpers, without mercy or measure.

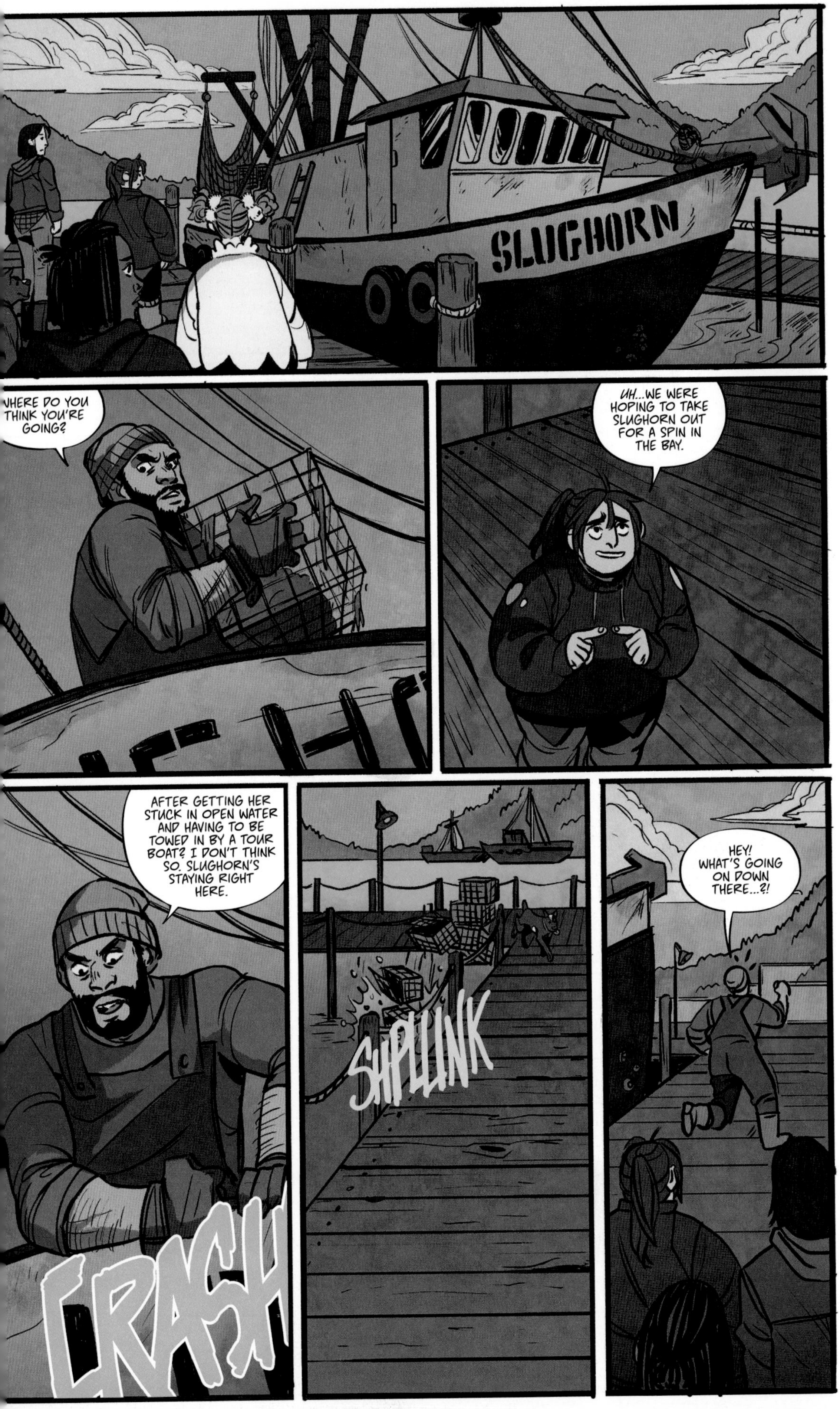
SLUGHORN
WHERE DO YOU THINK YOU'RE GOING?
UH...WE WERE HOPING TO TAKE SLUGHORN OUT FOR A SPIN IN THE BAY.
AFTER GETTING HER STUCK IN OPEN WATER AND HAVING TO BE TOWED IN BY A TOUR BOAT? I DON'T THINK SO. SLUGHORN'S STAYING RIGHT HERE.
CRASH
SHPLLINK
HEY! WHAT'S GOING ON DOWN THERE...?!

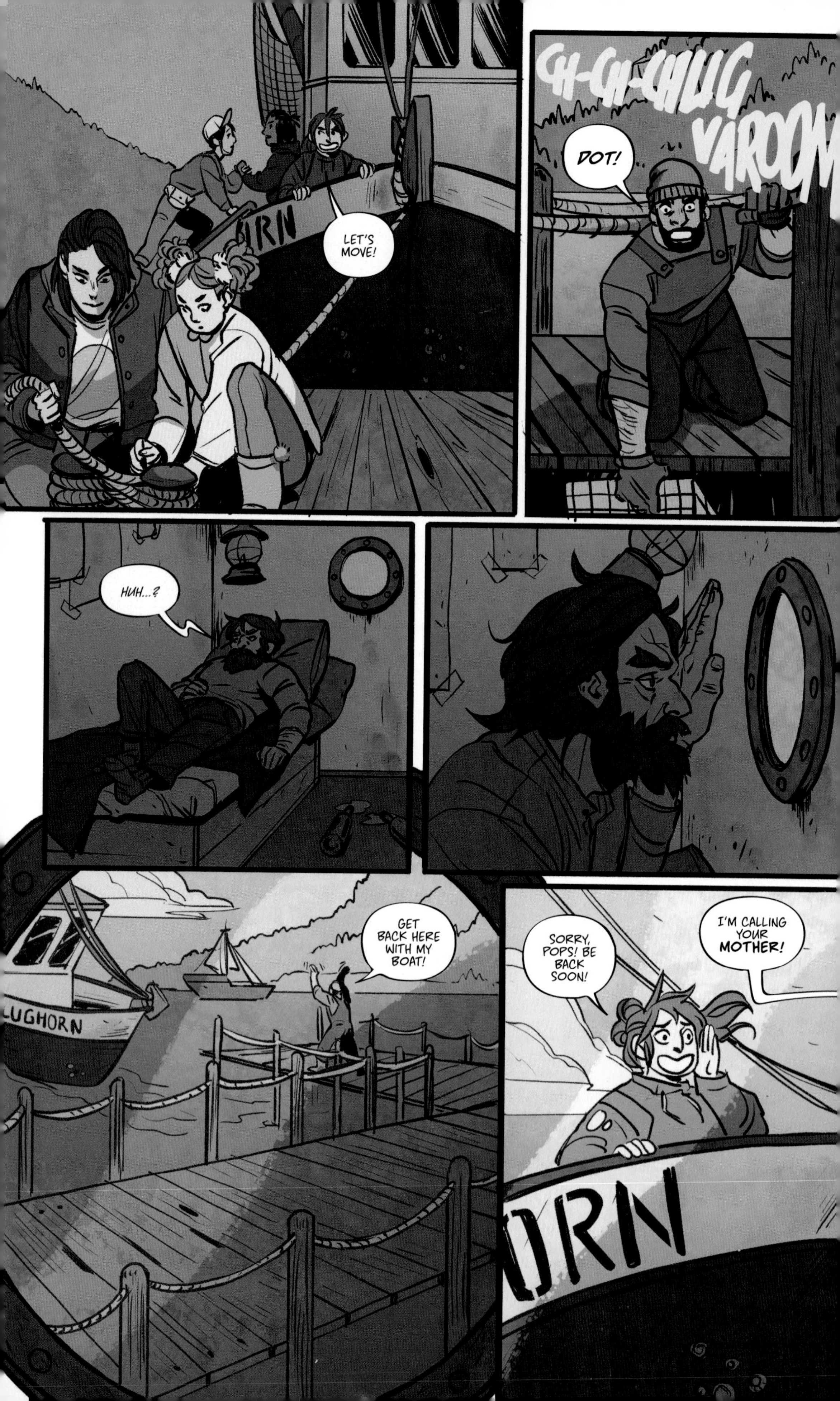

LET'S MOVE!
CH-CH-CHUG
VAROOM
DOT!
HUH...?
GET BACK HERE WITH MY BOAT!
SORRY, POPS! BE BACK SOON!
I'M CALLING YOUR **MOTHER!**

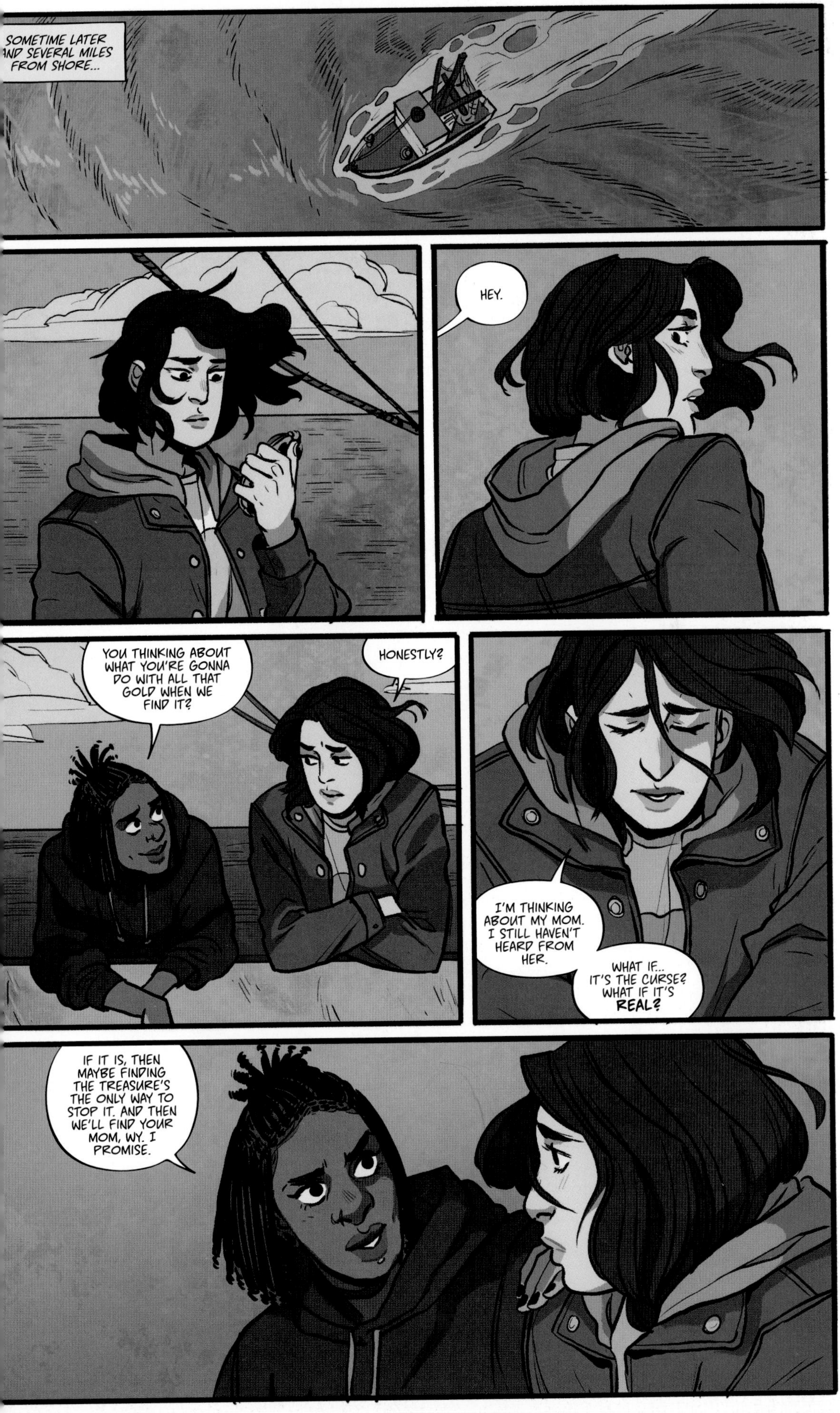
SOMETIME LATER AND SEVERAL MILES FROM SHORE...
HEY.
YOU THINKING ABOUT WHAT YOU'RE GONNA DO WITH ALL THAT GOLD WHEN WE FIND IT?
HONESTLY?
I'M THINKING ABOUT MY MOM. I STILL HAVEN'T HEARD FROM HER.
WHAT IF... IT'S THE CURSE? WHAT IF IT'S REAL?
IF IT IS, THEN MAYBE FINDING THE TREASURE'S THE ONLY WAY TO STOP IT. AND THEN WE'LL FIND YOUR MOM, WY. I PROMISE.

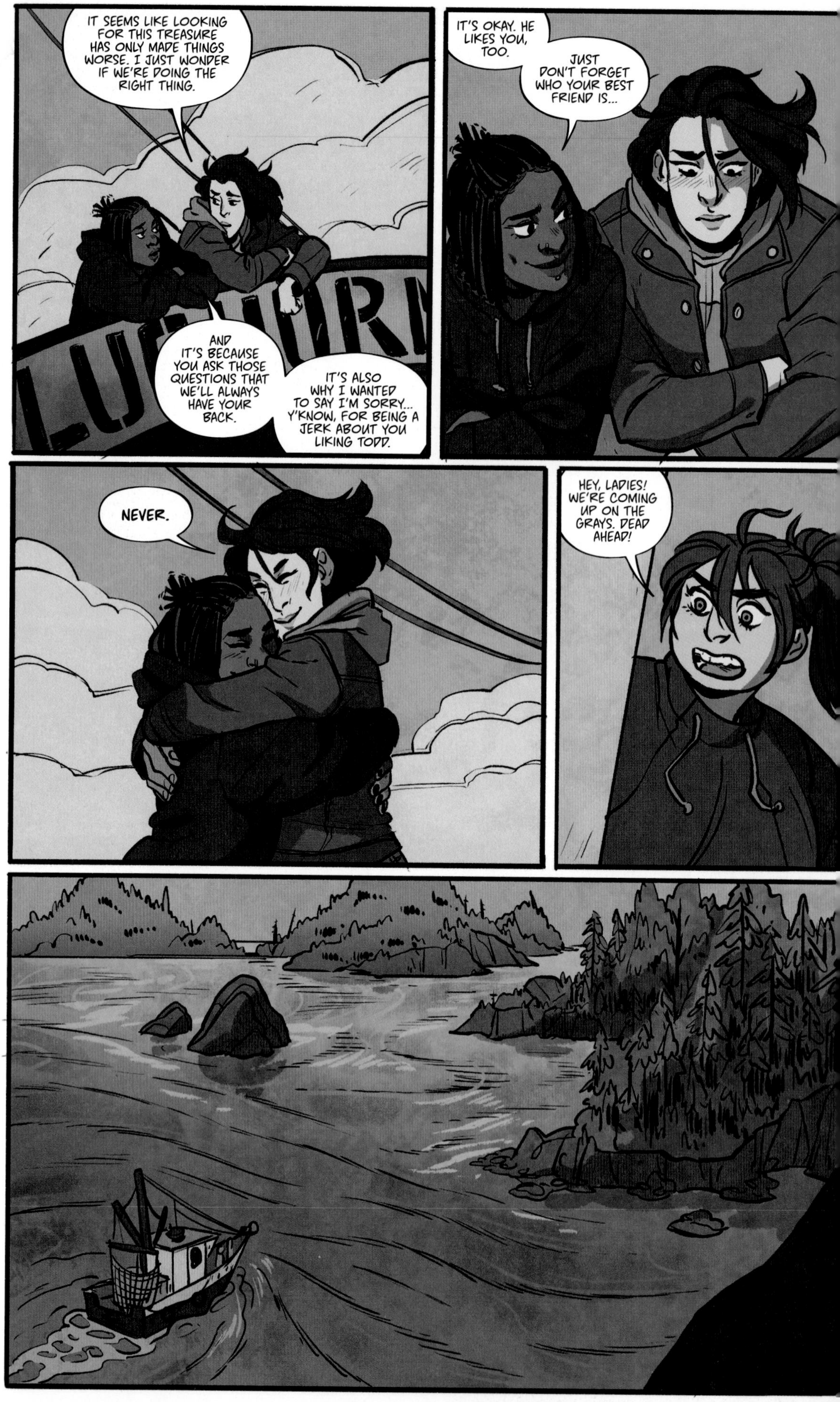

IT SEEMS LIKE LOOKING FOR THIS TREASURE HAS ONLY MADE THINGS WORSE. I JUST WONDER IF WE'RE DOING THE RIGHT THING.
AND IT'S BECAUSE YOU ASK THOSE QUESTIONS THAT WE'LL ALWAYS HAVE YOUR BACK.
IT'S ALSO WHY I WANTED TO SAY I'M SORRY... Y'KNOW, FOR BEING A JERK ABOUT YOU LIKING TODD.
IT'S OKAY. HE LIKES YOU, TOO.
JUST DON'T FORGET WHO YOUR BEST FRIEND IS...
NEVER.
HEY, LADIES! WE'RE COMING UP ON THE GRAYS. DEAD AHEAD!

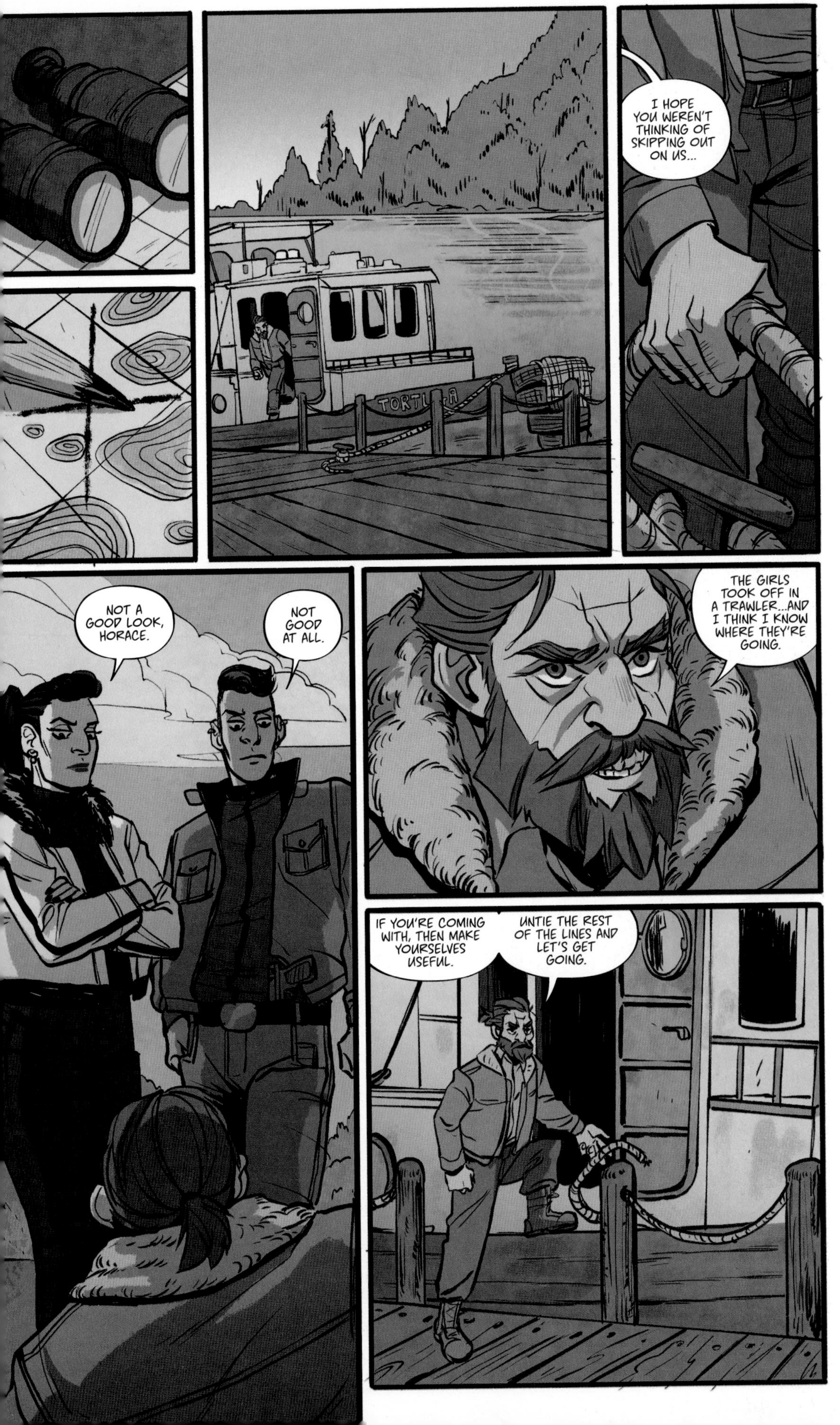
I HOPE YOU WEREN'T THINKING OF SKIPPING OUT ON US...
TORTUGA
NOT A GOOD LOOK, HORACE.
NOT GOOD AT ALL.
THE GIRLS TOOK OFF IN A TRAWLER...AND I THINK I KNOW WHERE THEY'RE GOING.
IF YOU'RE COMING WITH, THEN MAKE YOURSELVES USEFUL.
UNTIE THE REST OF THE LINES AND LET'S GET GOING.

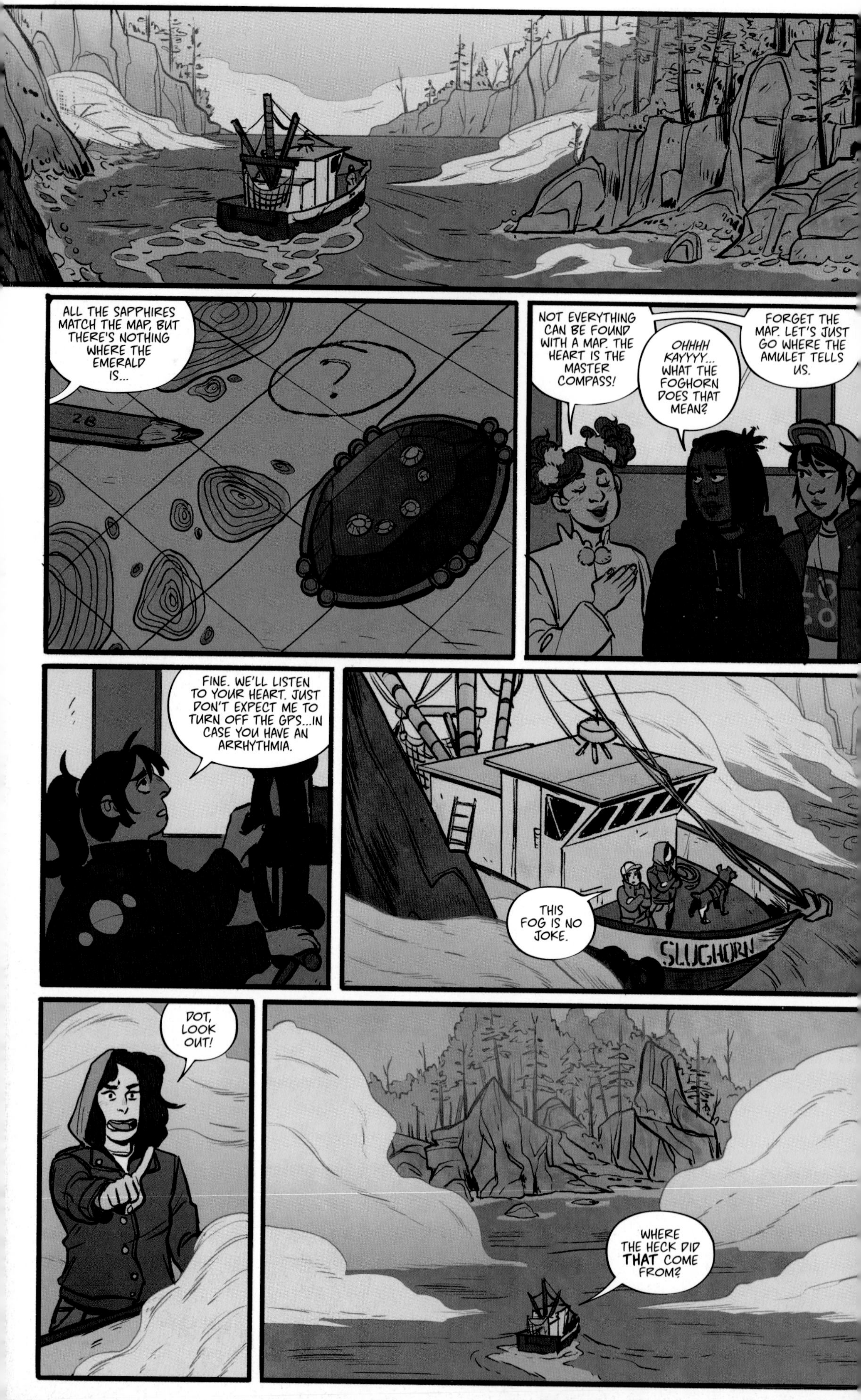

ALL THE SAPPHIRES MATCH THE MAP, BUT THERE'S NOTHING WHERE THE EMERALD IS...
2B
NOT EVERYTHING CAN BE FOUND WITH A MAP. THE HEART IS THE MASTER COMPASS!
OHHHH KAYYYY... WHAT THE FOGHORN DOES THAT MEAN?
FORGET THE MAP. LET'S JUST GO WHERE THE AMULET TELLS US.
FINE. WE'LL LISTEN TO YOUR HEART. JUST DON'T EXPECT ME TO TURN OFF THE GPS...IN CASE YOU HAVE AN ARRHYTHMIA.
THIS FOG IS NO JOKE.
SLUGHORN
DOT, LOOK OUT!
WHERE THE HECK DID **THAT** COME FROM?

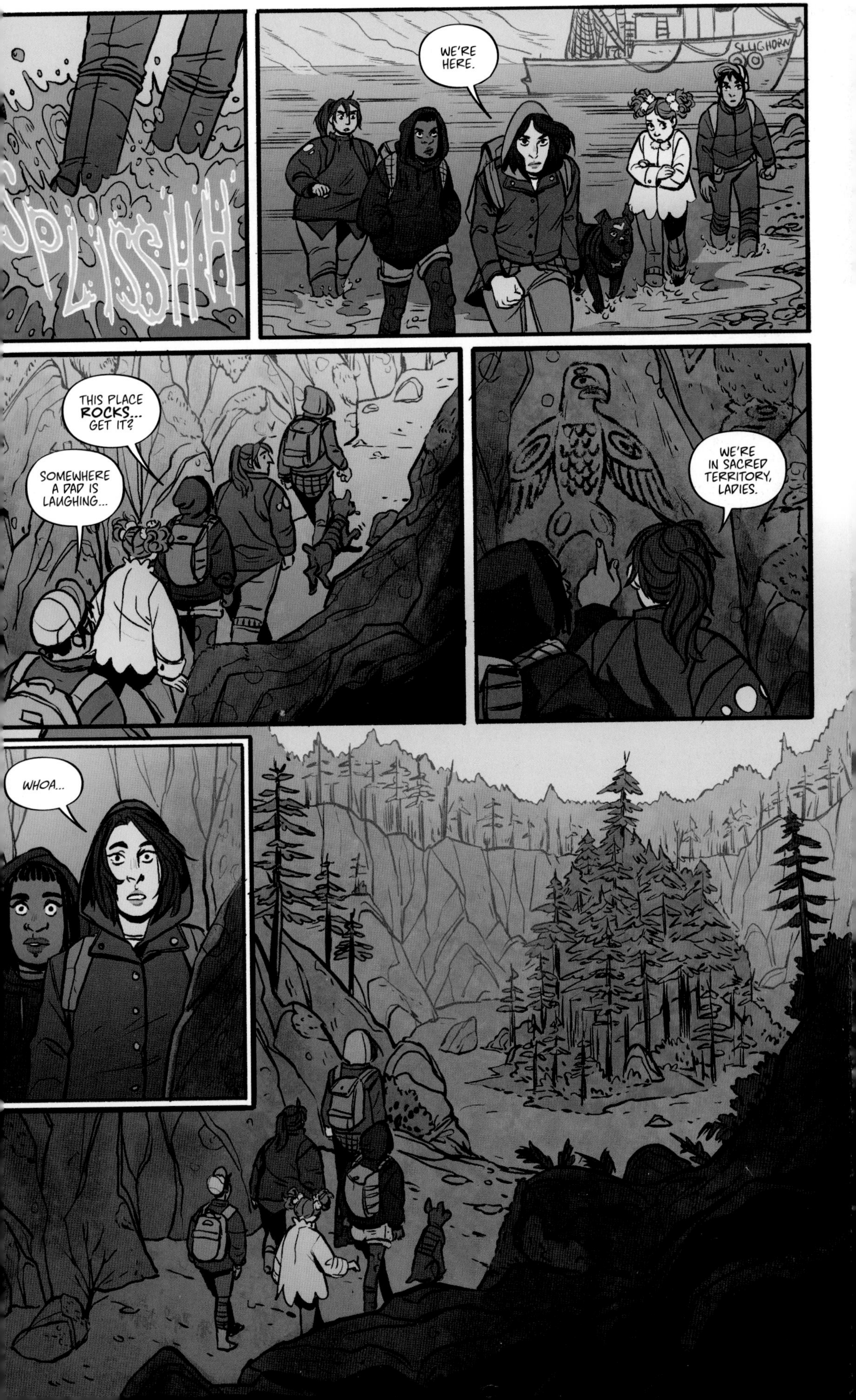
SPLISHH
SLUGHORN
WE'RE HERE.
THIS PLACE ROCKS... GET IT?
SOMEWHERE A DAD IS LAUGHING...
WE'RE IN SACRED TERRITORY, LADIES.
WHOA...

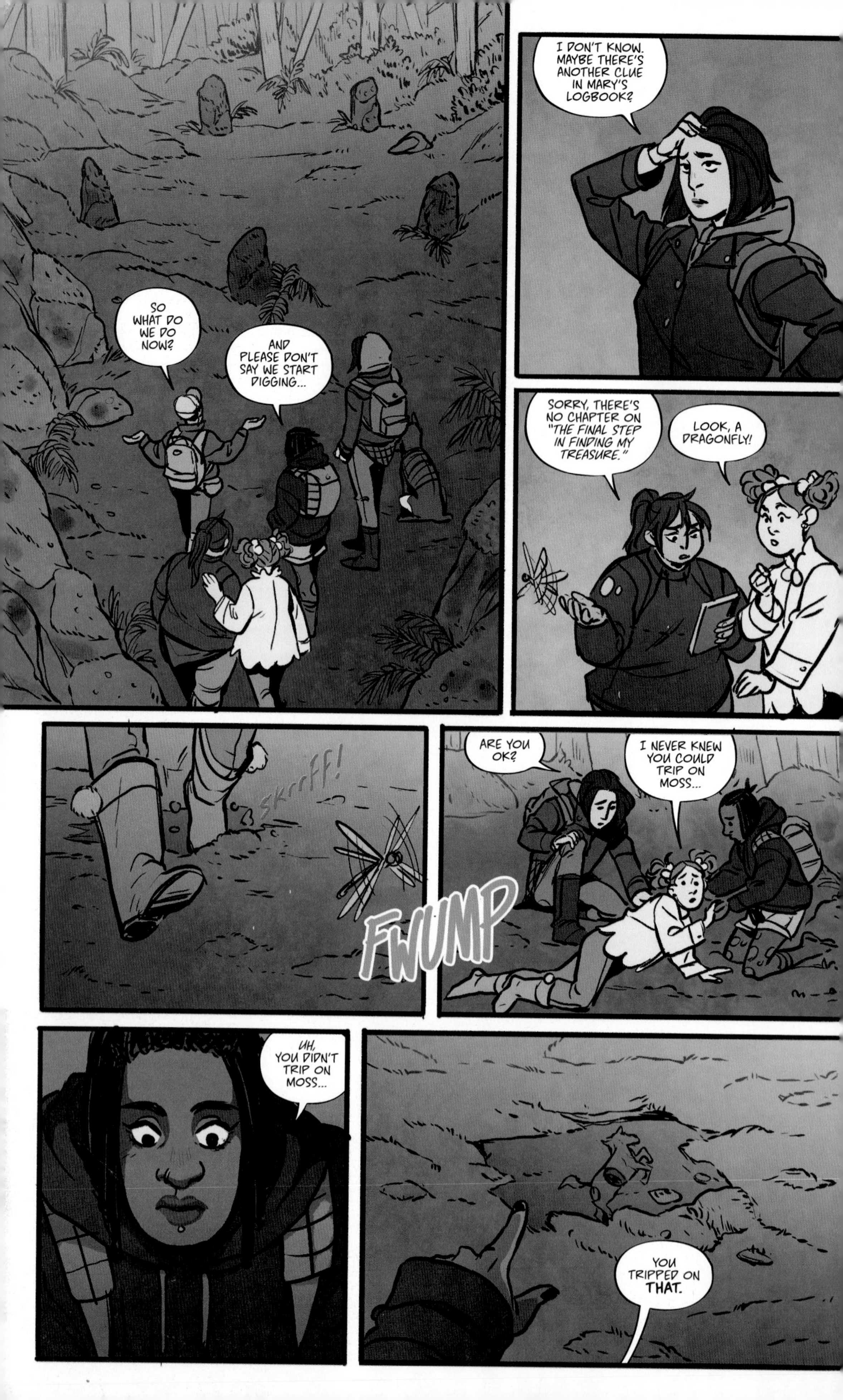
SO WHAT DO WE DO NOW?
AND PLEASE DON'T SAY WE START DIGGING...
I DON'T KNOW. MAYBE THERE'S ANOTHER CLUE IN MARY'S LOGBOOK?
SORRY, THERE'S NO CHAPTER ON "THE FINAL STEP IN FINDING MY TREASURE."
LOOK, A DRAGONFLY!
SKRRRFF!
FWUMP
ARE YOU OK?
I NEVER KNEW YOU COULD TRIP ON MOSS...
UH, YOU DIDN'T TRIP ON MOSS...
YOU TRIPPED ON THAT.

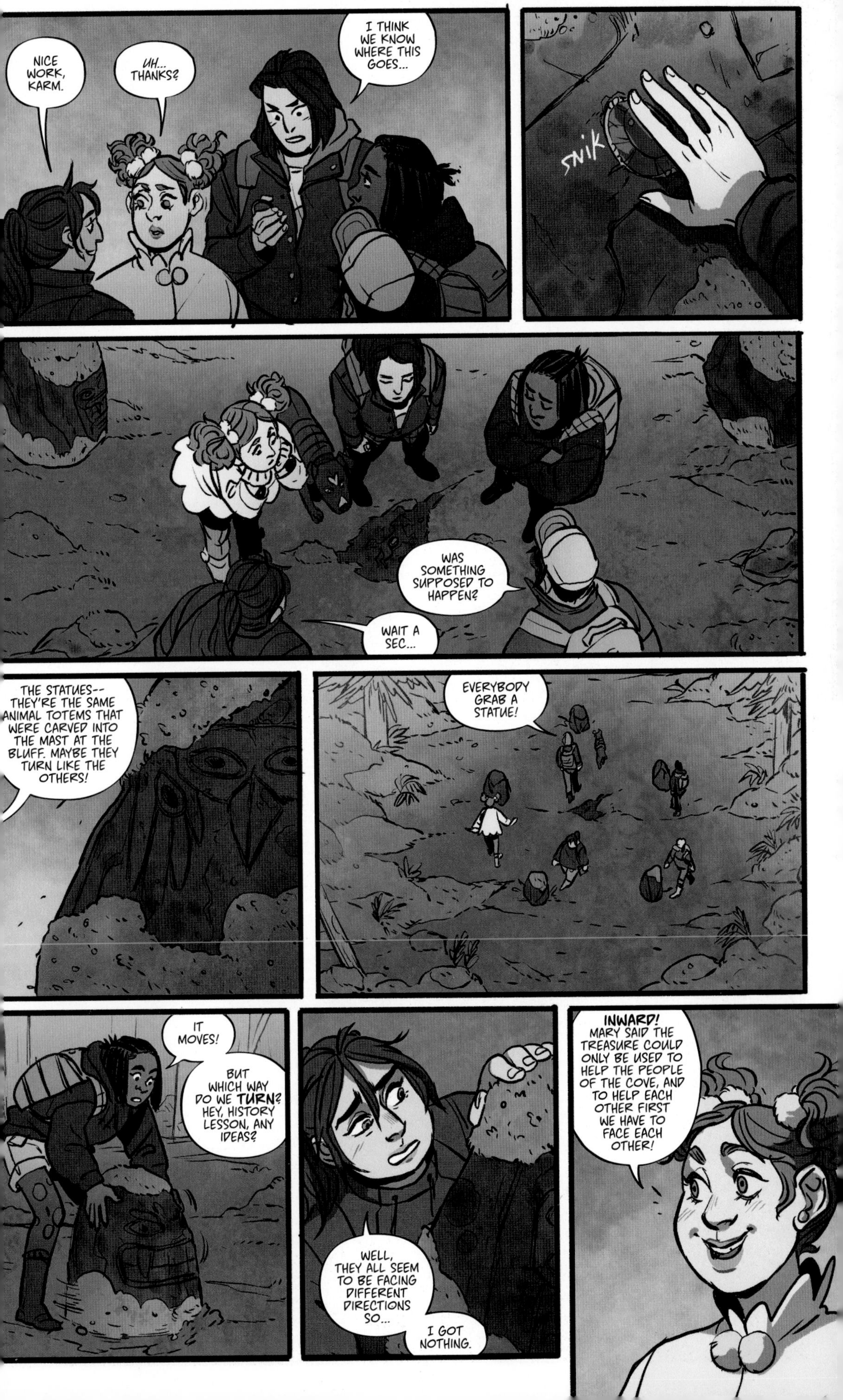
NICE WORK, KARM.
UH... THANKS?
I THINK WE KNOW WHERE THIS GOES...
SNIK
WAS SOMETHING SUPPOSED TO HAPPEN?
WAIT A SEC...
THE STATUES-- THEY'RE THE SAME ANIMAL TOTEMS THAT WERE CARVED INTO THE MAST AT THE BLUFF. MAYBE THEY TURN LIKE THE OTHERS!
EVERYBODY GRAB A STATUE!
IT MOVES!
BUT WHICH WAY DO WE TURN? HEY, HISTORY LESSON, ANY IDEAS?
WELL, THEY ALL SEEM TO BE FACING DIFFERENT DIRECTIONS SO...
I GOT NOTHING.
INWARD! MARY SAID THE TREASURE COULD ONLY BE USED TO HELP THE PEOPLE OF THE COVE, AND TO HELP EACH OTHER FIRST WE HAVE TO FACE EACH OTHER!

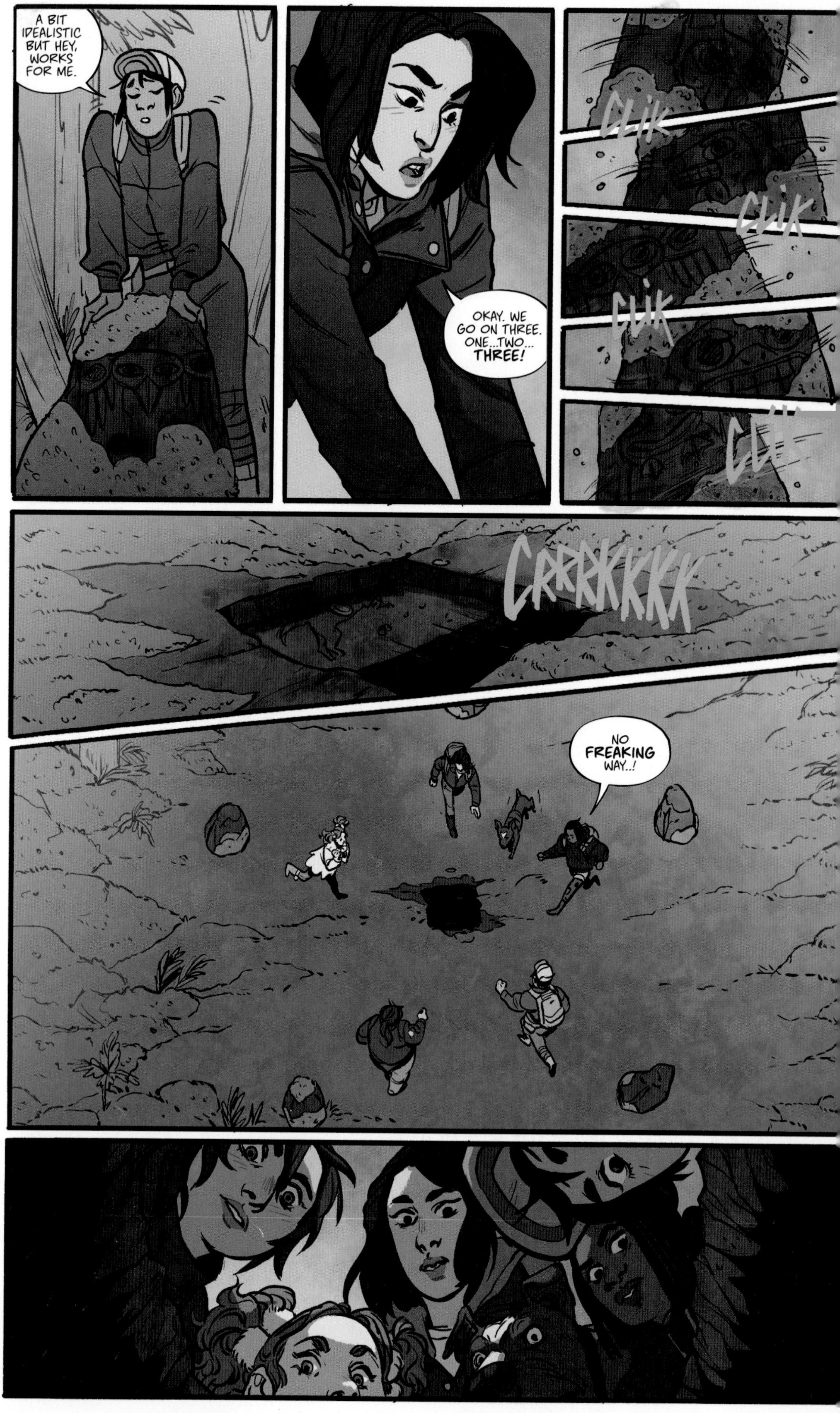
A BIT IDEALISTIC BUT HEY, WORKS FOR ME.
OKAY. WE GO ON THREE. ONE...TWO... THREE!
CLIK
CLIK
CLIK
CLIK
CRRRKKKK
NO FREAKING WAY..!

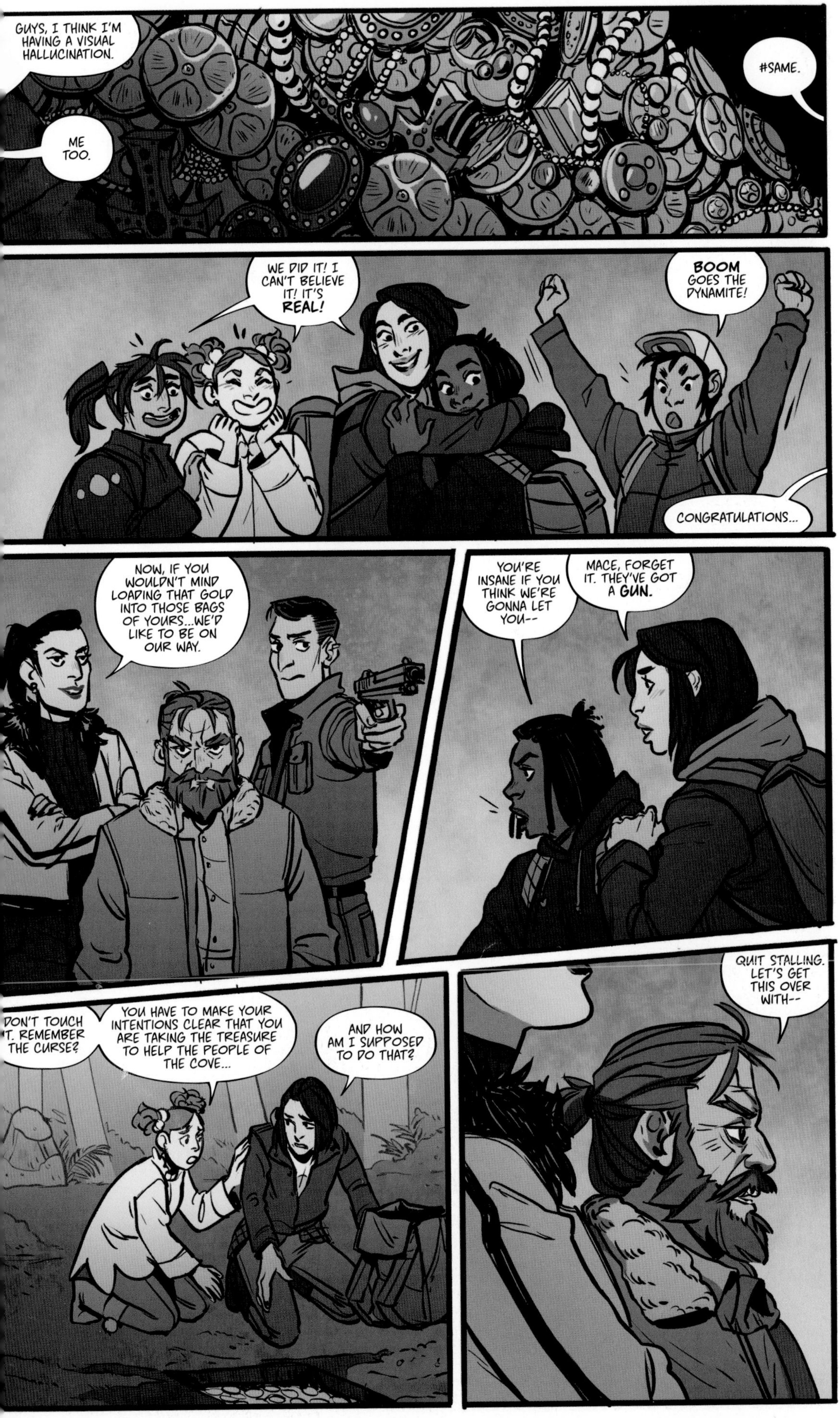
GUYS, I THINK I'M HAVING A VISUAL HALLUCINATION.
ME TOO.
#SAME.
WE DID IT! I CAN'T BELIEVE IT! IT'S REAL!
BOOM GOES THE DYNAMITE!
CONGRATULATIONS...
NOW, IF YOU WOULDN'T MIND LOADING THAT GOLD INTO THOSE BAGS OF YOURS...WE'D LIKE TO BE ON OUR WAY.
YOU'RE INSANE IF YOU THINK WE'RE GONNA LET YOU--
MACE, FORGET IT. THEY'VE GOT A GUN.
DON'T TOUCH IT. REMEMBER THE CURSE?
YOU HAVE TO MAKE YOUR INTENTIONS CLEAR THAT YOU ARE TAKING THE TREASURE TO HELP THE PEOPLE OF THE COVE...
AND HOW AM I SUPPOSED TO DO THAT?
QUIT STALLING. LET'S GET THIS OVER WITH--

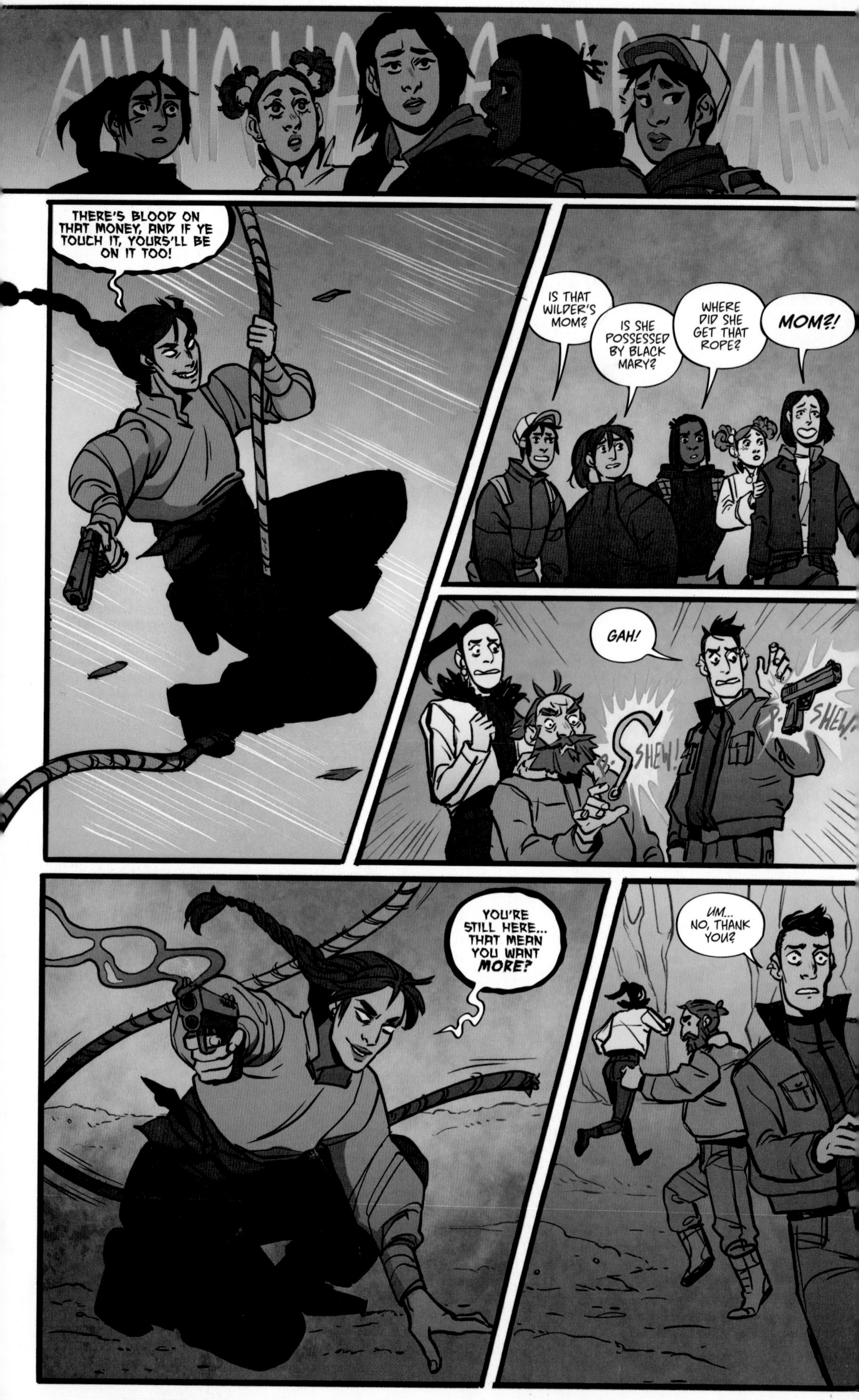
THERE'S BLOOD ON THAT MONEY, AND IF YE TOUCH IT, YOURS'LL BE ON IT TOO!
IS THAT WILDER'S MOM?
IS SHE POSSESSED BY BLACK MARY?
WHERE DID SHE GET THAT ROPE?
MOM?!
GAH!
SHEW!
SHEW!
YOU'RE STILL HERE... THAT MEAN YOU WANT MORE?
UM... NO, THANK YOU?

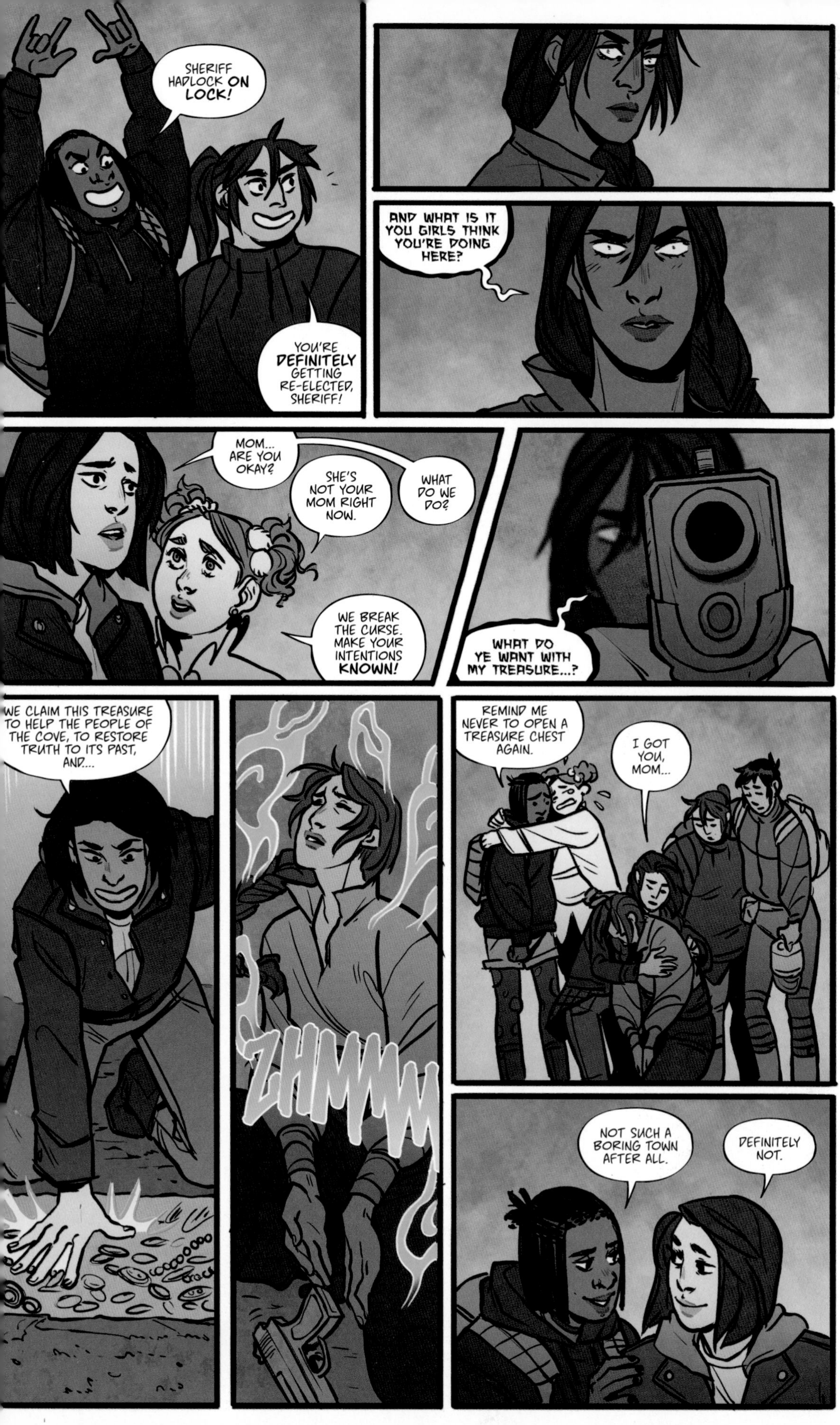
SHERIFF HADLOCK ON LOCK!
YOU'RE DEFINITELY GETTING RE-ELECTED, SHERIFF!
AND WHAT IS IT YOU GIRLS THINK YOU'RE DOING HERE?
MOM... ARE YOU OKAY?
SHE'S NOT YOUR MOM RIGHT NOW.
WHAT DO WE DO?
WE BREAK THE CURSE. MAKE YOUR INTENTIONS KNOWN!
WHAT DO YE WANT WITH MY TREASURE...?
WE CLAIM THIS TREASURE TO HELP THE PEOPLE OF THE COVE, TO RESTORE TRUTH TO ITS PAST, AND...
ZHMMMM
REMIND ME NEVER TO OPEN A TREASURE CHEST AGAIN.
I GOT YOU, MOM...
NOT SUCH A BORING TOWN AFTER ALL.
DEFINITELY NOT.

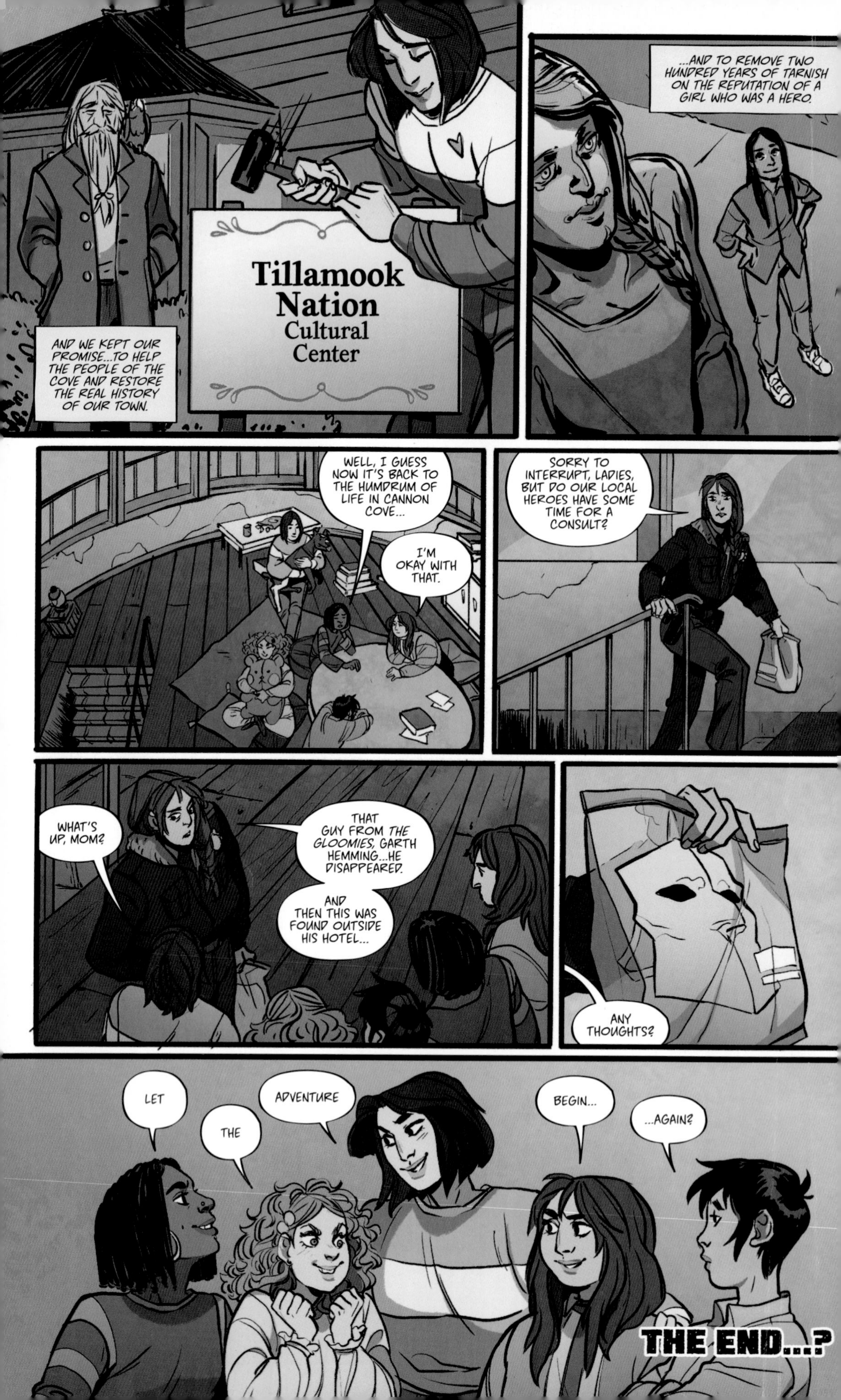
AND WE KEPT OUR PROMISE...TO HELP THE PEOPLE OF THE COVE AND RESTORE THE REAL HISTORY OF OUR TOWN.
Tillamook Nation Cultural Center
...AND TO REMOVE TWO HUNDRED YEARS OF TARNISH ON THE REPUTATION OF A GIRL WHO WAS A HERO.
WELL, I GUESS NOW IT'S BACK TO THE HUMDRUM OF LIFE IN CANNON COVE...
I'M OKAY WITH THAT.
SORRY TO INTERRUPT, LADIES, BUT DO OUR LOCAL HEROES HAVE SOME TIME FOR A CONSULT?
WHAT'S UP, MOM?
THAT GUY FROM THE GLOOMIES, GARTH HEMMING...HE DISAPPEARED.
AND THEN THIS WAS FOUND OUTSIDE HIS HOTEL...
ANY THOUGHTS?
LET
THE
ADVENTURE
BEGIN...
...AGAIN?
THE END...?

COVER
GALLERY

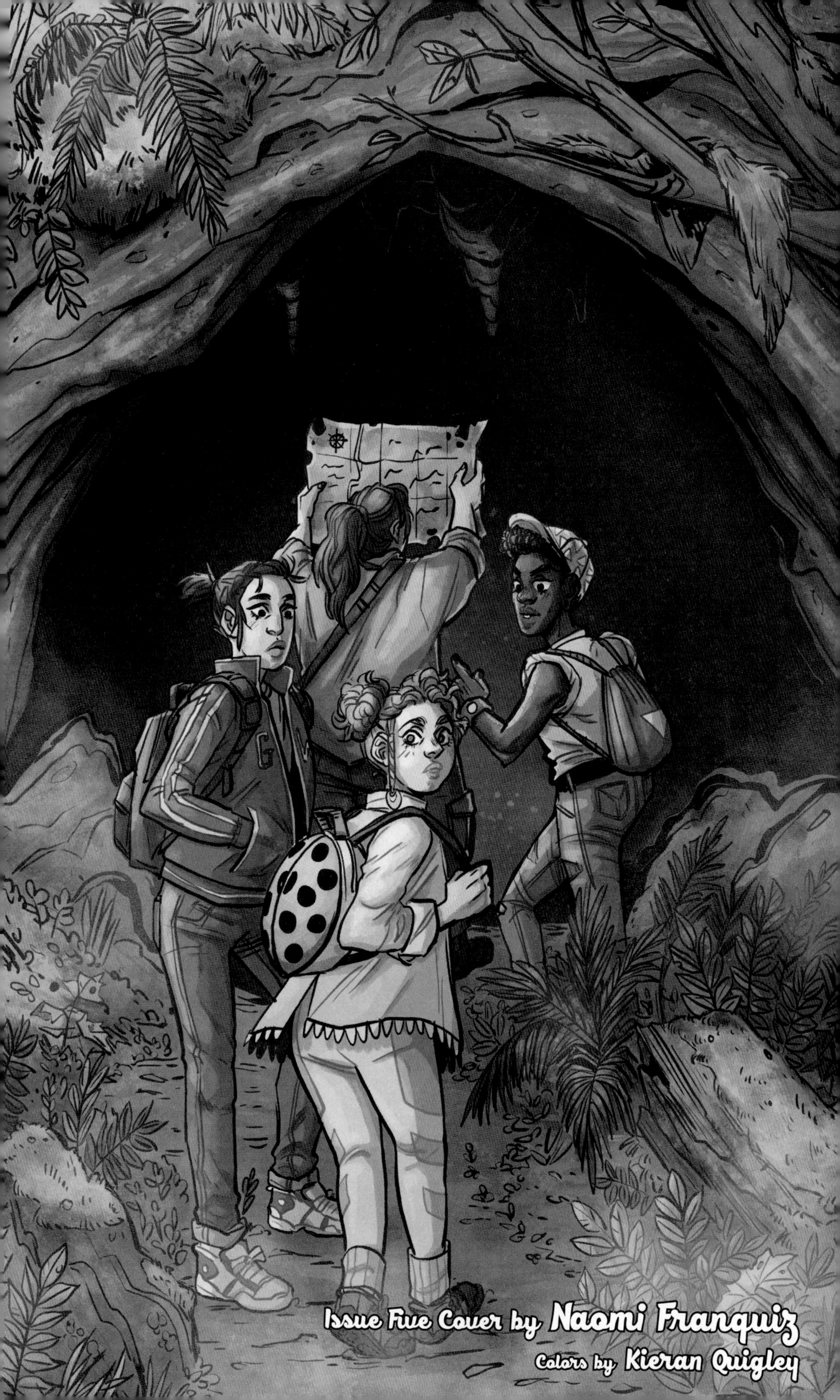
Issue Five Cover by Naomi Franquiz
Colors by Kieran Quigley

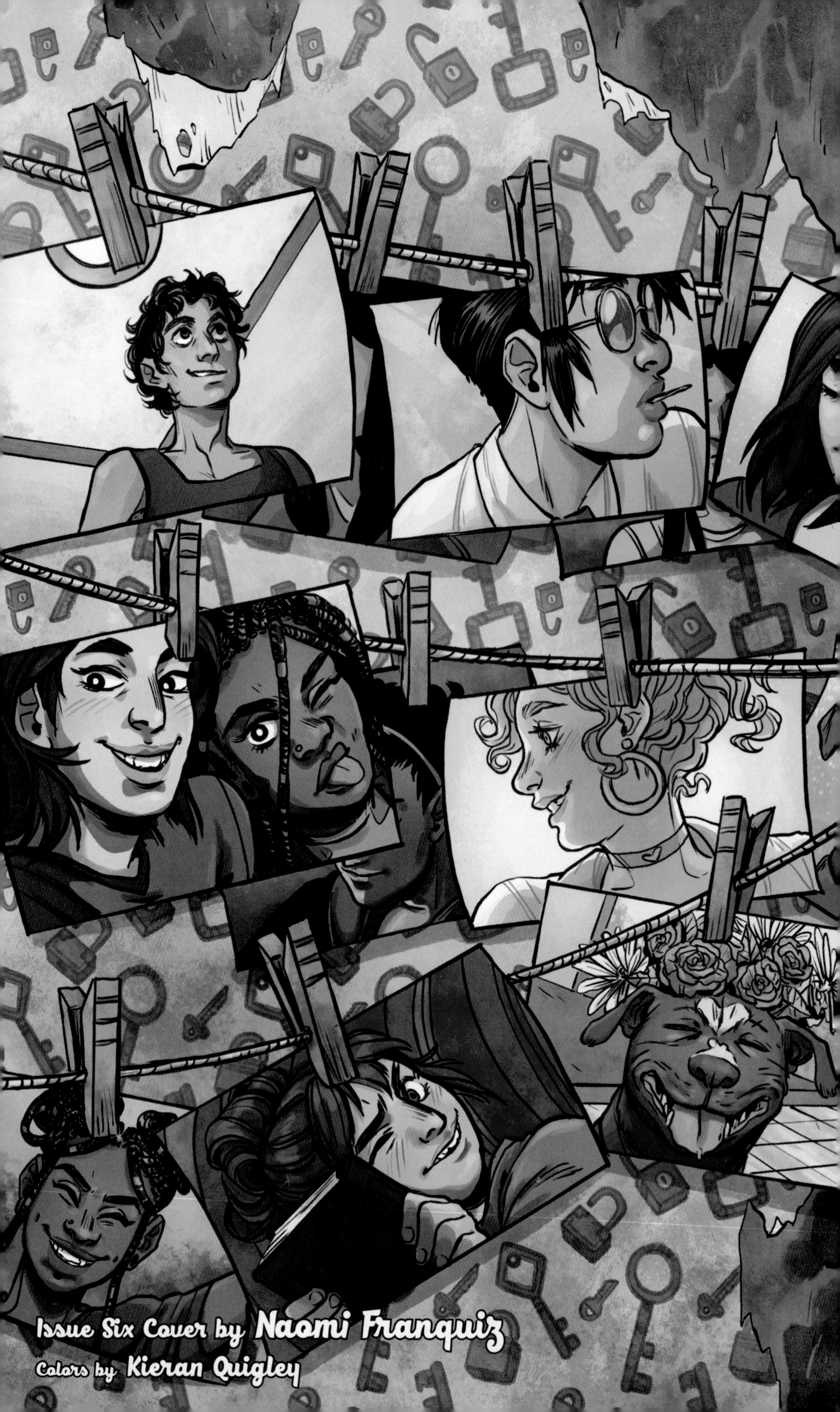
Issue Six Cover by Naomi Franquiz
Colors by Kieran Quigley

Issue Seven Cover by **Naomi Franquiz**

Colors by **Brittany Peer**

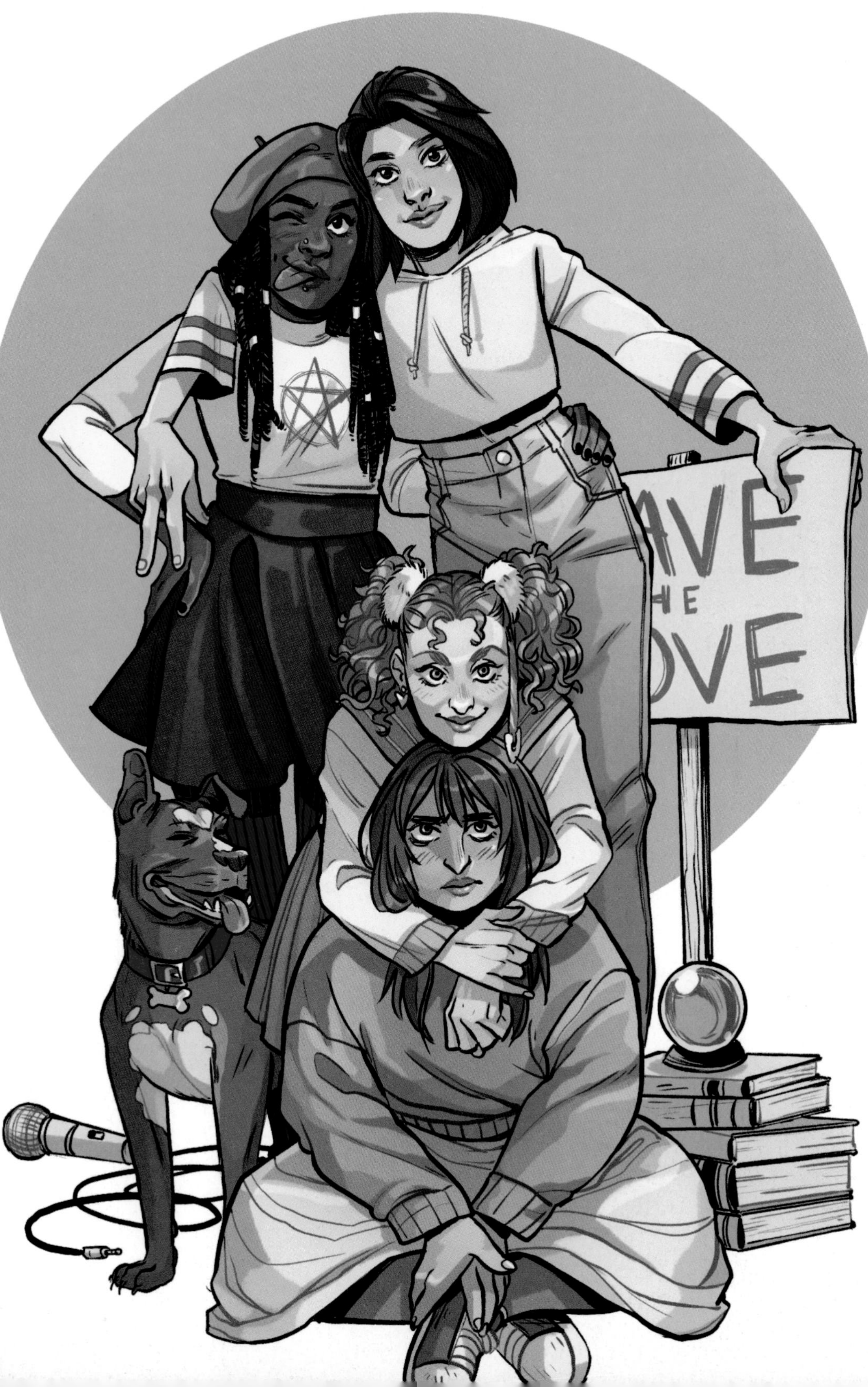
AVE
HE
OVE

Issue Eight Cover by **Naomi Franquiz**

Colors by **Brittany Peer**

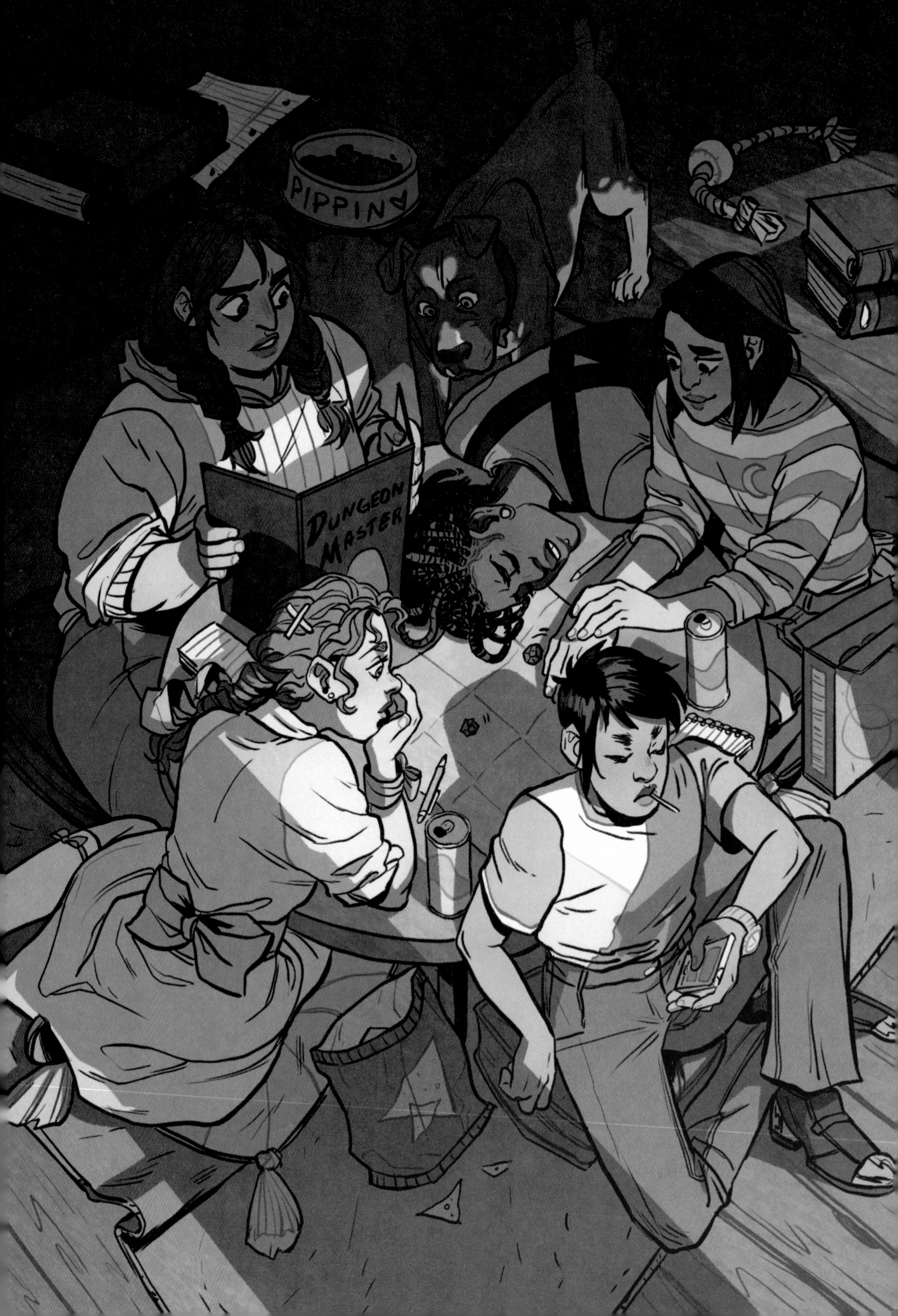
PIPPIN
DUNGEON MASTER

EXPLORE THE ORIGINS OF
MISFIT CITY!

Creators Kurt Lustgarten and Kirsten 'Kiwi' Smith sit down with artist Naomi Franquiz, and Leonardo Faierman of *BLACK GIRL NERDS* to talk about treasure hunting, the Pacific Northwest, and *MISFIT CITY*.

LEONARDO FAIERMAN, BLACK GIRL NERDS: How did you first get into reading comics? And following that, when did you decide to start creating your own and/or enter the industry?

KIWI SMITH: I'm relatively new to comics, beginning with a few years ago, when I was sent *Lumberjanes* to consider a possible screenplay adaptation. It was so vibrant and funny and femme-powered; I got really intrigued by the creators and the world and it led me to meet Shannon Watters (co-creator of *Lumberjanes*, and also an editor at BOOM! Box) on Twitter. Shannon emailed me to ask if I'd ever thought of writing a comic or graphic novel, and it had always been something I'd fantasized about, although had no idea how to do it. Fortunately, she gave me tons of examples of scripts so I could learn the format, and was very patient with me as I bounced ideas at her for a good long time before we finally landed on *Misfit City*.

KURT LUSTGARTEN: We were doing a little road-tripping up in Washington state, and we passed through Astoria, Oregon, where *The Goonies* was filmed. I'm a massive fan, so I shouldn't make it sound like we "passed through" by accident. We drove into town blasting the Cyndi Lauper theme from the movie and we had this thought: What if everyone who comes to this town does this exact same thing? Do these people have to put up with *Goonies* fans doing this all day long?

KIWI: We got really inspired by the idea of telling a story about kids who live in a place famous for being the location of a classic kids treasure hunt movie. They're really jaded about treasure hunting...until then they get pulled into a treasure hunt themselves.

Of all the ideas I pitched to Shannon, this felt the most comic-friendly and cinematic at the same time. And it had the bonus of Kurt and I being able to write it together. I could bring my female friendship/lady power obsession and he could bring his adventure-seeking, comic book-loving expertise.

KURT: I love comics and grew up reading Batman/Detective Comics and Eastman and Laird's *Teenage Mutant Ninja Turtles*.

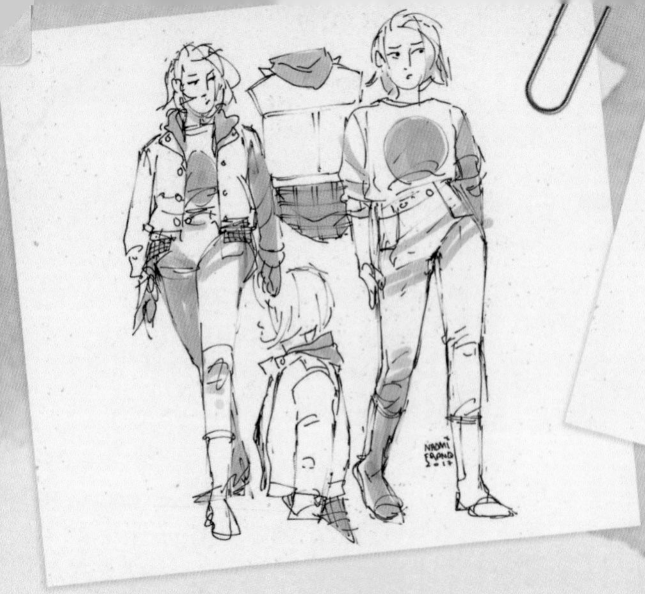

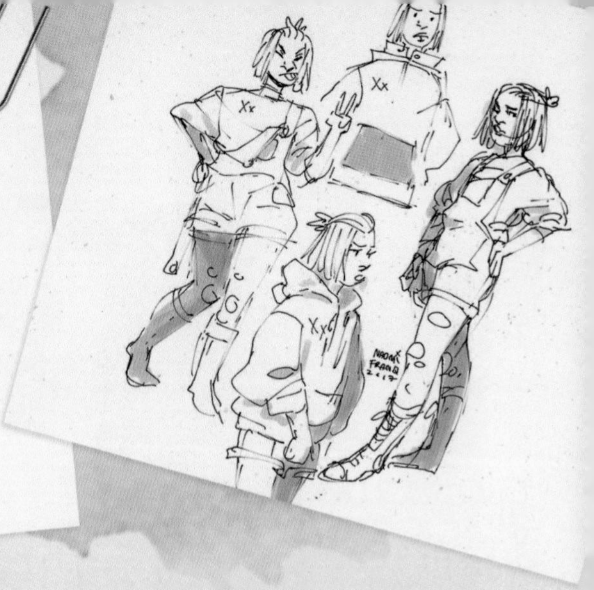

NAOMI FRANQUIZ: I first got into reading comics as a kid—*Archie*, *Shonen Jump*, any and every comic that my older brothers brought home (so a lot of *Spawn*, so much *Spawn*). I fell in love with the medium, and I used to make my own little homemade comics and zines in middle school with my best friend (whose dad was a huge comic book geek, too, and taught me a lot about it). It wasn't until after university and leaving the bitter criticism of the fine arts world (wherein "illustration" and "comic books" were treated like four-letter words) that I started to try and make some mini-comics and get my work out there. For as long as I've been an artist, it's only been within the last few years that I've solidly considered myself a comic book/sequential artist thanks to group anthologies like [editor Joamette Gil's] *Power & Magic*.

BGN: Can you describe your collaborative writer's process in *Misfit City*? It's relatively unusual—though not unheard of—for comics to feature two writers. Is the writing work equally divided between you? Does someone "run point" on the bulk of the narrative while the other supports and edits the text, or is it an organic process front-to-back? Are there fistfights over who gets top billing?

KIWI: We pass the outline back and forth and then break story out loud a bit, then we'll divide up scenes. I'd say Kurt runs point on big picture treasure hunt stuff, whereas I love writing anything relationship-y or anything involving Karma, Pippin, or Macy singing rock songs. Kurt generally takes first crack on anything involving action set pieces, obscure knowledge from Dot, and/or scrimshaw. I'll do a final pass which usually involves a small "fistfight" or two... especially since we live together as well as write together. We've tried to instill spaces or times to NOT talk about the story and the characters, but we invariably break those rules because we love our characters so much and we're always coming up with ideas that we can't help but pitch the other person in the

most inopportune moments. "I love that idea, but do you mind? I'm peeing."

BGN: *Misfit City* features a wide range of characters (mostly women) on the page, including characters with varying body-types. Has representing body diversity been an emphasis in your work? Do you use photographic references and, if so, are there individuals you referenced for the main characters in the comic?

NAOMI: A huge pet peeve of mine in comics and character design is the lack of design and variety in character body shapes. So many silhouettes look too similar, and I am surrounded by far too many wonderful and amazing people of all sizes to not want to try and represent them (and myself) in my work. I use photo references a lot (as no artist should be ashamed to admit), but the body types in *Misfit City* are really inspired by some of my closest friends that I grew up with. Wilder's height, for instance, is based on one of my best friends, a tall, gangly, wonderfully bold

and charismatic woman who once attempted to hide herself behind me, a 5'3" chick. It, uh... it didn't work.

BGN: Do you find that working on comics aligns conveniently with your film-writing/production background? Are there greater challenges or benefits to writing a story with the comics medium in mind? Do you think *Misfit City* is just the start of your work in this space?

KIWI: It's been a perfect alignment because I love breaking story and building an outline in collaboration with a partner, and that's what I've been doing as a screenwriter for 20+ years. So, Kurt and I map out the arcs in advance obviously, in both macro and micro ways. Sometimes in the writing it changes, and our editors Shannon and Sophie [Philips-Roberts] at BOOM! have been really lovely and supportive about those digressions, whereas in film you have less leeway. And Kurt's commercial directing background, in terms of storyboarding and framing, has been super helpful in terms of us learning to write in panels.

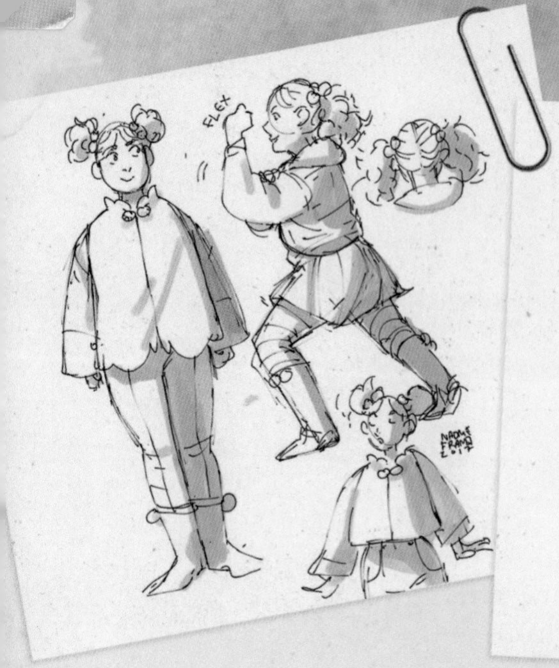
FLEX

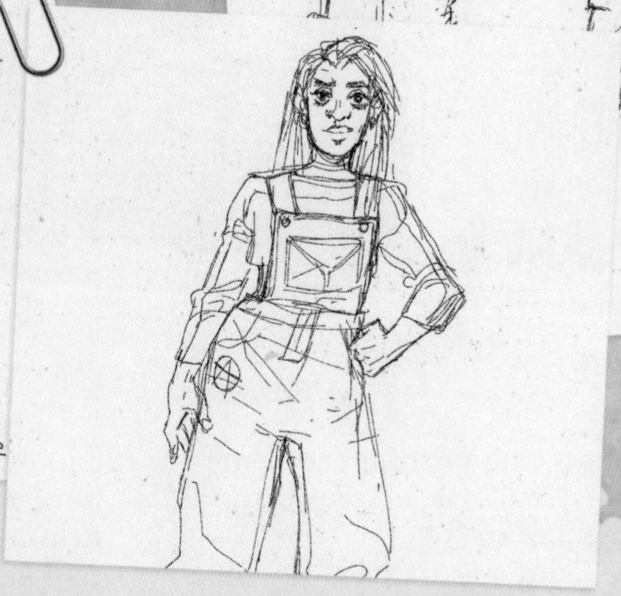

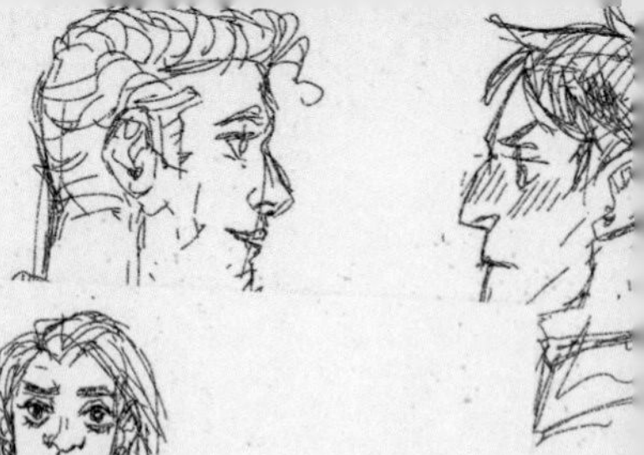

For the first few issues, I had to write in Final Draft and then translate it into a comic script, but then Kurt talked me out of that, and now we write like Real Comic Writers.

KURT: We're getting better at paneling as we go, and thinking in a static image, and because this past year has been such a big learning curve, we'd love to continue in comics because we finally feel like we're getting our footing. So, we're keeping a running list of graphic novel and comic ideas. We're itching to create a new series.

BGN: What are your backgrounds in terms of the places you grew up in, and does this play a part in the *Misfit City* story at all?

NAOMI: I'm as far away from the Pacific Northwest as you can get in the States—Florida. My family members, however, are island folk and many of my influential memories come with coastlines and the ocean, so certain recurring gags in *Misfit City* (fishing puns, pesky seagulls, and remarkably salty old men) are things I'm very familiar with.

KURT: Kiwi grew up in the Northwest, primarily in Washington on the Olympic Peninsula, and it's one of the most beautiful places on Earth. I grew up in the Northeast watching *The Goonies* and dreaming of growing up in a place like that. So, the setting is both grounded in experience but still carries a feeling of nostalgia.

BGN: Naomi, in your Twitter bio you self-identify as "queer ace." I feel like we're slowly seeing more prominently presented ace characters in fiction and media—would you agree with this statement? Are there any characters you see in contemporary media that represent these aspects, or that you feel a kinship with? Are any of the characters in *Misfit City* ace (even if this is only in your head-canon)?

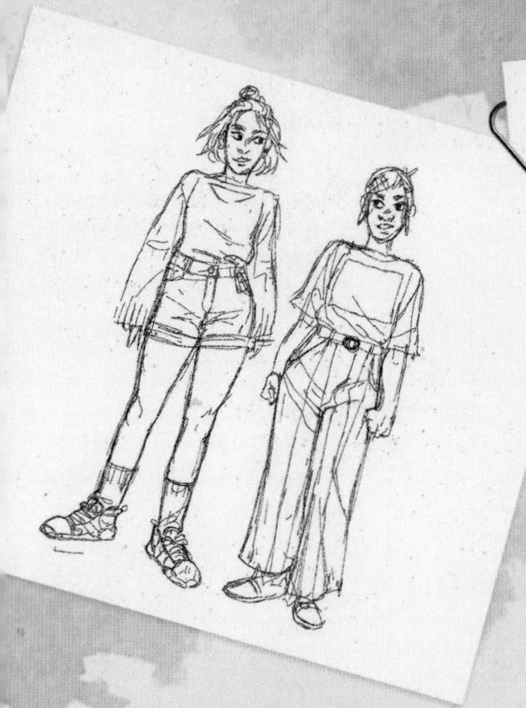

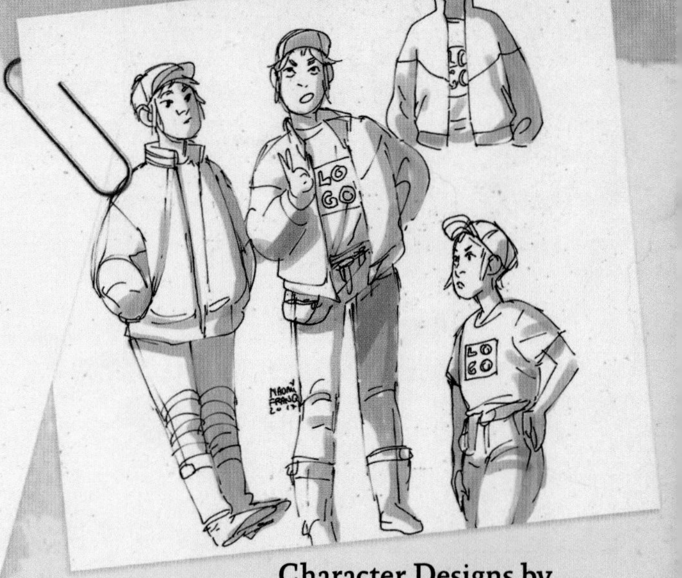
LO GO

Character Designs by
NAOMI FRANQUIZ

NAOMI: I do agree that there's definitely more ace/aro characters slowly cropping up and owning it in stories these days, some of which I feel like I knew was canon all along. Jughead Jones is the first major name I can think of. I grew up reading those *Archie Digest* books you pick up in the grocery check-out, and Jughead was always my favorite and who I connected with most. He wasn't bothered with dating or making out or looking hot. Dude just wanted a burger, and I felt that on a real level so seeing it made canon made me really excited.

Haruhi Fujioka in *Ouran High School Host Club* is another great example. The US version of the British TV series, *Sirens*, also introduced a canonically ace character (nicknamed "Voodoo"), and thoroughly rebuked the ignorance most people have about aces. She's not "waiting for the right person," like everyone keeps insisting. As for *Misfit City*, I completely head-canon that Dot is the Major Ace of the group. She's my Jughead, but instead of being in love with food, she's in love with books and mystery.

BGN: What else might you recommend to readers who really enjoyed *Misfit City*?

NAOMI: BOOM! Box is putting out a lot of great projects like *Lumberjanes*, but outside of them, *Gotham Academy* would be another great dig for more adventure and intrigue.

KURT: Everything Kiwi mentions below plus *Gotham Academy*, *Rat Queens*, and *Monstress*.

KIWI: *Lumberjanes*, *Giant Days*, *Paper Girls*, the graphic novel *Lucky Penny*, and anything Naomi does in the future. She is an incredible talent, and we feel so lucky to have been teamed with her by BOOM! Her work is a gift to this series in so many ways. We love you, Naomi!

DISCOVER
ALL THE HITS

STEVENSON • ELLIS • WATTERS • ALLEN
LUMBERJANES
BEWARE THE KITTEN HOLY
NEW YORK TIMES BESTSELLING SERIES

Allison + Treiman + Cogar
GIANT DAYS
VOLUME ONE

RIBON • FISH • PEER
SLAM!
VOLUME ONE

Hope Larson • Brittney Williams • Sarah Stern
GOLDIE VANCE
Volume One

THE BACKSTAGERS

TYSON HESSE'S
DIESEL
IGNITION

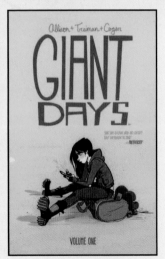

Lumberjanes
Noelle Stevenson, Shannon Watters, Grace Ellis, Brooklyn Allen, and Others
Volume 1: Beware the Kitten Holy
ISBN: 978-1-60886-687-8 | $14.99 US
Volume 2: Friendship to the Max
ISBN: 978-1-60886-737-0 | $14.99 US
Volume 3: A Terrible Plan
ISBN: 978-1-60886-803-2 | $14.99 US
Volume 4: Out of Time
ISBN: 978-1-60886-860-5 | $14.99 US
Volume 5: Band Together
ISBN: 978-1-60886-919-0 | $14.99 US

Giant Days
John Allison, Lissa Treiman, Max Sarin
Volume 1
ISBN: 978-1-60886-789-9 | $9.99 US
Volume 2
ISBN: 978-1-60886-804-9 | $14.99 US
Volume 3
ISBN: 978-1-60886-851-3 | $14.99 US

Jonesy
Sam Humphries, Caitlin Rose Boyle
Volume 1
ISBN: 978-1-60886-883-4 | $9.99 US
Volume 2
ISBN: 978-1-60886-999-2 | $14.99 US

Slam!
Pamela Ribon, Veronica Fish, Brittany Peer
Volume 1
ISBN: 978-1-68415-004-5 | $14.99 US

Goldie Vance
Hope Larson, Brittney Williams
Volume 1
ISBN: 978-1-60886-898-8 | $9.99 US
Volume 2
ISBN: 978-1-60886-974-9 | $14.99 US

The Backstagers
James Tynion IV, Rian Sygh
Volume 1
ISBN: 978-1-60886-993-0 | $14.99 US

Tyson Hesse's Diesel: Ignition
Tyson Hesse
ISBN: 978-1-60886-907-7 | $14.99 US

Coady & The Creepies
Liz Prince, Amanda Kirk, Hannah Fisher
ISBN: 978-1-68415-029-8 | $14.99 US

BOOM! BOX

AVAILABLE AT YOUR LOCAL COMICS SHOP AND BOOKSTORE
To find a comics shop in your area, call 1-888-266-4226
WWW.**BOOM-STUDIOS**.COM